BEN FINE
ZAVAREH RUSTOMJEE

The Political Economy of South Africa

From Minerals–Energy Complex
to Industrialisation

WestviewPress
A Division of HarperCollins*Publishers*

338.968
F49p

Published in 1996 by
C. Hurst & Co. (Publishers) Ltd.,
38 King Street, London WC2E 8JZ

Published in the United States by
Westview Press
A Division of HarperCollins Publishers
5500 Central Avenue
Boulder, CO 80301-2877

Printed in Spain by G. Z. Printek

Library of Congress Cataloging-in-Publication Data

Fine, Ben.
   The political economy of South Africa: From minerals-energy complex to industrialisation / Ben Fine, Zavareh Rustomjee,
      p.   cm.
   Includes bibliographical references and index
   ISBN 0-8133-2789-X. -- ISBN 0-8133-2790-3
    1. South Africa -- Economic conditions. 2. South Africa-- Economic policy. I. Rustomjee, Zavareh, II. Title
   HC905.F56   1996
   338.968--dc20   96-19858
                                       CIP

CONTENTS

Part III. THE SOUTH AFRICAN FORM
OF INDUSTRIALISATION

FIGURES

TABLES

ABBREVIATIONS

AAC	Anglo American Corporation
ABSA	Amalgamated Banks of South Africa
AECI	African Explosives and Chemical Industries
AMCOAL	Anglo American Coal Corporation
AMGOLD	Anglo American Gold Corporation
AMIC	Anglo American Industrial Corporation
Anglovaal	Anglo-Transvaal Group
Alusaf	Aluminium Development Corporation of South Africa
Armscor	Armaments Corporation of South Africa
BTI	Board of Trade and Industries
CEAS	Central Economic Advisory Service
CSIR	Council for Scientific and Industrial Research
EO	export-oriented
Escom	Electricity Supply Commission
ESRs	effective subsidy rates
Fedvolks	Federale Volksbeleggings
Foskor	Phosphorus Corporation of South Africa
GDFI	gross domestic fixed investment
Gencor	General Mining and Union Corporation
Genmin	General Mining Corporation
GFSA	Gold Fields of South Africa
HCI	heavy and chemical industries
IDC	Industrial Development Corporation
Iscor	Iron and Steel Corporation of South Africa
ISI	Import-substituting industrialisation
ISIC	International Standard Industrial Classification
ISP	Industrial Strategy Project
JCI	Johannesburg Consolidated Investment
JSE	Johannesburg Stock Exchange
MEC	minerals-energy complex
NBS	Natal Building Society

NFC	National Finance Corporation
NICs	newly industrialised countries
NP	National Party
OFS	Orange Free State
PIC	Public Investment Commission
PWV	Pretoria–Witwatersrand–Vereeniging
SAICCOR	South African Industrial Cellulose Corporation
Sanlam	South African National Life Assurance Company
SARB	South African Reserve Bank
Sasol	South African Coal, Oil and Gas Corporation Ltd
TCOA	Transvaal Coal Owners Association
TNC	Trans Natal Coal
UBS	United Building Society
Ucor	Uranium Enrichment Corporation
VFTPC	Victoria Falls and Transvaal Power Company

PREFACE

Research for this book was funded from October 1990 to October 1992 by the UK Economic and Social Research Council under grant R000232411 to study the South African minerals-energy complex and the capital goods sector. But the book's history runs longer and deeper than the term of funding. For one author it began in the mid-1980s when he was asked on behalf of the African National Congress (ANC) to assess and make policy recommendations for the South African mining and energy sectors. These recommendations emerged as discussion papers under the now defunct group Economic Research on South Africa. For the other author, the second half of the 1980s, when he was directly experiencing the role of the MEC through his work as a chemical engineer in South Africa, was the crucial time.

Our paths crossed and eventually ran together in order to undertake this research, which began at Birkbeck College, University of London, and then removed to the newly-founded Centre for Economic Policy for Southern Africa at the School of Oriental and African Studies, also part of the University of London. Throughout this time we have continued to have close working relations with the South African democratic movement, with one of us acting as a contributor to the Industrial Strategy Project supported by the Congress of South African Trade Unions, the other as a contributing editor to the Macroeconomic Research Group report, *Making Democracy Work*, and both of us serving in an advisory capacity at various times to the ANC's Department of Economic Planning. Once again, our paths have now taken their separate courses: one of us is continuing as an academic with strong ties to Southern Africa and the democratic movement while the other has served as policy adviser to the new South African Minister of Trade and Industry, before appointment as Director-General for Trade and Industry.

Throughout our collaboration, daily and close at hand or less frequently and at a distance, we have benefitted from critical support from a host of colleagues and friends, whether they be attached to the institutions listed above or otherwise. Special thanks to John Sender, who commented on the whole manuscript, and to the originating publishers, Hurst and Co. Others are too numerous to list. We dedicate this book to them and the spirit of debate that they have inspired. Hopefully this spirit will continue and even intensify, as it must if political economy is to make a lasting contribution to the effective formulation of policies necessary to meet the basic needs and economic empowerment of the majority of South Africans.

London, 1995   BEN FINE
                                                       ZAV RUSTOMJEE

1

INTRODUCTION AND OVERVIEW

The research and first drafts for this book were undertaken as the apartheid regime was undergoing what ultimately turned out to be its final political death throes. At each stage up to the election itself in April 1994, potentially insurmountable obstacles appeared to stand in the way of the election, not the least of which was threat of non-participation and intensified violence from Inkatha in the last few weeks of campaigning. In the event, the electoral process was completed and a remarkable political transition has been realised. Whatever the consequences may be for the longer-term material well-being of the majority of the population, now enfranchised, the extent of political change could hardly have been anticipated a few years ago even by those who reasonably, if cynically, question the degree to which there have been fundamental shifts in economic power.

It is such issues that we seek to address. The acclaim with which democratisation is greeted has to be tempered by the recognition, gained from experience elsewhere, that it is compatible with continuing, even deepening, economic inequalities. This is all the more disturbing given the extreme forms already taken by inequality in South Africa, the excessively low absolute standards of well-being currently experienced by much of the black population and the occasional correlation between democratisation and economic instability and collapse, such as that seen in eastern Europe. Further, the process of negotiating a political settlement has explicitly involved a series of compromises that have weakened the commitment to, or practicability of, significant shifts in economic power. The collectivist, potentially socialist content of the Freedom Charter first gave way to the more guarded commitment to a mixed economy. This in turn has witnessed the erosion of much official ANC support for public ownership. Consequently, the position of large-scale private capital seems to have been securely safeguarded, in part as a result of its own and the apartheid regime's frenetic pressure and campaigning during the pre-election period. In addition, the continuing occupation of the civil service and key posts in ministries by the 'old guard' in areas such as economic affairs and mining and energy casts doubts on the weight of momentum

3

pushing progressive economic policies forward. Some might welcome these cautious developments as securing economic stability and the limited economic change compatible with it; others might regret them as enforced but pragmatic compromises. But none can doubt that the political transition, however much it may have been completed, has yet to be complemented by a corresponding economic transition.

We do not believe that South Africa's economic prospects can be satisfactorily broached in the simplistic terms already outlined – in which the impetus, or lack of it, for economic change can be read off in general terms from the potential released by democratisation and its associated economic policies. Although it may be important to make overall assessments about the shifting balance of economic and political forces, these can only be adequately understood on the basis of a more complex analysis of the structure and functioning of the economy itself. Only then can political change be related to the prospects for economic change and the issue addressed of whether there has or can be an economic transition, or break with the past, corresponding to the political transition that has already occurred.

Consequently, we are concerned not only with the performance of the economy over the past decade or so but also with its longer-term economic history. We delve back into the inter-war period in order to identify the economic and political factors that were to determine the path of the post-war economy which is the current inheritance. In this task, we have been both assisted and obstructed by the existing literature for two separate reasons. First, the focus of the literature has itself moved very quickly; over the past decade, there has been a shift from exploring why the apartheid economy should be in crisis to one of formulating policies for the post-apartheid economy. Quite apart from their lack of overlap in focus, there has been a dramatic change in analytical emphasis and method, from critical political economy to policy-oriented assessment.

One of our broad conclusions is that the political economy and economic and social history of South Africa has unduly suffered from the exclusive attention that has been paid to economic and political agencies. This is apparent in the race-class debate and in the study of Afrikaner as opposed to English interests. It has meant a sore neglect of the expression and formation of those interests in economic activity itself – what has been the structure, composition, interaction and mode of functioning of the commercial world? In classic Marxist terminology, the forces of production have been overlooked in a one-sided emphasis upon class or other relations, whatever the sophistication with which these have themselves been revealed.

Over the past five years, these features of the literature have been extensively abandoned, especially within political economy, in the search for technical solutions to the economics of transition. Questions of what is good for growth, distribution, investment or the balance of payments, etc. (which should also have been more prominent in the earlier period) have displaced the focus upon class structure and, equally important, how it is changing and liable to change. In short, to employ the vernacular, social relations of production have been set aside in seeking to advance the forces of production. It is most notable in the extent to which the entrenched inheritance and structures of apartheid, in income and wealth, infrastructure, health, education and welfare and employment, etc. are now perceived as problems rather than the continuing basis on which society functions irrespective of political democratisation – which itself is open to serious interrogation beyond what has been achieved through the franchise.

While understandable in formulating policies for a prospective government (and in defending them against the assaults of entrenched interests), the new 'post-apartheid' literature suffers considerably from the failure to incorporate, even if critically, the insights to be gained from the earlier literature concerning who holds economic power and how it has been exercised. For otherwise how can the most perfectly formulated policies be guaranteed any chance of implementation, let alone success? It is remarkable that the dichotomy between these two literatures is often bridged by individual authors who seem to have been able to shift seamlessly from critics of apartheid to post-apartheid policy making, despite the disjuncture in the form and content of the analysis involved.

The second deficiency in both groups of literature concerns its failure to be rooted adequately in the realities of the South African economy. The central theme of our argument is that what will be termed the Minerals-Energy Complex (MEC) lies at the core of the South African economy, not only by virtue of its weight in economic activity but also through its determining role throughout the rest of the economy. Consequently, we have been astonished by the ease with which economic analyses and policies have been formulated and debated without reference to this simple and central fact. Indeed, many have overlooked and even consciously resisted the notion of the MEC both theoretically and empirically in order to be able to propose policy as if free from its influence. Both strategically and in many detailed policies, let alone in more academic exercises, this is a dangerously misguided approach. More specifically, there is a persistent view that South Africa has industrialised through import-substitution, stimulated by protection of consumer goods. In reality, this has proved less important than the growth of manufacturing around primary production. This has to be recognised as the appropriate starting point if policies are to be designed for the future direction of manufacturing. In addition, the economic and political factors that have prompted South Africa's industrial trajectory need to be identified.

Nonetheless, despite these reservations about the existing literature and its relation to our own broad stance, elaborated later in this introduction, there is much common ground concerning certain features of the most recent performance of the South African economy. It is generally recognised to have experienced what has been termed an economic impasse. Throughout the 1980s, economic growth has been negligible, levels of investment have scarcely been high enough to replace depreciation, and unemployment, officially recognised if under-counted, has risen as falling levels of employment, especially in manufacturing, have confronted an ever-expanding labour force. The extent to which these symptoms of chronic economic failure reflect the gathering together of the endemic weaknesses of the apartheid economy as opposed to the costs of transition itself is a moot point. The past decade has witnessed internal conflicts, political instability and economic sanctions and an apparently bewildering pace of social change. These are not the conditions conducive to business confidence through which the economy can prosper. Yet their actual or prospective removal following democratisation has not done enough to restore such confidence.

Thus the symptoms of South Africa's economic malaise are now recognised to have been more deeply rooted. Previously, the distinction between liberal and radical understandings of the apartheid system has had its counterpart in explanations of the economic impasse. For liberals, the denial of economic and political freedoms and benefits to the majority of the population has obstructed the efficacy of market forces and condemned the economy to dependence upon the low productivity of an unskilled labour force. For radicals, the apartheid economy has only been able to function profitably for capital while the level of resistance and the costs associated with it were sufficiently contained. Whether it be market forces or class struggle that is the operative agency, the apartheid economy is perceived to have lost its *modus vivendi*.

Subsequently, a more sophisticated understanding of the workings of the economy has emerged. It focuses on the poor performance of the manufacturing sector. While this sector is perceived to have been successful in the narrow sense of having increased its share of the economy at the expense of mining and agriculture, its overall performance over the past two decades is considered inadequate by a number of criteria. This is all the more striking given the previously held view that South Africa had successfully industrialised. However, it is apparent that manufacturing has been confined to a limited number of activities, relying upon import substitution for finished consumption goods and, even in these, has not proved to be competitive on world markets. In particular, the South African economy has been deficient in developing capital and intermediate goods. Consequently, whenever the economy is subject to expansion, there is an immediate flood of imports in order that producers can meet higher levels of domestic demand. This places strains on the balance of payments, particularly in the context of limits on foreign borrowing. Thus economic policy has to deflate the economy to prevent a widening imbalance on the foreign exchange account. Essentially, we do not dispute this diagnosis of the problems of the economy. However, we do consider that, by its emphasis on and understanding of the manufacturing sector, a considerably distorted image of the realities of the economy is projected to the forefront. Most striking is the lack of prominence accorded to what are arguably, the three most crucial features of the economy leaving aside the labour system: the mining and energy sectors, the financial system and the economic role of the state.

These factors constitute our starting point but we do not treat them as independent of one another. For it will be shown that they are bound together through the functioning of the MEC. Only by unravelling its mode of operation is it possible to address the issue of the weakness of manufacturing which other analyses take as their starting point. But what is meant by the MEC? Before continuing we must outline its essential features, how its various aspects and implications are examined in greater detail in the remainder of the book, and how it operates as a specific system of capital accumulation.

To do so, we utilise the broader analytical framework, provided in Part I. Here we are concerned with the issue of what makes economic development successful or not and what form that economic development takes. We argue that these problems can be addressed in terms of linkages and agencies; the first refers to the (potential) connection between one economic process and another, the second to the active entities that do or do not bring them about. This broad approach is capable of accommodating a variety of different theoretical approaches, assessing the ways and the extent to which they recognise economic development as dependent upon linkages, agencies and the dynamic between them.

In Chapter 2 we specifically review the literature on the South Korean economy from this perspective in order to highlight the extent to which development economists have been more concerned with linkages than agencies. In particular, the debate over South Korea's success has turned upon whether the state or the market has been the decisive agency. While the verdict has increasingly swung in favour of the state as progenitor of effective industrial policy and industrialisation, the issue of why it should have been able and willing to perform that role and perform successfully, has been sorely neglected. But it is this question that is of particular importance for the South African economy since we consider that the potential developmental linkages that it could have fostered were sorely neglected, in contrast to the South Korean state. The reasons for this must be uncovered through the economic and political forces that operate through the state (and market).

This is the subject of Chapter 3, where the literature on the developmental state is reviewed for its relevance for the South African economy,
as is some of the most recent literature on the prospects for the South
African state, given its change of government. We specifically reject the
idea that the state can be developmental through being autonomous from
class or other economic and political interests or through pursuing a
separately defined interest of its own (or of its personnel). Rather, the state
is subject to the economic and political forces and interests that operate
through and upon it. These do not translate readily and transparently into
specific policies nor does this imply the institutional forms and personnel
of government are unimportant, but the significance of each of these is
different according to their sphere of application. In short, because class
or other interests cannot be read off immediately from state policies, this
does not imply the need for an alternative approach based upon the
potentially autonomous or developmental state. A further factor is that of
the role of the state as the class structure and structure of economic
interests are themselves subject to transformation. This issue is taken up
specifically in the context of the shifting relations between Afrikaner and
English capital in Chapters 6 and 7, even as these fractions of capital shift
in content and in their relationship to one another.

Before employing this framework more fully and with more detail
drawn from the South African economy, Part I is concerned to establish
the presence of the MEC on a more mundane, empirical level. In identifying the MEC as lying at the core of the economy, there is at its own core
those sectors associated with minerals and energy in the narrow technical
sense. The role of gold as a key sector in the South African economy is
well known. Its importance has declined in recent years with the declining
price of gold, the fertility of reserves and the emergence of other sources
of supply in the world market. However, other metals have gained in
prominence, especially platinums. The same is true of coal: it is responsible for 80 per cent of the country's primary energy needs. It also provides
for 20 per cent of the country's exports and one-third of all non-gold
exports. But very little coal is used for direct energy needs. The vast
majority is either converted into electricity (over 50 per cent) or into oil
(over 30 per cent). On a global scale, the South African economy is
uniquely dependent on electricity and is uniquely electricity-intensive,
with levels of consumption per capita comparable, for example, to those
of the UK, despite limited domestic consumption by the majority of the
population. This is primarily due to its use in mining and mineral processing, which accounts for 40 per cent of consumption. Even though
manufacturing accounts for a slightly greater proportion, the industries
concerned are closely related to and, as will be argued, form part of the
MEC, with electricity heavily used in a small number of plants in engineering, iron and steel and base metals and chemicals. Thus, coal is

produced to generate electricity which acts as a major direct and indirect input to the production of gold. In this light, it is not surprising that one estimate puts gold as having generated as much as 40 per cent of GDP through its direct and indirect effects.

Chapter 4 establishes these linkages more thoroughly through detailed calculations from input-output tables. First, however, it is necessary to posit what constitutes the core sectors of the MEC in order to examine its size and the flow of inputs from it to the rest of the economy and vice versa. We include within the MEC a number of sectors which have traditionally been allocated to manufacturing. We do so because they are so directly attached to mining and energy, as in metal fabrication directly following on from ore-processing, that it is misleading to do otherwise. On this basis, it is demonstrated that, contrary to popular opinion and much assumption in academic inquiry, the economy's dependence on mining and energy and directly related activity has increased and not decreased. Consequently, the idea that manufacturing has increased in importance and now overshadows primary production is erroneous. In other words, the application of standard industrial classification schemes to the South African economy has given a false picture of the extent and form of the industrialisation that has been achieved. Through this statistical exercise, we establish the continuing importance of the MEC in the narrow technical sense of the weight of its constituent sectors within the economy while also suggesting why its continuing significance has been overlooked or even denied by less careful empirical summaries of the economy's sectoral composition.

Chapter 5 is also primarily empirical in character and equally concerned with establishing the existence and nature of the MEC. It examines the institutional character of the MEC, in particular the structure of ownership of its constituent activities. Mining in general is primarily controlled by the six private corporations, mining houses known as the group producers. This extends to coal mining, with the major exception of the coal produced by the state-owned steel company, Iscor, which is now privatised, and the predominantly state-owned coal-to-oil conversion plant, Sasol, now partially privatised. These two organisations have primarily served their own coal needs. Sales of coal for domestic consumption are almost exclusively to the state electricity utility, Escom. This coal is from mines tied to particular power stations with a guaranteed profit. Coal exports are licensed by the state through a quota system and depend crucially on the newly-built railway line to the recent development of Richards Bay Harbour, both of which are run by the state-owned transport company, Transnet – formerly the South African Transport Services (SATS). The users of electricity within mining are the group producers who own and operate the gold and other mines.

As is already apparent from this pattern of ownership structure and economic activity, there is close integration between the state and the private, group producers and this is entrenched institutionally. The interests of the group producers are coordinated through the century-old Chamber of Mines. Government policy towards the MEC is formulated through close co-ordination with the private sector. In addition, the state depends heavily on tax revenue derived from the mineral sector, this reaching as much as 26.4 per cent from gold alone when the gold price was at its peak in 1981.

In addition, the mining houses are at the centre of a much wider set of activities than of mineral production alone. There is an extensive pattern of interpenetrating directorships and ownership of shares between them and a highly concentrated ownership of other companies within the economy as a whole and abroad. For example, the conglomerate Anglo-American Corporation (AAC) is reputed to own over 70 per cent of the shares on the Johannesburg Stock Exchange (JSE) and to be the single largest foreign investor in the United States. This conglomerate structure of the MEC depends upon and is reflected in a close integration with South Africa's highly developed financial institutions. For each mining house, there is not only a corresponding holding company for its industrial activities but also a matching set of financial institutions.

Such are the immediate parameters that trace out the body of the MEC as a core of functioning private and state capital. But the MEC is much more than this, for it has given and continues to give rise to a much wider range of economic as well as of political and social phenomena. As mentioned above, the MEC is to be seen not merely as a core set of industries and institutions but also as a system of accumulation and one that has varied in its nature over time. Indeed, the apparent decline in the importance of mining to the South African economy over the past fifty years, as it increasingly, if not smoothly, comes under the shadow of manufacturing, is in sharp contrast to its literally golden era of the previous fifty years. It indicates the changing character of the MEC, not its eclipse. In this light, which fragments of capital do or do not belong to the MEC or its core is of lesser significance than how any capital is subject more or less directly to its influence.

What then is the system of accumulation which is to be associated with the MEC today, over and above the individual parts already identified? First, despite its origins and productive basis in the mining and energy sectors, the MEC revolves around a separate but intimately related epicentre – that of finance. Consequently, this has imparted a dynamic of its own to the path of accumulation. In particular, so powerful and concentrated have been the finance houses that there has been a tendency for acquisitions and mergers to take on a prominent role so that corporate restructuring and financial speculation have occurred at the expense of providing funds for investment for the expansion and restructuring of production itself. This process has itself been compounded and influenced by a number of factors. As there have been foreign disinvestments in response to the crises of apartheid and sanctions campaigns, so foreign subsidiaries have become available for acquisition. In addition, various sorts of restrictions on foreign exchange movements out of South Africa have to some extent confined investment funds to the domestic economy. These have been used to seek out and acquire established companies. The lack of commitment to use investment funds as the basis for a vibrant expansion within the domestic economy is reflected in the extent of capital flight from South Africa in the form of the illegal export of capital, predominantly by firms of domestic origin. As much as 7 per cent of GDP per annum has been subject to such international movements of capital, which occur at the expense of the resources made available for domestic investment. Their magnitude indicate the extent to which South Africa's corporate and financial structure is global in its operation.

The extent of such capital flight is a stunning indictment of large-scale South African capital, particularly in light of its unprecedented ideological offensive to blame the economy's poor performance on what it claims to be unreasonable demands for real wage increases and public expenditure programmes. It has itself been responsible both for the low levels of investment and for the allocation of finance to speculation and acquisition rather than productive employment. But this reflects more than a self-interested and often illegal use of finance; it begs the question of why large-scale capital should have formulated its self-interest in this way. If there were domestic opportunities for profitable investment, surely they would have been exploited by private capital?

Considering the issue in this way is misleading, however, since it leaves aside the central issue of the role of the state. For whether one use of funds rather than another is profitable is highly dependent upon state policy. We show throughout the book that the state has played a major part in fostering unproductive investment and capital flight, both by the way in which it has built up the financial system in South Africa as well as through its failure to develop coherent policies for industrialisation. Moreover, in line with the discussion of the theory of the state, we demonstrate how this has corresponded to the shifting balance of economic and political interests that have acted upon and through the state.

Part III begins by identifying in Chapter 6 the configuration of capitalists' interests operative in the 1930s, a period in which there was considerable disjuncture between economic power (held by English, foreign or mining capital) and political power (held by Afrikaner capital). The impact of this is shown to have been diverse, sector-by-sector and policy-by-policy, depending upon the balance and structure of economic and political forces. This was because the state depended upon the sources of revenue that could be generated from the MEC and how it could intervene to obtain and to employ them. However, a crucial consequence of the disjuncture between economic and political power was to preclude a strategy for industrialisation based on diversification out of the economic strengths (technical, financial, managerial and economies of scale and scope) to be found in mining. Mining capital itself was short of a guarantee that collaboration with the state would not lead eventually to policy penalties from a hostile government, even to nationalisation. Government could not secure its re-election if it was revealed to be pursuing policies overtly collaborative and supportive of mining capital which, in turn, could not be certain that the returns from an industrialisation strategy would be secure from government appropriation.

Thus, private capital was insufficiently secure politically to eschew a strategy of importing inputs and exporting profits. Nor could the state appropriate sufficient resources for industrialisation without prompting a flight of capital, thereby endangering access to the surplus that mining was able to make available. This is not to suggest that a greater harmony between economic and political interests would have sufficed to have enhanced South Africa's industrialisation. Such counterfactual assumptions presume transformed economic and social conditions under which conflicts would have been resolved. Firmer political support for mining might well have prompted it to have drained the economy even more of the surpluses that it generated and transferred abroad.

However, the purpose of Chapter 6 is not so much to speculate on what might have been. It seeks to set the scene for the following examination of post-war developments where, with the election of the National Party in 1948, the disjuncture between economic and political power appeared to have been considerably *sharpened*. Yet significantly the erosion of the disjuncture between economic and political power, between English and Afrikaner, has today become so much a feature of the past that its passing is almost unacknowledged. While a standard point of reference for economic, political, social and ideological commentary on the pre-1948 period, the issue has nowhere near the same degree of prominence today, especially concerning economic issues. No doubt this reflects a shift of attention from conflict over the formation of apartheid policies within the white community to conflict over their abolition. Equally, it reflects not the passing of distinctions between Afrikaner and English capitals but their supersession by the dominance of large-scale over small-scale capital and the interpenetration of ownership and interests between large-scale Afrikaner and English capitals.

If, then, the analyses of the inter-war and the contemporary period are correct, an analytical conundrum is created in terms of the post-war transition from one to the other. What were the historical processes by which the economic and political disjunctures of the inter-war period were eroded rather than sharpened? What impact did they have on the economy and on industrialisation in particular? In order to answer these questions, it is necessary to identify both some continuities with the past and some breaks. The apartheid labour system continued to serve as the major form of exploitation, although it did not remain unchanging. Commercial, white agriculture continued to receive substantial state support and subsidy, although the share of the sector in the economy has declined substantially.

On the other hand, the process of change within the capitalist class is shown to have exhibited three overlapping phases in what is essentially a history of the creation and empowerment of large-scale Afrikaner capital, its interpenetration with English capital and, ultimately, their combined collaboration through the state. The first phase in the 1950s witnessed the state's successful encouragement of the development of large-scale Afrikaner finance capital. The second phase (the 1960s) witnessed the interpenetration of large-scale Afrikaner finance capital into mining, with the active collaboration of both the state and mining capital itself. As a result, there was by the 1970s no longer a political obstacle within the capitalist class to the adoption of a concerted economic strategy on the part of the state.

Indeed, one was adopted. But economic conditions had changed, both through the collapse of the Bretton Woods system and the associated rise in the price of gold, as well as through the oil shock which similarly enhanced all energy prices. Consequently, the state and private capital drew upon policies to strengthen the MEC in its core activities. Thus, the third phase, which emerged in the 1970s, consolidated the collaboration between MEC capital and the state with extensive, if not comprehensive, co-ordinated polices for the economy emerging for the first time in South Africa's history. They were directed at the MEC through the expansion of public and private investment to promote mineral, heavy chemical and energy production, both for domestic and foreign markets.

By the 1980s, both the boost to core MEC activities was eroded and the apartheid system as a whole was in crisis. With increasing sanctions, disinvestment and labour and social unrest, it is hardly surprising that a coherent industrial strategy continued to remain far off the agenda. These adverse conditions might be considered sufficient reason but they were reinforced by the mode of operation of the economy, particularly of its previously developed financial system, this being geared more to speculation than to long-term provision of investment finance to industry. Further, the policy priority of the financial system has been oriented around macroeconomic objectives rather than those of industrial development.

This account of the development of South African industry in the post-war period is elaborated in detail in Chapter 7 and is complemented by two further chapters. Chapter 8 concentrates on the three main instruments of industrial policy that have been employed: the creation of state corporations and their joint ventures with private capital; the extensive use of tariffs; and industrial decentralisation. The conduct of these industrial policies is traced and shown to have been mediated by the role of the MEC as a system of accumulation, in particular by eroding the disjuncture between English and Afrikaner capital that was the economy's inheritance from the inter-war period. Although the MEC's impact has differed over time and across sectors, it has effectively led to policies which both supported its core sectors and precluded the adoption of other industrial policies of diversification away from economic dependence on South Africa's resource base. This was despite numerous recommendations to the contrary by official Commissions of Inquiry into industrial performance. Further, it is demonstrated that the industrial policies that were actually pursued, particularly by the two key institutions of the Industrial Development Corporation (IDC) and the Board of Trade and Industries (BTI), followed a separate path from that of promoting industrialisation.

In reviewing past debates over industrialisation and industrial policy, Chapter 9 considers how these have changed in parallel with more general shifts in the theory of industrialisation and development. In addition, it shows how the themes of the debates and their interpretations of industrialisation have remained remarkably unchanged, these often being resurrected from time to time. The rhythm of the debate is revealed and is shown to have been based on false perceptions of the patterns of industrialisation and on a partial, even false, recognition of how industrial policy has been adopted and implemented in practice. Two specific examples are used to illustrate this. First, the commonly accepted past and prospective trajectory of import-substituting industrialisation (ISI) (backward from consumption goods to intermediate and then capital goods) is shown to be contrary to the actual form taken by post-war industrialisation in South Africa, as in fact it ran in the opposite direction. Secondly, reflecting earlier themes, a false analytical dichotomy has been drawn between mining and manufacturing activities, masking the evolution of the MEC that straddles both.

In Part IV there is a single chapter drawing together the implications of our research in two different respects. First, our analysis of the MEC has, beyond identifying it, primarily focused upon its impact upon South Africa's industrialisation. But as a system of accumulation, the MEC has had a pervasive effect on almost every aspect of the economy, whether directly or indirectly. Consequently, we briefly point to further areas of research that might be conducted or revised in the light of our MEC-led historiography. These include the South African 'military-industrial complex', the structure and functioning of labour markets, the character of research and development, privatisation and the role of specific sectors such as agro-industry and capital goods.

Secondly, we employ our analysis of the MEC less as a means of making policy proposals and more as a way of highlighting the policy and strategic issues that need to be addressed. In particular, we place the goals of meeting basic needs at the forefront, alongside the peculiar economic structure attached to the MEC. While identifying the scope for substantial progress on the basis of the economy's existing strengths, we are also mindful that policy proposals must stand the test of being rooted in the productive capacities as they currently exist and are organised, together with the political capacity to carry them out. Indeed, the control and exercise of state power is liable to be of central importance in the future as in the past and will depend upon a conflict between the interests attached to different classes, some of which are still in the process of formation.

While this might all seem to be overly abstract and uncontroversial, it is remarkable how much it has been overlooked in practice. Too often policy stances have been and continue to be formulated on the basis of perspectives which, however appropriate these were originally, have been developed for other countries or contexts. This is not simply a matter of World Bank and IMF laissez-faire dogma, possibly the easiest example to display, but is also true of other approaches, such as that of the flec-spec strategies associated with the Industrial Strategy Project (ISP) research programme. Consequently, we critically assess the analytical foundations of this particular strategy as a typical case in which policy is both unrooted in the material realities of the South African economy and fails to address adequately the implications of its proposals for the formation of classes and the representation of their interests.

It is thus our intention that this book performs a number of different functions. First and foremost, it is the presentation of the results and implications of detailed and wide-ranging academic research on both the history and the current dynamic of the South African economy. Secondly, we hope that it presents this research so that as much of it as possible falls within the range of understanding of those with an informed knowledge of economic principles and the basic contours of South African society. Thirdly, it seeks to assess the more general theoretical arguments involved in the propositions that we and others have posited. In this respect, it is intended that the book can in part serve as a text both of political economy and of the political economy of South Africa. For this reason we have tried to make each chapter as self-contained as possible, even if with some cross-referencing and at the expense of limited repetition, so that particular topics can be studied in isolation from others as required.

Finally, we hope to have contributed to the policy debate, not in the sense of proposing a blue-print for South Africa which would inevitably be rendered redundant before it had appeared in print but, rather in laying out strategic alternatives and how they relate to the shifting balance of economic and political power.

This is an ambitious set of tasks and we do not doubt that we have been deficient both in the scope and depth of what we have covered. But we will be more than satisfied if we succeed in initiating further thought and debate, whether it supports or challenges the framework of analysis that we have proposed and which places the MEC at the centre of South Africa's political economy.

Part I. LINKAGES, AGENCIES AND THE STATE

2

ASIAN MIRACLES: LESSONS
FOR SOUTH AFRICA

The main substance of this chapter is a discussion of South Korea's industrialisation.[1] This topic might be thought to sit uncomfortably within a book predominantly concerned with the South African economy. But the intention is to bring to the fore a number of methodological issues arising from the study of South Korea that have proved central in our investigation of economic and political change. At the general level, it is suggested that development and theories of it can be understood in terms of linkages and agencies, as elaborated in the following section. We will first examine this approach for its potential for comparative analysis of relevance to South Africa, before moving on to a detailed consideration of South Korea. An array of factors and arguments are assembled, of which the full significance and interaction should emerge later.

Much more attention has been paid to highlighting the linkages underlying South Korea's economic success than to the agencies that have brought them about, except that the state has often been seen as a principal instigator of success. This in part reflects the literature's wish to confront the World Bank's world view of the primacy of the role to be played by market forces, in that the South Korean state's interventions are shown to have been decisive for its industrialisation. A corollary of the state versus market approach has been to reinforce the idea of the autonomy of the state, both as a theoretical possibility and as a precondition for developmental success for latecomers. The following chapter disputes this stance and argues for a theory of the state that locates its policies in terms of the complex outcome of the class interests that act upon it and which in turn lead to the strengthening, weakening and even transformation of the underlying class structure. This is particularly important in understanding the evolution of industrial and other economic policy and its impact.

---

[1] This chapter is heavily based on Fine (1992a), on which Chris Edwards and anonymous referees made valuable suggestions.

The relevance of all this for the South African economy follows from parallel, if distinct, deficiencies within studies of its industrialisation. It is rare to find balanced treatments of the impact of both linkages and agencies upon the formulation and implementation of policy. Emphasis is usually upon one at the expense of the other. In addition, the understanding of industrial policy and its associated linkages has been confined to too narrow a plane, comprised predominantly of protection and state enterprise, while insufficient attention has been paid to detail in the differences across sectors when exploring the policies of the state in acting as an economic agency. The misunderstandings or incomplete understandings that result for the inter-war period are outlined in Chapter 6. These deficiencies are no less significant in many assessments of the subsequent path and future prospects of the South African economy, as detailed and, hopefully, at least partially remedied in much of the remainder of this book.

Consequently, the richness of the detail to be found in studies, whatever their deficiencies, of the South Korean economy serves as a lesson for those who seek to address the South African economy. The purpose is not to set South Korea as a standard from which South Africa has diverged or which it could emulate but to highlight some of the theoretical and empirical elements involved in understanding economic change. We begin, then, with the the problem of how to approach the peculiarities of the South African economy.

Those wishing to understand the workings of the South African economy are faced with the problem of how to proceed methodologically. Perhaps more than for any other economy, the difficulty is posed of combining abstract or general propositions and theoretical insights with those that are appropriate to the apparent uniqueness of the apartheid system. The economics of racism has always proved especially elusive, possibly because of its interdisciplinary demands. In the context of South Africa, it cannot be ignored or glossed over.

The relationship between abstract theory and empirical application is not unique to the study of South Africa. But the virulent form taken by its racism within the bounds of a predominantly capitalist economy has cast considerable doubt on the simple expedient of examining South Africa's development in terms of hypotheses derived from ready-made analytical frameworks. Yet the alternative extreme of granting casual and conceptual priority to racial categories is equally unpalatable because of its insensitivity to the economic powers and processes that are not defined exclusively in racial terms. This is true not only of the relations between the two great classes of capital and labour but also of the relations within these classes. Different fractions of the capitalist and labouring classes may be divided by material interests, comprising factors other than those synonymous with race.

Again, just as for race and the economy, the relationship between class and race and the analytical problems that it poses is not unique to South Africa. But it has occupied the central stage both in the political economy and the historiography of apartheid even as these have gone through a number of stages.[2] There has been a major analytical divide between the liberal and revisionist traditions. The first, wedded to a more or less well-defined theory of capitalist development or modernisation, perceives labour market and other restrictions as an obstacle to economic progress. Consequently, such obstacles will inevitably be eroded as the forward momentum and rationale of economic, predominantly market, forces roll over what would otherwise increasingly become politically and socially anomalous structures and vested interests. The virtue of the alternative, Marxist revisionism has been to emphasise how inequality in production relations before the market is entered has formed part and parcel of capitalism, even if such inequality is made all too transparent by the economic conditions of the apartheid system, where property relations have been explicitly racially exclusive. Far from holding back the economy, this system is perceived positively to have promoted profitability and accumulation by its extreme forms of exploitation.

As has been pointed out all too frequently, the distance between these two positions is enormous both in methodology and in conclusion, but they also have a common thread in counterposing the relative priority of race and class against the performance of the economy. In this respect, they are like two sides of a well-worn coin which, as is well-known, drives the better out of circulation – at least until it is no longer acceptable currency. Till recently, preoccupation with the race-class dichotomy has tended to preclude other, more sophisticated approaches to the relationship between South African capitalism and apartheid:[3]

> When defined in antithesis to this liberal stance, revisionism amounts to a simple reversal of the purportedly liberal priorities: class now has primacy over race, and segregation and apartheid are seen as functional, rather than dysfunctional, to the development of South African capitalism. (Posel 1983 p. 6)

The most apt testimony, possibly testament, to this observation is Lipton's (1986) culminating contribution to the liberal tradition, into which it falls mainly by virtue of its sympathy with the idea of the ultimate efficacy and triumph of market forces. For her work might be more

---

[2] Exploring South Africa's own historiography has proved an extremely popular pastime. See for example, Bozzoli and Delius (1990), Cell (1982), Mabin (1986), Marks (1986), Marks and Rathbone (eds) (1982), Morris (1987), Murray (1982; 1988), Saunders (1988a; 1988b), Smith (1988), Wright (1977)

[3] See also Bonner *et al.* (eds) (1993)

accurately described as a synthesis between the two schools, providing an examination of the interests of different classes/strata which are often realised at the expense of one another's and of overall economic efficiency.[4] In short, the liberal view of apartheid is one that sees it as a distortion from an ideal, whether laissez-faire, welfare or modernising capitalism. By contrast Marxism views apartheid as an extreme example of conformity to the capitalist system of exploitation. In many respects, the substance of the two analyses need not differ too much from one another; they are separated more by way of their standards of comparison.

Whatever its limitations, the race-class debate has inevitably been dependent for its stimulus on the specificity of South African society. This has not, however, been the only influence on intellectual developments. New approaches and objects of analysis have followed in response both to the unfolding of internal events and according to the intellectual fashions of the outside world. Thus, revisionism in different ways appropriated the insights of the various strands of the structural Marxism of the 1960s onwards, such as its articulation of modes of production at the economic level and to hegemony and power blocs at the political level. Such fashions have subsequently given way to the new social history, which has drawn its inspiration from the work of E.P. Thompson, in which rural struggles have figured prominently as case studies. Here there is considerable antipathy to reductionism, functionalism, structuralism and many other-isms. Instead is offered rich empirical detail and an emphasis on the many-sided making of history in terms both of the different aspects of struggle and participants in it. But there is precious little explicit theory.

In response to the more recent gathering crisis of the apartheid regime, much attention has been shifted to explaining this turn of events. Ironically, this is possibly a greater problem for what had been the triumphant Marxists revisionists than for the predominantly vanquished liberals, given their respective positions on the functionality of apartheid for South African capitalism. Neatly illustrating the point of the dual dependence of South African intellectual development on internal events and external theory, Gelb's (1991) collection marries French regulation theory, with its notions of modes, social structures and regimes of accumulation, to an explanation of the crisis of the South African economy: the collapse of 'racist Fordism'.[5]

However, any analytical stance organised around explaining the crisis of apartheid has already been rendered redundant to some extent by the pace of internal events. It is too backward-looking. Now there is less

---

[4] For an illustration of how such issues can be accommodated within the framework of neoclassical economics, see Lundahl (1992).

[5] Regulation theory originated in the Marxist work of Aglietta (1979). It has since become increasingly eclectic. For a critique, see Brenner and Glick (1991) and Mavroudeas (1990).

emphasis upon the causes of the current crisis and more upon the shape of future economic policy and developments in a post-apartheid society. It is no longer enough to look back and see how what was favourable to accumulation came to be unfavourable; it is also necessary to see how conditions can be made conducive to economic growth once again, albeit in serving very different needs and constituencies. Policy considerations, rather than class or other struggles and laws of development, have now become the leading edge along the analytical cutting tools.[6]

These opening remarks are critical but not dismissive of past contributions. We accept that scholarship is necessarily influenced and biased by current events and intellectual fashions. It is a product of its time and milieu and should be recognised and assessed as such. Indeed, we are only too well aware of and indeed welcome the dependence of our own analysis on the wish to confront the problems of the transition from the apartheid economy. We do so through a critical dialogue not only with past analyses of the South African economy but also through insights gained from political economy more generally and from comparative experience. The South Korean experience offers us that opportunity at this point in our study. Other chapters draw on other comparative experience and lessons from political economy.

It is also our intention to persuade the reader of the importance of the considerations that we bring to bear, even if the theoretical framework we adopt is not fully accepted. Our methodology for doing so is informed by the idea of economic development as dependent upon the interaction between linkages and agencies and this provides a central if, at times, implicit thread throughout this book. As such, any originality does not derive from the use of these concepts, which have been commonplace in development economics. However, they have been little used explicitly in analyses of the South African economy. For example, the race-class debate is primarily concerned with agency, whether one or the other or some combination of the two has been instrumental in determining and benefitting from the path of the economy.

In addition, both liberals and revisionists have referred to the disjunctures between economic and political power, that different sections of the workforce or of capital have unduly influenced state policy. For example, in the inter-war period, Afrikaners (whether white farmers, industrialists or various sections of the white workforce) are perceived to have displaced imperial capital in the exercise of political power. But these and other propositions concerning classes and strata, certainly within a historical

---

[6] This subordination of analysis to the dictates of policy needs carries certain dangers with it, especially when policy is technically conceived in terms of economic stability. It tends to undermine the representation of certain interest groups, usually the impoverished, and to neglect confrontation with previously developed analytical positions.

context, have only been pursued to a limited extent in detailing economic outcomes. There have been frequent and broad references to industrialisation, and the mining and agricultural sectors are perceived to have been of particular importance. But these particular sectors serve primarily as the terrain on which different economic interests are played out; they only have breathed a limited life of their own. In Marxist terms, more attention has been devoted to the social relations of production than to the forces of production.

Such observations are much less germane to the most recent literature concerning the crisis of the apartheid economy, which is more pre-occupied with economic linkages. In particular, emphasis is placed upon the inability of the economy to expand without sucking in imports of intermediate and capital goods, thereby inevitably resulting in balance of payments problems. The economy's weakness is perceived in terms of lack of productive capacity in goods other than at the extremes of primary production and final consumption goods, the latter, themselves, having been heavily protected.

Interestingly, such diagnoses are divorced from the previous considerations of the disjuncture between economic and political power.[7] Much greater emphasis is placed on the economic and social crisis of apartheid, although this may be complemented by reference to the constraints on economic performance imposed by labour market imperfections and low levels of skills, education and training amongst the black workforce. Nonetheless, the focus of most recent literature is primarily, if often implicitly, upon the poorly developed linkages in the current South African economy and less upon the exercise of economic power through agencies, even if there is an underlying motif that, in so far as these are attached to the apartheid system, they are increasingly moribund.

In short, literature on the South African economy has often proved to be one-sided, either emphasising historically the exercise of particular economic interests or pointing to weaknesses in the economic structure. In our own work, we have sought to strike a balance between these two aspects and to incorporate and add to the insights of the existing literature through the following elements. First, despite claims that South Africa has industrialised, the economy remains heavily dependent upon core activities organised around minerals and energy. Secondly, the role of the state is a crucial factor in economic development and, thirdly, this is particularly so for the formation and implementation of industrial policy. Fourthly, it is necessary to encompass a greater level and breadth of empirical detail, not least because the interaction of different economic

---

[7] This is sharply illustrated in the evolution of the work, for example, of Kaplan (1977 and 1990).

interests necessarily expresses itself unevenly, in a variety of ways and with a variety of effects.

Further, conflicts within the capitalist class have been more prominent in discussion of the inter-war and, to a lesser extent, of the immediate post-war period. This is because of primary interest for the earlier period in the determinants of apartheid policies and whether the particular forms of oppression of the black majority were subject to, and hence influenced by, conflicts between different sections of capital or whether they were due to the interests of white labour or to non-economic factors, such as the political ideology of racial superiority. Such divisions within the capitalist class have been less prominent in the examination of the more recent period. This corresponds to the previously observed shift in emphasis to the economic weaknesses of the present as opposed to the structure of economic interests when examining the past. In our view, there is a deeper rationale underlying this shift of emphasis, reflecting the erosion of the disjuncture that existed between (imperial) economic power and (Afrikaner) political power in the inter-war period.[8] A compromise had long had to be forged between different fractions of capital, despite the presence of fundamental conflicts of interests. Accordingly, the history of the South African economy can in part be understood as the simultaneity of two processes: a shifting and complex short term resolution of conflicts of capitalists' interests and a longer-term integration and interpenetration of those capitals as they became increasingly large-scale and diversified. In both processes, the state has played a central, mediating role.

The adoption of these analytical starting points is, however, the outcome of a process of investigation involving a continuing confrontation between existing studies of the South African economy, various elements of political economy and comparative experience. For the latter, a critical assessment of some of the literature on South Korea provides the means for developing analysis based on linkages and agencies. But before turning to the specific literature on South Korea, it is worthwhile exploring the notion of linkages and agencies themselves in slightly more detail.

Linkages and agencies

The term linkage is used broadly and informally, focusing on the impact of one or more economic variables upon others, usually through time. Naturally, forward and backward linkages, upstream and downstream activity, immediately spring to mind. But this is to confine linkages to the input-output table of technical coefficients. It could equally apply to

---

[8] It has been standard in the literature, especially of the pre-war period, to use a terminology involving, for example, the economic and political 'disjunctures' between 'imperial' and 'Afrikaner' interests. For the moment we comply without expressing reservations.

broader issues of how production gives rise to the introduction of new technology or restructuring between regions or sections of the economy, between town and country or formal and informal sectors, for example.[9] Stewart and Ghani (1991) see externalities as a particular type of linkage, of which environmental effects and the dynamics of technical change are significant examples, potentially negative and positive, respectively. They look for such linkages as externalities in the semi-conductor industry of the United States and in the relationship between agriculture and industry in the Punjab. A more general approach is taken by Sender and Smith (1986), drawing upon Hirschmann's (1977) wider definition of linkages:[10] 'A linkage exists whenever an ongoing activity gives rise to economic or other pressures that lead to the taking up of a new activity.' (p. 10) They emphasise transport, for example, as part of a developmental process oriented towards and providing infrastructure for exports. More generally, they point to a 'complex array of linkages which resulted from the activity of producing export commodities on a massively expanded scale.' (p. 9)

Hirschmann's own generalisation of the notion of linkages focuses on those derived from the production, consumption and fiscal opportunities for the state to generate and employ revenue, especially out of 'enclave capital', presumed to be more readily taxed in view of its limited political leverage. He points to the significance of not only those linkages associated with static input-output tables but also those induced dynamically through ISI, especially for 'staples'.

However, in pushing forward the analytical role of linkages, Hirschmann is forced to press against the boundaries of their explanatory scope and where he steps over those frontiers, he is subject to inconsistency. At one point, he characterises his contribution as purely heuristic and one in which he seeks to avoid being overly deterministic (p. 89 and p. 98 respectively). Yet at other times, he argues as if the mere presence of potential linkages suffices to realise them.[11] Specifically:

[9] For a penetrating analysis of the relationship between agriculture and industry in the context of development which draws upon a number of case studies, see Karshenas (1995). One of the main pre-occupations in this context – the transfer of surplus from agriculture to industry as a resource for investment – has been entirely absent in consideration of South Africa, so much is it taken for granted that mining takes on this role.

[10] Hirschmann's own definition is given as follows:
Development is essentially the record of how one thing leads to another, and linkages are that record...They focus on certain characteristics inherent in the productive activities already in process at a certain time. These ongoing activities, because of their characteristics, push or, more modestly, invite some operators to take up new activities. Whenever that is the case, a linkage exists between the ongoing and the new activity (p. 80).
Note that there is already a tension here discussed below between 'push' and 'invite': are agencies spontaneous or automatic in the presence of linkages?

[11] This occurs more or less favourably according to their nature, since different linkages

As an economist, I preferred to simply assume an insufficiency of entrepreneurial motivation and then to systematically search for such constellations of productive forces as would move private or public decision makers to 'do something' through special pressures that are more compelling than those that are expected to move the rational decision maker or received economic theory. (p. 70)

Despite the use by Hirschmann of a much wider motivational and causal calculus than that of neoclassical economics, which is restricted to utility and profit maximisation, it remains the case that the supply of appropriate linkages appears to call forth a corresponding supply of agencies to implement them, much as in Say's Law, supply creates its own demand. This is explicit in some instances, as in the quotation above; it is implicit in other instances in the presumption that the demand for infrastructure as a public good tends to induce its provision by the state.

In pressing the study of linkages to their limits, Hirschmann increasingly bumps up against the problem of explaining what are the mechanisms by which linkages do or do not materialise. This issue is specifically addressed by Smith and Sender, who are concerned with the classes that forge linkages and how class interests are brought to bear. Class is an example of agency, although the notion is less well-developed in orthodox economics than in the disciplines of the sociology and politics of development.[12]

More generally, the atomised, optimising individual is the fundamental agency within neoclassical economics, even though the terms capital, labour and land may be generically employed as representative of aggregated classes of agents. Macro-behaviour is analysed as a complex system of supplies and demands, simultaneously harmonised more or less efficiently through the linkages provided by market forces, depending upon the presence of natural or artificial market imperfections. Here, both the notions of linkage and agency are, in their different ways, extremely simple. Agency is limited in scope, behaviourally through optimisation and substantively through individuals. Linkage as demand and supply is broad in scope, potentially encompassing the whole economy in a general equilibrium system, but it is shallow in analytical depth. On the other hand, orthodox Keynesianism tends to have an equally shallow view of agency, but linkage is primarily felt through the transmission of aggregate effective demand, most notably in the multiplier effect.

A particularly common form taken by agency is in institutional analysis. Chandler (1990) provides a striking example in his comparative

---

may be more or less compatible or balanced with one another. This perspective reveals a degree of technical determinism in Hirschmann's work.

[12] But see Hindness (1987) for the case against class or agency.

study of corporate performance. For whereas linkages are explicitly forged as a consequence of economies of scale and scope, agency is a consequence of the managerial organisation of the firm. Hirschmann offers other instances, although his primary concern is with linkages. Dependency theory as a theory of underdevelopment is criticised for too one-sidedly deploying the negative impact of core-periphery relations but equally, surplus transfer and appropriation requires a role for agencies along the chain of imperialism. And Marxist theory is sympathetically interpreted, accurately or not, as integrating the forces (linkages) and class (agencies) relations of production.

What these examples across a diverse range of schools of economic thought are intended to illustrate is that any economic analysis typically has, at least implicitly, three components. There is the role of linkages and of agencies, together with a theory that unites them. The relative emphasis placed on linkages and agencies is often uneven. For example, a popular explanation for Britain's poor economic performance of late is the role of the City: it is seen as an agency with interests that predominate over those of others and, in particular, at the expense of domestic industry.[13] Here an identification is made of *who* is responsible but *how* is often left unexplored. Similar arguments have been made for the South African economy, given its highly developed financial system.[14] On the other hand, the equally popular view of Britain's weakness through de-industrialisation and constraints on growth through balance of payments deficits is strong on the linkage side (from trade to economic performance) but relatively silent on the agencies and interests involved.[15] Again, there is a parallel with the South African economy, although the balance of trade problems arise out of the imports of capital and intermediate rather than consumption goods.

Consequently, there is a case for examining the content of different analyses for their use of linkages and agencies, in part to uncover the extent to which they have explained both the how and the who of economic change. This approach will be adopted here to examine some of the research on South Korea, since it both illustrates the linkage-agency (or, in our shorthand, 'linkagency') approach and calls forth issues of relevance for our subsequent analysis of the South African economy. Despite differences of focus and theoretical framework, much of the recent literature has shared a number of common features. First, it has rejected the explanation of South Korean success based on the virtues of

---

[13] This is part of an explanation put forward by Fine and Harris (1985) for Britain's industrial weakness, although they complement it by examining the role of other agencies and by the use of greater detail in specific sectoral studies.

[14] See Chapters 7-9 for further discussion.

[15] See Singh (1977).

purely market-led progress. Secondly, in doing so, it has highlighted a number of economic linkages in the growth process. Thirdly, these linkages are forged primarily or with heavy influence through the agency of the state. This, however, leaves unresolved the relationship between the state and the classes or other interests and agencies that it represents other than to see some of these as advantaged but, paradoxically, over-ruled by the autonomous state. This is a matter taken up in the next chapter, where the role of the state and of industrial policy is considered. In short, the literature proves to be strong in identifying both economic linkages and, by way of reaction against the laissez-faire orthodoxy, the agency of the state in implementing them. However, this somewhat unsatisfactorily leaves the state as an agency independent of or at least able to free itself from class interests, a condition taken as necessary for the adoption of developmentally successful policies.

As should be apparent, our use of the linkagency approach is primarily heuristic in the first instance. The patterns of development or the content of an economic or other form of analysis can be examined within this framework without explicitly favouring one school of economics or political economy. The approach is equally compatible with a variety of methodologies, with atomised individualism at one extreme, as in neoclassical economics and Marxist or other emphasis on class relations and interests at the other. Our own position favours the latter methodology, although it is anticipated that the less narrowly focused linkagency perspective will still prove useful or challenging to those who are not or cannot be persuaded of the virtues of our stance.

Nonetheless, we do not here attempt to justify our more general methodology that economic development can only be satisfactorily ad-dressed analytically through a focus upon social forces, relations and interests. Essentially, dispute over this issue is a corollary of the debate over the meaning and significance of (social) structure and agency. In particular, those committed to methodological individualism deny the possibility that agency can be concretely examined or that the scope of freedom for individual agency is unduly restricted by the imposition of propositions derived from social structures or agencies. Callinicos (1987), for example, has reviewed these arguments in depth and has convincingly shown a commitment to social theory does not preclude analysis of the role of individual agency. Indeed, social theory is necessary to explore the constraints and influences upon the horizons within which the individual roams.

More important for our purposes is to point to the substitution of linkage for structure in the concepts employed. This is more than a matter of terminological convenience, for the notion of a structure inevitably gives rise to the understanding of something as fixed and rigid around which movement takes place. By contrast, the notion of linkage is intended to suggest a relationship and movement between structures which are themselves fluid. It is more dynamic in content.

Perhaps an example will help. Most economic theories recognise the distinction between market and non-market activity, even if only implicitly. There is the separation between the spheres of production and circulation in Marxist theory as opposed to the internalisation of transactions costs in the Coasian theory of why the firm exists at the expense of the market. Within Marxist theory, the economic *structure* is one which is essential for the functioning of capitalism, in order that profit can emerge in production and be realised through exchange. The positing of this structure, however, does not imply an automatic nor a fixed content within the two structures and between them. This is most evident either from periods of rapid growth or from their interruption through crises and stagnation. On the other hand, the neoclassical theory of the firm and the more general treatment of market and non-market activity as constituting essentially equivalent arenas of optimising behaviour, as in the new household economics, for example,[16] is liable ultimately to reduce structures to aggregate atomised individualism because of the absence of an effective dynamic within and between structures.

In short, this abstract digression has sought to have enriched the notion of linkage and to have attached it to a content that includes more than social structures and the dynamics within and between them. The significance for this and economic development, in which societies change their character over time, should be transparent.

Linkages. The role of linkages in economic development can be studied in the context of the success of the Asian newly industrialised countries (NICs) and of South Korea in particular.[17] The source of South Korea's success is a contested ideological terrain, although the contest in the academic arena has become extremely one-sided. From one corner the World Bank claims that the NICs' growth and industrialisation is a triumph of free enterprise and of an orientation towards export growth at world prices rather than the result of a subsidised and protected domestic market. Underlying this is a static analysis around allocative efficiency. However, as it can hardly explain sustained growth at a higher rate, it tends

---

[16] See Fine (1992b) for a critique and, in this context, how the dynamic of structures is related to the social forces that act upon them.

[17] As will be clear, the following references in particular have been pillaged: Alam (1989), Amsden (1989), Deyo (ed.) (1987a) and Lee and Yamazawa (eds) (1990). See also Cho and Kim (eds) (1991), Enos and Park (1988) and the special issue of *World Development* (1988, issue 1). Usually page references will be given only for quotes. For an early account raising many of the themes taken up by later writers, see Jones and Sakong (1980) and Mason *et al.* (1980). For a more recent emphasis on the role of the state, see Kawakami (1992).

to be supplemented by appeals to the dynamic impact of the market, especially where it is biased by policy towards exports. Thus there is presumed to be greater potential for economies of scale and scope, and hence for capacity utilisation, by entering the world market, the elimination of featherbedding in domestic industry and the easing of foreign exchange constraints. This is seen in Alam's (p. 35) critical assessment of Krueger (1981; 1984). In the free-marketeers' neat combination of neoclassical and neo-Austrian views, then, there are fairly simple and immediate linkages between exports (rather than import-substitution) and growth with the agents of growth perceived to be those filling and creating the opportunities previously occupied or pre-empted by the 'rent-seeking' activity generated by state economic intervention.[18]

In the opposite corner to the World Bank's stance are those who collectively comprising an overwhelming intellectual momentum, totally reject not only this explanation but also the implied empirical account of the NICs' economic history. For Alam

> The analysis presented here provides no support for the frequently voiced contention that the superiority of neoclassical policies is demonstrated by the success of the EO [export-oriented] regime in countries like Korea. The evidence accumulated here on the interventionist character of Korean policies prevents us from taking this claim seriously. Instead, a much more convincing account of Korea's growth record would proceed in terms of the dynamic advantages that flowed from its interventionist policies. (p. 49)

Alam also notes that the degree of state intervention in practice is liable to be much the same under export-orientation as under import-substitution. Although the overall balance between these two strategies appears to have swung towards the former in recent years, this conceals continuing subsidies and orientation to the domestic market and production in many sectors.[19] Alam (p. 34) finds that for effective subsidy rates (ESRs) in South Korea:[20]

---

[18] Nonetheless, these two schools of thought are fundamentally incompatible with one another, one seeking the removal of market imperfections and the creation of perfect competition for static efficiency, the other the removal of obstacles to freedom (of capital) within the market even at the expense of monopolisation in order to guarantee dynamic efficiency. For a critical assessment in the context of the economics of the 'New Right', see Fine and Harris (1987).

[19] And, as Luedde-Neurath (1986) emphasises, trade liberalisation has not been general but oriented to cheapening imports that can contribute directly or indirectly to export drives.

[20] See also Wade (1990, p. 308). Predominantly concerned with Taiwan, Wade's notion of 'governing the market' seeks a synthesis between market-led and government-led approaches, in which industrial policy by sector induces certain industries to be successfully developed through the market.

A similar ranking of industries was observed in 1978 [as 1968], with the highest incentive rates accorded to import competing industries (34.8), followed by export-and-import competing (22.4), exporting (6.2), and non-import-competing industries (– 12.4). The dispersion of incentive rates is even more impressive when we take a more disaggregated look at the industries. In 1968 there were 23 industries (out of 150) whose ESRs exceeded 100 per cent. The dispersion of incentive rates across major groups was even greater in 1978 than in 1968... With the exception of agriculture, the pattern of effective incentive rates across industries reveals a general bias toward infant industries in intermediates, and consumer and producer durables.

Much to the chagrin of those who propose reliance on market forces to get the prices right, this implies that state intervention did much to get them wrong. Moreover, support to industry is multi-faceted and cannot be reduced to trade and subsidy policy alone.[21] For Auty (1991):

> Although the South Korean planners pursued the outward-oriented trade policy favoured by agencies like the World Bank, they also intervened strongly to create competitive advantage. Their policy has been accurately defined as dual industrial development...in which import substitution industrialization proceeds alongside export promotion. The Korean government intervened to create competitive advantage in HCI [heavy and chemical industries] via tariff protection, infrastructure provision and, most important, cheap finance. (p. 18)

It is very important to recognise how much of the literature takes as its starting point a critical assessment of the laissez-faire orthodoxy.[22] This leads to the adoption of an alternative approach which emphasises how NICs have historically depended and continue to depend upon state economic intervention. The role of the state as an agency will be examined later in this chapter, as well as in the next.

Initially, consider the economic linkages that are implied. First, the role of trade and the relative emphasis on generating growth through domestic as opposed to export markets has been central. Japan is often taken as the

---

[21] Alam points to preferential interest rates, export targeting, wastage allowances for exports, investment rationing and the influence of public investment. See also Luedde-Neurath (1985), who details with references the role of industrial policy, financial policy and price controls.

[22] See Luedde-Neurath (1986, p. 23), van Liemt (1988, p. 50), Wade (1985). Recognising the significance of and need for state intervention is of course possible within neoclassical theory in the presence of market failure. This can be perceived to be informational as when two infant industries with scale economies need to be established together because of reciprocal externalities. See Pack and Westphal (1986, p. 117). H. Evans (1990, p. 47) reasonably claims, however, that state economic intervention is more than 'a clearing house for information and technology in the face of market failure'.

early-comer in Asian development, both for the purposes of emulation as well as for cross-country comparison. Its early post-war growth was not export-led[23] and its heavily protected domestic market is a well-known and continuing bone of contention now that its exports have become so crucial and competitive. Thus, the preference of the World Bank orthodoxy for export-led growth is found to be totally misplaced on the basis of past experience of success. As C. Lee (1990) concludes:

> The conventional characterization of Japanese development as export-led growth is incorrect. It is domestic demand...that has driven the growth of the Japanese economy...Japan has followed the flying geese pattern of successive stages of trade and production: the introduction of a new product through import, then import-substituting production, and the eventual export of the product.

For South Korea, Alam argues growth passed from import-substitution to export orientation between 1955–63 and 1963–73. This transition was achieved through sectorally sensitive and detailed trade targets linking permitted imports to domestic manufacturing performance and promoted exports; controls on imports, despite some liberalisation, have continued into the latter phase.[24] In terms of the flying geese strategy, or linkage through broadening diversification, C. Lee (p. 186) finds: 'This pattern is also observed in Korea. But Korea has a much higher import and export dependency, as it has a smaller domestic market and has yet to develop a full-fledged capital-goods and intermediate-goods sector.' Amsden also notes the high trade dependence of the South Korean economy, with exports rising from 5 per cent to 35 per cent of GNP between the 1950s and 1980s, with import growth lagging slightly behind. This represents twice the level of trade dependence attained by Japan at a comparable stage of development.

Crucial in export performance have been the sectoral shifts involved. Typically, a linkage is forged by extending existing comparative advantage and spreading it to new sectors. Again, Japan proves instructive by way of comparison: as Kohama (p. 12) indicates, the share of textiles in exports declined from 37.5 per cent in 1955 to 3.6 per cent in 1985 while over the same period, the share accounted for by machinery rose from 16.2 per cent to 72.1 per cent. For South Korea, comparative advantage is initially identified with the export of an agricultural surplus and then with textiles. Although there is a forward linkage from cotton spinning for the latter, as Amsden notes, further linkages were not realised as diversification or economies of scope proved limited (presumably a machine manufacturing sector was required for them to materialise).

[23] See Kohama (1990).

[24] Alam also finds similar trade controls for Taiwan.

More important to South Korea has been the development of a steel industry to support both shipbuilding and shipping and, subsequently, the auto industry.[25] According to Amsden, finance and technology for steel was initially provided by the Japanese and it was supported by high levels of training, quality monitoring and dumping in export markets in phases of world recession. As a state-owned industry, subsequently privatised, it did not reside within the conglomerate system of huge corporations known as *chaebols* but paid high wages to secure jobs and with a high R&D subsidy. It served the export market indirectly via shipbuilding:[26]

> Hyundai Heavy Industries (HHI), a subsidiary of the Hyundai Group, began building its first ship, a very large crude carrier, in March 1973. Less than a decade later, HHI had become the world's largest ship-builder, with cumulative deliveries exceeding 10 million deadweight tons (DWT) by 1984. South Korea's share of world orders for new ships vied with Japan's, having reached 17.4 per cent by the mid-1980s – a 15 percentage point increase over ten years. (Amsden, p. 269)

Similarly, the electronics industry has been built up extremely rapidly without any substantial, previously existing domestic linkages:

> As late as the mid-1970s, Korea's industrial structure was dominated by textile manufacturing, and advanced technology industries were a negligible part of its industrial sector. Electronics only emerged as the dominant export industry by the end of the 1970s, while large-volume production of semi-conductors did not start until the mid-1980s. Today, Korea ranks as the world's third largest producer of micro-chips and, in 1988, its production of sophisticated electronic components, including semi-conductors, surpassed that of consumer electronics. (Suarez-Villa and Han 1990, p. 273)

Thus, export growth in South Korea has been dependent both upon forward linkages, established from a base in labour-intensive production, and success in sectors predominantly technically free of linkages to pre-existing manufacturing. Even within sectors, continued momentum has been sustained only by the renewal of spurts of innovation:

> Essentially, what has occurred in Korea's case is that several 'take-offs' have propelled electronics to the most important position among this nation's industries. Each of these take-offs has been characterized by significant changes and new learning curves in productive organiza-tion, technology, and work processes. What is remarkable is the rapid

[25] For the development of the South Korean steel industry in a global context and by comparison with the UK, see Y. Lee (1992).

[26] See also Auty's (1991) study of the South Korean steel and petrochemical industries.

succession of these takeoffs, demonstrating Korea's ability to absorb and adapt foreign technology and to change its productive structure to accommodate the needs of each new wave of industrial activities. (Suarez-Villa and Han, p. 275)

In short, in terms of the flying geese analogy, Korea seems to have enjoyed a variety of flock formations, these at times being unrelated to each other. While the initial dependence upon domestic markets and subsequent shift into export markets seems a well-established pattern, the sectoral routes and linkages by which such shifts are achieved are by no means pre-determined. But they do have to be forged and the state has played a significant role in bringing them about.

Rather than looking to inter-sectoral movements in the composition of output to explain economic success, the latter might be partially explained by reference to an economy-wide factor such as the operation of and conditions within the labour market. As heavily emphasised in the literature, the initially low level of wages helped to establish international price competitiveness, even though wage rates have risen relatively quickly in response to and in order to induce productivity increase. Between 1970 and 1984 there was an almost threefold increase in real wages:

> By comparison with English data, the following is striking: while it took English workers seventy years [from 1781 to 1851] to raise their real earnings by roughly 150 per cent, Korean manufacturing workers achieved a comparable gain in about twenty years from 1955 to 1976. In just one decade, 1969–79, real wages in Korea rose by more than 250 per cent. (Amsden, p. 197)

While manufacturing wages have been higher than for agriculture, the general dispersion of wages has been high within manufacturing, with women earning about half as much as men. So there has been the possibility of exploiting low wage female labour in the absence of adequate productivity increase to sustain international competitiveness. Clearly, conditions in the labour market reflect the role of economic agents. But this does not explain the direction taken by manufacturing nor is it free of consideration of linkages. For it is acknowledged that the supply of cheap labour has been provided by agriculture. Again Japan (perhaps Arthur Lewis's theory of surplus labour) provides the model; Hara (1990) explains that for Japanese agriculture: '...first, it provided a large amount of economic surplus through budgetary transfer (land tax) to the nonagricultural sector. Second, it contributed to industrialization by supplying cheap food. Third, it supplied the labor force necessary for industrialization.' (p. 134)

This model has to some extent been followed by South Korea.[27] Although agriculture provided the surplus population for manufacturing employment, with the share of labour in agriculture falling from 79.5 per cent to 32.3 per cent between 1962 and 1985 and agriculture's share of national income fell from 36.7 per cent to 16.3 per cent, only limited surplus has been transferred to industry. Agriculture provided a surplus for export under Japanese rule and the terms of trade turned against the countryside in the 1960s.[28] Burmeister (1990) analyses the relations between agriculture and industry as being highly articulated through state intervention.[29] High levels of fertilizer provision from the chemical sector have been crucial. However, self-sufficiency in food has not been sustained because of the precipitous decline of the young, educated, rural labour supply and the import of food from the United States.[30] Absentee landlords have become more common as dual incomes are sought from both town and countryside. As has been traditionally recognised in development economics, the shifting relationship between agriculture and industry plays a crucial role across a number of dimensions: in labour supply, food provision (with balance of payments implications), in generating a financial surplus, and in determining distribution of income and well-being (of significance to social and political stability).

In the case of finance more generally, emphasis is placed on the pervasive role of differential interest rates and credit rationing to favoured borrowers. As Alam points out, subsidised credit was extended in the 1960s not only to particular sectors but even to specific firms and projects. Paradoxically, Tajika and Yui (1990) see this as evidence of a lack of coherence in industrial policy, as finance is not made available to all capitals on equal terms, rather than as definite industrial targeting. As Choi and Lee (1990) report:

> Using the industrial development plan as its guide, the government also directly allocated financial resources. Funds were mobilized through deposit money banks and the National Investment Fund and allocated to different industries. In addition to these loans, the government provided the heavy and chemical industries with so-called 'policy loans' at a preferential low interest rate. (p. 57)

Amsden shows how this was done through borrowing from abroad to finance domestic industry: to finance investment in the heavy industries

---

[27] For discussion of the role of agriculture in promoting industry, see Karshenas (1995). His emphasis, however, is mostly upon improved performance of both broad sectors rather than transfer from one to the other.

[28] See E. Lee (1979) and also Moore (1985).

[29] See also Nam (1990).

[30] See Chung (1990) for a detailed account.

and increase its share of manufacturing from 40 per cent in 1971 to 56 per cent in 1980, South Korea employed foreign loans so that total debt rose from \$4.3 billion to \$20.5 billion. Thus, as a linkage to investment, finance has been used for targeting through the agency of the state. [31] Linkages through access to foreign technology have been part and parcel of this process.

Thus one result of state mediation in finance has been to limit the role played by direct foreign investment as an agency of growth. As Haggard and Cheng (1987) observe: 'In East Asia, in contrast to Latin America, direct foreign investment played a negligible role during the ISI phase.' (p. 87)

As its peak in 1972–6, direct foreign investment in South Korea still lay below 10 per cent of all foreign loans and investments.[32] Alam reports that only extremely limited competition has been permitted with domestic manufacturers, domestic credit and export finance have been denied to foreign firms, ownership of real estate is barred and, where these obstacles to foreign investment do not prove absolute, pressure is exerted to engage in joint ventures. Where foreign capital has been most important is in the provision of the linkage through technology transfer. Amsden points to the role of foreign technical assistance. C. Lee and Yamazawa (p. xxi) show that the weight of licensing imports have, apart from the oil industry, been heavily concentrated in electric, electronic and other machinery, their share rising from 44 per cent to 52 per cent between 1962–76 and 1977–80. Choi and Lee argue that initial technology transfer came through the import and use of machinery. Now South Korea relies more upon adaptability but does not have great capacity for indigenous innovation:[33]

> Despite these advances and the progress made in adapting foreign technology, Korea nevertheless relies substantially on technology imports in virtually all electronics activities. Like Taiwan and, initially, Japan, Korea has built its electronics industry on foreign technology...by directing its efforts toward the adaptation of foreign technology. This reflects its strategic emphasis on competitiveness,

---

[31] For particularly strong emphasis on the role of the state in controlling and providing access to finance, see Woo (1991).

[32] See van Liemt and Haggard and Cheng for some comparisons with other NICs.

[33] For C. Lee:

In the case of Korea, foreign technology was introduced in the 1960s mainly through imports of machinery and equipment, since the standardized technology easily embodied in machinery and equipment was required. In the early 1970s, technology transfer through direct foreign investment and licensing became important as Korea started building its heavy and chemical industries...governments intervened in technology, restrictive marketing clauses, the possible impact on the development of new industries, and royalty payment arrangements. (p. 187)

emphasizing marketing and user requirements rather than the origins of technology. (Suarez-Villa and Han, p. 281)

Amsden also emphasises the need for latecomers in industrialisation to rely upon indigenous innovation rather than invention. For this, education as an input into economic growth is seen as important, although Amsden stresses that it should not be deified.[34] For R & D policy, both Korea and Japan are seen as targeting sectors where innovation is rapid rather than maintaining heavy expenditure on mature industries as has occurred, by contrast, in the United States. In electronics, for example:

> This VLSI [very large-scale integrated circuits] project is one of many high-priority 'national projects' involving collaboration between private sector R & D labs and public sector research institutes, to which the government allocates organizational capability and subsidized credit. In 1983 some 182 research projects of 131 industrial firms were selected as national R & D projects and the government contributed about $28 million to these projects...To stimulate R & D generally, the government sets a lower tariff rate on equipment imported for R & D purposes. This provision is important for technology-intensive firms and tells something about the extent to which the machinery sector is protected in general (fairly well). (Amsden, p. 83)

There are many other policies which encourage R & D, such as tax exemptions, state aid to venture capital and government procurement of supplies.

The review of the literature on South Korea has so far shown how varied and extensive are the linkages that have promoted its economic success. At almost every stage, the role of the state has been extensive in bringing those linkages to bear in practice. Not surprisingly, this should have come to the fore analytically in those analyses committed to undermine the free market ideology of the World Bank and other international agencies. It is as if the state versus the market is the key issue in deciding whether agencies are available to bring about favourable linkages.

Agencies. So much, then, for the role of a number of linkages that are to be found discussed in the literature. How do they relate to corresponding agencies? At one level, there is a superficial answer. The agency immediately responsible for a particular linkage is identified, whether it be the industrialist, financier or trade minister. This is not, however, liable to provide any causal content unless, following Hirschmann, there is an erroneous tendency to rely upon potential linkages to call forth corresponding agencies. The agency is then being reduced to the linkage

---

[34] See also Choo (1990).

itself, unless it is revealed why it is able, willing or forced to perform its designated function. While the literature is in some respects now outstanding in giving a sense of the nature of industrialisation as an often implicit changing structure of linkages, it is less successful in explaining why these came about and why they succeeded (when they did).

We are, therefore, provided with an account of the possibility of industrialisation and growth but not a decisive explanation of why that potential materialises. In part, this may reflect the inherent difficulty of the task; it may also show a perspective oriented towards demonstrating the fallacy of the laissez-faire ideology of the NICs' performance for which the very identification of extensive state economic intervention suffices. Agency might also be thought to be more appropriate to political science or sociology, although the danger there is to neglect economic linkages in exploring the detailed exercise of power in the economy in practice.

The problem of identifying agency is illustrated in a rather different way by reference to three commonly cited factors in South Korea's development. The first is the role of the military which Alam sees as not being aligned to any earlier economic and social elite that would have imposed a continuing policy of protection over its own particular vested interests. By contrast Lee and Yamazawa assign a more positive developmental role to the army through its positive influence on the functioning of government bureaucracy.[35] The second is Japanese colonialism, which is perceived to have provided institutions and an ethos, as in the merit of education, that has been conducive to growth. Barrett and Deyo (1987) place this within a dependency framework in which the United States, Japan and South Korea and Taiwan, respectively, are located at the core, semi-periphery and periphery in the world system.

The third commonly cited factor in South Korean development is the crucial role of the United States. Amsden notes its support for the most conservative political party, redistributive land reform and the Korean army, and its granting of substantial aid. Alam reveals that South Korea only financed 11 per cent of its own imports in 1955 and 22 per cent in 1960, although such US aid declined between 1957 and 1965.[36] However,

---

[35] Thus Black (1992) sees national unity as an important factor in preventing the developmental state from degenerating into bureaucratic failure, placing this alongside centralised and targeted decision-making, close consultative links between government and business and the exercise or imposition of wage restraint. On these other factors see below, but appeal to national unity does itself leave open whose representation of the nation prevails and how it is formed and imposed over those with alternative notions of national interests and culture. This might be of particular significance for South Africa, given that it is currently tied to a government of national unity, with the latter's content open to different and shifting interpretations.

[36] See also Hamilton (1986, p. 40).

overall US aid to South Korea from 1946 to 1978 totalled $6 billion, compared to just $6.9 billion to the whole of Africa over the same period.[37]

Consequently, the army, the Japanese and the United States are perceived as direct or indirect agencies promoting growth. But their exact relationship to specific linkages is scarcely elaborated and why they should or should not have intervened in the way that they did tends to remain unexplained. The United States backed land reform, for example, with the effect of breaking up the concentrated ownership of landed property which was the heritage of the Japanese occupation. Yet, elsewhere in the world, the United States is notorious for its aid serving to bolster political and military regimes and landed oligarchs that have been far from conducive either to economic development or to the exclusion of its own direct foreign investment. Alam sums this up:

> During the 1960s Korea was favored by several factors contributing to its potential for capitalist growth. Among these may be included its strategic importance to the United States; the destruction of the *ancien régime* and foreign capital (largely Japanese) as a result of Japan's defeat and US occupation; the emergence of governmental attributes (relative autonomy, commitment to development, 'strong' state, and so on) favorable to economic growth; and the legacies of industrialization under Japanese occupation, which include a start in industrial entrepreneurship, a sizable accumulation of modern skills, and an industrial labor force. (p. 43)

In short, South Korea's inheritance from Japan, the United States and its own high level of militarisation are usually seen as having endowed it with weak class influences over the state which has consequently been committed both strongly and efficiently to a strategy of economic development.

Thus we find that the major agency in critical accounts of South Korean growth is undoubtedly the state and perhaps the most important feature of those agencies already considered is that they support the state in its designated role or allow the state to act independently of them or even against their immediate interests. The emphasis is upon state economic intervention in promoting land reform, creating dynamic comparative advantage through education, R&D and technology policy and in manipulating credit and both domestic and foreign commodity markets to distort prices and interest rates and even to allocate quotas and finance at a detailed level. There has also been extensive state ownership and investment. The number of public enterprises increased from 36 to 108 from 1960 to 1972, with output growing from under 7 per cent to over 10 per cent of GNP, with their share of gross domestic investment reaching

[37] See also Woo (1991, pp. 45-6).

levels of 30 per cent.[38] In addition, there have been controls over capital flight and all commercial banks were nationalised.

The role of the state has been particularly emphasised by Amsden:

Late industrialisation in Korea was retarded by a state too weak to intervene and stimulate capital expenditure...when industrialisation began to accelerate, it did so in response to government initiatives and not the forces of the free market...these processes can be thought of as general propositions applicable to similar countries. (p. 27)

This analysis leads Amsden to locate the role of other agencies as being mediated by the state; most notably, in accordance with other writers, the working class is seen as having been acquiescent, partly through repression and partly through low but growing wages, even with a long working week and limited welfare benefits.[39] Labour relations have been closely monitored by the police and the equivalent of the CIA, leading Johnson (1987, p. 164) to declare that the cases of Japan, South Korea and Taiwan: '...illustrate how economic performance is related to political arrangements, to argue for the essential rationality of the soft authoritarianism-capitalism nexus in terms of comparative development strategies.'

Amsden also observes the role of the middle-classes as a tax base but the key relationship is between the state and big capital. As an agency on its own, the latter is characterised as having familial origins, a limited hierarchy within management with low overheads and an emphasis on engineering control from the shop floor rather than through a separate business administration. From this class has been built up a close relationship with the state in which highly concentrated levels of ownership have resulted both within individual sectors and across the economy as a whole. This occurred as the conglomerate or chaebol, the equivalent of the Japanese *zaibatsu*, gained cumulative experience in diversification and an ability to break into new industries rapidly and cost-effectively. While it is recognised that the state-capital relation is neither simple nor free of corruption, it is perceived to have been dominated by developmental goals rather than self-enrichment at the expense of accumulation. Most significant has been the high concentration of control of industry. Amsden notes that in the early 1980s, the average share of the three largest firms across manufacturing was 62.0 per cent in South Korea, 56.3 per cent in Japan, and 49.2 per cent in Taiwan. The combined share in GNP of the

---

[38] Mason *et al.* report:
Enterprises operating in the public sector are characterised by high forward linkages, high capital-intensity, large size, market concentration and the production of non-tradeables or import substitutes rather than exports. (p. 274)

[39] On the South Korean labour movement, see Ogle (1990).

top ten chaebol in South Korea increased from 15.1 per cent in 1974 to 67.4 per cent in 1984 (p. 116).[40]

This analysis of industrial concentration raises two issues: first, the underlying economic theory of growth; secondly, the relationship between this theory and of that between the state and capital. For the theory of growth, all commentators lay stress on the creation of dynamic, rather than reliance on static, comparative advantage:

> Changes in the pattern of trade and industrial structure have been guided not by the actual but by the potential comparative advantage in both countries. General trading companies have played this guiding role in Japan with the assistance of the government's industrial policy. In the case of Korea, the government has been more active in guiding the development of new industries. (C. Lee, p. 187)

Amsden positively places the emphasis on the need for credit and commodity markets to be distorted away from international price levels, as well as internal uniformity, in order that successive industries can be entered and provide a foundation for further diversification. She also points to the continuing commitment to growth during periods of macro-economic instability, although the success of the strategy is dependent upon continuing growth potential; otherwise instability would worsen.

For Alam, a growth theory in this context is provided less positively and more by way of rejection of neoclassical thinking in emphasising the presence of market imperfections. Thus:

> Support of exporting activity is also justified by the presence of several externalities...The economic arguments for selective promotion of infant industries have been rehearsed many times...the realization of these economies depends on several interventions...Neoclassical economists also take a limited view of dynamic external economies...There are other market failures that may derive from imperfect information...Financial institutions may fail to bring about an optimal allocation of resources...It is well known that markets for technologies are characterized by informational asymmetries favoring the seller. (pp. 10–15)

This then leads to a theory of the state in which a positive role has been identified for it to intervene and this needs to be done without undue influence from any one pressure group. In short, it needs to be politically autonomous in acting in the interests of growth:

> But probably the most decisive part in the transition to export orienta

---

[40] This level of concentration is disputed by Chang (1991). See also Chang (1994).

tion in Taiwan and Korea was played by a set of factors that greatly increased their governments' power to determine policies independently of various reference groups...the complete elimination of the power of landed interests, the suppression or co-option of the labor movement and the elimination of foreign (mostly Japanese) capital that preceded the entry of Taiwan and Korea into import substitution, permitted these governments a much greater latitude in the determination of their economic policies. Moreover, this power was exercised resolutely in support of policies that prevented the trade unions from gaining strength and forced private capital into co-operation with government policies. The presence of a national purpose, strengthened by the developmental commitment of the national leadership, also left its mark on the ability of the state to force sacrifices on particular groups as well as on society as a whole. (p. 20)

As such, Alam has not made a clear break from the orthodoxy for, apart from emphasising dynamic economies, the theory of the state is one in which it is potentially enabled to be neutral in correcting market imperfections.

A similar but less radical posture is adopted by Lee and Yamazawa. For they see state intervention as necessary only in the earliest stages of industrialisation to make up for the deficiencies in the trappings associated with modernisation, such as entrepreneurship. Thereafter policy can revert to greater reliance on the market:

> Initially, a developing country tends to lack, inter alia, entrepreneurs experienced in international trade and a well-developed financial system and thus can benefit from greater participation by the government in industrial and trade activities. As the private sector develops, the government should relinquish its role to private entrepreneurs, intervening indirectly with taxes and subsidies to correct externalities. (p. 186)

Pack and Westphal (p. 117) also question 'whether generalised market forces will lead to the timely creation of the requisite agents and markets. Neoclassical theory...simply assumes that responsive agents exist.' Where Lee and Yamazawa view this as a matter of developmental timing, for Pack and Westphal it depends upon the potential of the state to preoccupy itself exclusively with economic growth rather than its activities being captured by rent-seekers. The state must 'intervene selectively in pursuit of dynamic efficiency...most governments may lack this ability...where this ability does not exist, the government is probably well-advised to adhere rather closely to the strict neoclassical prescription for a neutral policy regime.' (p. 104)

The discussion of the state has so far been primarily concerned with its relations to capital and its presumed potential to be autonomous from it. Similar requirements are placed on its relations to labour, as in Johnson's desire for 'soft authoritarian-capitalism'. For Deyo (1987b)

> The political autonomy of technocratic planners, which has permitted the state to ignore political claims on development policy, has been rooted in the weakness and dependency of domestic social classes, in elite unity and in external support for authoritarian regimes. Internal unity and autonomy fostered exclusionary regimes at a very early point in industrialization, which pre-empted organizational efforts during the subsequent emergence of an industrial proletariat and assured that emergent trade unions were closely allied with ruling groups. The early political inclusion of Latin American industrial workers, by contrast, encouraged the development of strong labor movements that later were able to shelter a privileged segment of the labor force from repression. (p. 199)

For each of these views, with the partial exception of Amsden's, there is a problem. The theory of economic growth, presented here in terms of developmental linkages, provides a rationale for state intervention. It is then argued that the state is able to fulfil the role because of its independence from sectional interests. But how the state has arisen and why it does or does not act so altruistically remains a mystery. If it is free of sectional interests, then it is not clear why it should adopt goals other than those of its own personnel, however these may be determined, and they may not necessarily be coincident with policies to promote growth unless this is seen as a necessary condition for its own political and military survival. On the other hand, if the state is subject to competing interests, why have these been resolved in favour of a successful growth strategy?

These issues have occasionally been acknowledged but have rarely been addressed.[41] Luedde-Neurath (1986) recognises an unresolved issue in that:

> Neither have we tackled the critical question of why the State in Korea was able to intervene so decisively in economic development without causing chaos or provoking large-scale defiance among the business

---

[41] Thus, as Kohli (1994, p. 1269) puts it:

The prior question of why the South Korean state was able to do what it did, and the related genetic issue of the historical roots of the Korean political economy thus tend to be underemphasized.

In this and the following chapter, we refer a number of times to Kohli's outstanding study which corrects the imbalance that underestimates the role of Japanese colonialism in establishing the South Korean economic model. The imbalance is a consequence of the ideological and nationalist antipathy to ascribing what might be thought to be a positive role to Japanese imperialism. Note also that the first draft of this book was completed before Kohli's study was available.

interests keen, for example, to circumvent import controls, artificially prolong their 'infancy' or avoid export obligations. (p. 5)

White and Wade (1985) also recognise such a deficiency but, by way of contrast to the laissez-faire orthodoxy, it is one that is excused by establishing what the state has been doing and that it has been doing it:

> What none of the papers [in their edited volume] on Taiwan and South Korea say much about is the basis of state power, the way it is organised or the micro principles with which officials make allocation decisions...These are exceedingly important questions. To show why they cannot be ignored in an explanation of the industrial and agricultural success of these countries, it is necessary first to establish that the prevailing understanding, as presented by neoclassical economics, is misleading. (p. 9)

Like many others, Hamilton (p. 46) broaches these issues by arguing how independent the state has been of big business: 'The Korean state cannot be thought of as the instrument of big business – it has maintained a large degree of autonomy from the power of capital.' He finds that the Japanese destroyed the traditional ruling class and landed wealth was subsequently subject to a double transformation, first to merchant and then to industrial capital: '1976 found no less than 47 per cent of entrepreneurs' fathers had been "large-to-medium landowners".' (p. 31)[42] His economic analysis anticipates much of the literature already reviewed, emphasising the role of the state in distorting prices to create comparative advantage and establish linkages across the economy (although this is done empirically with a static general equilibrium model). Specifically, however, he sees the state as neither servant nor opponent of business. Indeed, he even goes so far as to suggest that the state is instrumental in creating the capitalist class: 'The recent history of South Korea, and of Singapore and Taiwan, identifies the central role of the state in the formation of a class of industrial capitalists and the dominance of industrial accumulation. In Korea, industrial capital is, in a sense, the creature of the state.' (p. 117)[43]

Consequently, while Hamilton pays closer attention than many other writers to the evolution and role of class structure, and hence agency, the net result is to enhance the position of the state as primary agent, since it acts to create the class structure and, not surprisingly in this light, appears able to act independently of it. It is a moot point whether the state is

---

[42] See also Eckert (1991, p. 254), quoted in Kohli (1994, p. 1285): '"60 percent of the founders of South Korea's top fifty chaebol" had participated directly in business under [Japanese] colonial auspices.'

[43] See also Woo (1991, p. 15) for whom:
> In reality, they [the Korean chaebols] are the creations – the productions and not reproductions – of the state and the Korean financial structure.

subsequently to become a victim of its own off-spring. For Steinberg (1988) 'corporations were more clearly in the government's iron glove than in the economy's invisible hand.' (p. 28) But, 'originally viewed as a mere instrument of government policy, the business sector is taking on a social and political role.' (p. 27) If, however, the state's power is being challenged by the rise of the business sector,[44] presumably it increasingly becomes in the state's interest to abandon and frustrate developmental goals that enhance the fortunes of such business opposition.

This unlikely prospect arises because of the construction of the state with an interest independent of, and over, the interests of other classes. By many accounts, Marxist as well as pluralist, this is to misrepresent the relationship between state and classes in which the interests of the latter are represented by or through the former. This is, of course, to enter the terrain of the theory of the state in which the problem of interests and agency is paramount. Amsden essentially avoids these conundrums by seeing the state as acting on behalf of large-scale capital as a whole without its being permanently captured by any one sectional interest within that class. It is, however, much easier to identify this outcome and its accompanying supports, such as working class acquiescence and US aid, than it is to explain it or to emulate it with or without more progressive policies for labour and with less authoritarianism. More detailed studies of specific sectors will shed light on these issues. For example, it is arguable that the land reform that proved so functional for economic development depended upon pressure from below from peasants, as opposed to the absence of a landlord class, particularly given the neighbouring demonstration of the North.[45] Similarly, the expansion of the steel industry served the interests of large-scale domestic capital and was not opposed by them, although, as has frequently been pointed out, it was strongly opposed by the World Bank. A central role played by the state was to discipline labour, particularly in imposing long hours of work, and to prevent the emergence of any countervailing worker organisation.[46]

Consideration of the oppression of labour is an open recognition of the class nature of the Korean state and its acting on behalf of capital. The analytical alternative of otherwise stressing the positive developmental role of the state as a consequence of its autonomy follows from an apparent inability to tie economic policies to the interests of specified capitalists, consciously acting through the state as its instrument. Such transparency in the relations between capital and the state are not unknown but they are not required to validate the notion of the state as being bound by ruling

[44] See also pp. 21–2.
[45] See also Kawakami.
[46] See Cumings (1981; 1990).

class interests, except in the crudest alternatives to the state as an autonomous agency.

We would, however, emphasise two further points, both in addressing the literature on South Korea in its own right and in drawing lessons for studying the South African economy. First, appealing to the weakness of internal classes, whether due to the Japanese, the United States or the indigenous military, as a basis for autonomising the state is misleading, even erroneous, in that it sets aside how these 'external' forces are themselves often predominantly instrumental through the state in allying themselves to particular class interests. Such is one lesson to be learnt from Cumings' studies of the origins of the Korean war (1981; 1990), where US policy functioned both to suppress anything that smacked of communism by the broadest criteria and to embrace anything pulling a ruling elite into the twentieth-century world of commerce. Kohli (1994) makes the strongest possible case for the influence of Japanese colonialism on the subsequent, if delayed, success of the South Korean growth model. He also does it in such a way that it sheds light on the nature of that model and, in particular, the early importance of the class interests of industrialists:[47]

> It is clear that Japanese colonialism in Korea established some basic state-society patterns that many now readily associate as integral to the later South Korean 'model' of a high-growth political economy. These patterns include a highly bureaucratized, penetrating and architectonic state, a state-dominated alliance of state and property owners for production and profits, and repressive social control of the working classes. (p. 1285)

Secondly, it follows that the state not only serves particular class interests but that it also actively intervenes in the restructuring of class composition. The circumstances that led the Korean state to promote capitalist development so successfully was simultaneously a process of creating and consolidating the presence of a class of large-scale capitalists. The previously mentioned conflicts among this class within the state represent its maturity rather than its gaining strength at the state's expense.[48] As Chang (1994, pp. 119–20) has put it in the vernacular of the World Bank approach, South Korean corporations cannot and do not claim to use bribery and corruption any less than elsewhere but they appear to engage in less rent-seeking activity and use less resources in

---

[47] See also Woo (1991, p. 15):
   We do notice something uncannily similar about the colonial experience and the later industrialization – the type of state and its role in the economy; the state's relationship to business, especially the conglomerates; the financial mechanisms peculiar to Japanese development, then, and Korean development, now.

[48] See Y. Lee.

doing so because of the limited, potentially successful, competition from outside the select elite of chaebols and because they are conglomerates able to bundle together a range of issues such as economies of scale and scope in rent-seeking, suggesting how closely integrated has been state policy and the pursuit of chaebols' interests.[49]

Nor does this involve an inconsistency when the state acts against the interests of an individual chaebol. Chang discusses this in terms of what persists in being an intense degree of competition between them, so that inefficiency in any one sector of the economy opens up the possibility for a state-aided transfer of control within the chaebol system, as has occurred through the instrument of the state's Economic Planning Board (EPB). The result is that the concentration of activity amongst chaebols has been complemented by frequent shifts in pecking order in their overall size. (p. 123) This stands in sharp contrast to the relative stability of the ranking of corporate power within South Africa and to the motives and impact of the state's economic interventions. But we anticipate.

From the preceding discussion it has been well established that the state has been instrumental in promoting South Korean industrialisation, as well as that of other NICs, and that by implication the World Bank's view has been undermined both analytically and empirically. Indeed, much of the literature reviewed has had the explicit aim of documenting the fallacies of the World Bank's stance.

This has, however, had the unintended and unfortunate effect of placing the World Bank perspectives at the centre of debate even if by way of rebuttal. It has encouraged authors to be satisfied with an empirical refutation of the World Bank's postures by demonstrating the centrality of the state's interventions. This has discouraged the development of more constructive analytical approaches to the role of the state, ones which do not simply posit themselves as not the World Bank view. In particular, this tends to leave open the question of why some economies and their associated state interventions have proved successful while others have not, an issue that has been side-stepped by the World Bank approach since it assigns success to the absence of state intervention. As observed earlier in the context of the South Korean literature, this issue has not been ignored altogether but it has been displaced by a separate set of conundrums; for example, when can the state be sufficiently autonomous to adopt and implement developmental goals?

While these matters are considered in the following chapter, we conclude here by referring to what at long last has been the response by the World Bank to its academic critics. By displaying an extraordinary

---

[49] See also Shin (1992, p. 78).

performance of analytical acrobatics, the World Bank manages to claim in *The East Asian Miracle* that it has been wrong in the past but has still been right all along!

First, it eschews a general model of successful development, despite having previously held to the notion that limited state intervention and maximum scope to market forces in the form of export-orientation, are universally the appropriate strategies to pursue. Thus:

> The eight countries studied used very different combinations of policies, from hands-off to highly interventionist. Thus, there is no single 'East Asian model' of development. This diversity of experience reinforces the view that economic policies and policy advice must be country-specific if they are to be effective. But there are also some common threads among the high-performing East Asian economies ...rapid growth in each economy was primarily due to the application of a set of common market-friendly economic policies...This report also breaks some new grounds. It concludes that in some countries...some selective interventions contributed to growth and it advances our understanding of the conditions for intervention to succeed. (World Bank 1993, p. vi)

Almost inevitably, the bias towards the market persists and it is analytically grounded in the idea that the normal economy functions in the relative absence of the state. So where there are identifiable successes, these are read off primarily from the role of the market even if supported occasionally, in a pre-determined secondary role, by the state's interventions. It is tempting to suggest that if the World Bank's bias were the other way about, it would be a simple task to find and replace the market by the state in the texts and vice-versa. This shows that the relationship between the state and market is unexplored in the World Bank's approach, except as an opposition.

Secondly, the World Bank accepts that the state can intervene and has intervened successfully in a few economies but suggests that the 'pre-requisites were so rigorous' (p. 6) that they were unlikely to be replicated elsewhere in the developing world. The rigour required is in governmental institutions with the capacity to monitor performance and limit the costs of interventions and the extent of price distortions. It is not clear why an economy incapable of such relatively simple functions, whether because of lack of bureaucratic resources or the interference of political interests, would be any more able or willing to serve market forces efficiently and effectively.

Thirdly, successful interventions are not surprisingly interpreted as those that are market-conforming or which have had the result of simulating what the market would have done if it had been working perfectly:

'Industrial policy in Japan, (South) Korea and Taiwan, China, produced mainly market-conforming results.' (p. 21) It is as if successful industrialisation and perfect market outcomes are one and the same thing so that the state can only intervene successfully when it corrects what the market would otherwise have achieved, if it were functioning ideally.

As Chang (1993) observes, the World Bank report draws upon a magnitude of unpublished background studies, each employing different and potentially erroneous and incompatible methodologies and techniques.[50] He questions, for example, whether the study of South Korean textiles based on total factor productivity is either appropriate or illustrative of the application of market-conforming interventions. In addition, sectoral studies of this type overlook the developmental gains accruing from the spin-offs between sectors. Nor is there any discussion of how the comparative advantage is created other than through the building up of 'human capital'.

What remains crucial to the World Bank's outlook is the polarity between state and market. The acceptance of this polarity by the Bank's critics, even if from the opposite extreme, may even have allowed the Bank both to incorporate and to reject the analyses of its opponents. However, this would be to credit the Bank with an honesty in and commitment to serious debate with both critics and evidence for which it has consistently shown scant regard. Thus, having set the terms of the debate over the role of the state and the market, as the one versus the other, it has refused to abandon them. The result is that the alternative of examining how state and market interact as a consequence of underlying economic and political interests remains underdeveloped.

---

[50] This also applies across World Bank postures. The recent re-assessment of housing, towards less state intervention, World Bank (1993), contradicts the East Asian study which strongly praises the heavy state intervention to provide low-income housing in Hong Kong and Singapore:

> By providing low-cost housing for the majority of residents, both programs have helped to decrease inequality and minimize social unrest, thus providing the long-term stability attractive to investors. Moreover, the massive effort created jobs when both economies faced high unemployment; subsequently, the wide availability of low-cost housing for workers helped to hold down wage demands, subsidising labor-intensive manufacturing. (World Bank 1993, p. 163)

This is of considerable importance to South Africa, where the option of a public housing programme seems to have been precluded from consideration at the outset. For a contrary view, see MERG (1993).

3

THE ROLE OF THE STATE

With the collapse of regimes in eastern Europe, moves away from both traditional concepts of socialist planning elsewhere and the policy and ideological hegemony of the Bretton Woods institutions in promoting the market, it is ironic that there should have been a resurgence in scholarship devoted to the state. Nothing apart from success seems to attract so much attention as failure. Studies of the state have been inspired by the apparent success of NICs, such as South Korea, and the apparent failure of state intervention in other developing countries. Not surprisingly, this raises two issues: first, what is the appropriate level and content of state economic intervention; secondly, under what conditions will this be realised? In many ways the second incorporates the first question, since it seeks an explanation for the role of the state in practice and consequently can be used to examine whether this will be conducive to development.

Much of the new literature does distance itself from the IMF/World Bank commitment to austerity and reliance upon the market. It accepts that the state can be 'developmental' through extensive intervention and, rather than precluding this at the outset on ideological grounds, honestly searches for the appropriate role for the state and the socio-economic and political conditions that allow it to be adopted. However, while the literature has successfully engaged and defeated laissez-faire dogma both theoretically and empirically, it has, possibly unwittingly, accepted the central theoretical framework upon which that dogma has been constructed. As this framework is itself open to question, it is essential both to identify it and to assess it critically.

It is very easily identified but, at least most recently, it has become so much a part of analytical common sense that it is simply taken for granted. Essentially, the state is seen as an integral agency or set of institutions and social structures so that it can be perceived in terms of its interaction with or relation to the rest of society. In this respect, the state is understood as autonomous, a separate entity, even if it is itself dominated by a particular hegemonic class or by economic imperatives, such as the preservation and promotion of profitability, as in radical theory. For our purposes this approach to the state is encapsulated in the common problematic of what is or should be the relationship between the state and the market.

Of course, this is expressed precisely and in pure form in the debate over the state versus the market. Once again, there is the implicit notion that the market is an integral entity with a relationship to the rest of society and to the state in particular. It is how the two separate entities, state and market, interact that has endowed most recent theories of the state with their particular analytical framework.

Our approach is different and explicitly rejects the dichotomy between state and market as an analytical starting point. Rather, it sees both the market and the state and their interaction as the complex product of the forces that are exerted upon them; most prominent of these are economic interests and imperatives attached to specific fractions of classes. To return to the organising theme of the previous chapter, the state and the market are both forms (specified relatively abstractly at this level of discussion) through which agencies function and linkages can be formed. Neither one is itself an agency for a linkage; the market never bought or sold anything on anybody's behalf, although this is done through the market. However, in common parlance the state and the market are often viewed as if they were agencies, by reference to market forces, for example, or the state's role. This is best seen as a shorthand for functioning through the market or the state, although in some approaches, the state is seen as having an interest of its own as embodied in that of its leading personnel, institutions or bureaucracy.

To highlight the difference in the position adopted here, consider privatisation, especially in the context of denationalisation. From a variety of theoretical perspectives based on state versus market, this would be considered as a shift in favour of the market and against the state. This is, however, arguably both incomplete and potentially misleading. From our perspective, privatisation is a particular form of state intervention, as was the creation of state industry previously. What is privatised, how, why and to whom together make up an irreducible combination of economic and political factors through both state and market institutions and reflect underlying interests. Paradoxically, the very same class interests can potentially be served as much by privatisation as by nationalisation, even of the same company at separate times. Thus when a particular fraction of capital, even a privileged family, holds secure political power, it can use the state and state-owned assets to promote its material interests, although profits may be transferred to them as private property at the expense of overt corruption. Privatisation might follow from the threat of loss of political power.

Such an example is crude but far from unknown,[1] and it serves to illustrate that substantial shifts between state and market may reflect considerable continuity in underlying determinants. More complex instances,

[1] President Banda's interest in Malawi's Press Holdings is a classic case.

more readily accepted as legitimate, are no less susceptible to similar interpretations. Thus, the privatisation programme in South Africa was clearly motivated, at least in part, by the wish to remove state-owned assets beyond the control not of the state as such, but of those interests that were about to adopt state power. In this case, then, withdrawal of the state from ownership was designed to perpetuate the economic power of large-scale capital. More generally, it has been argued that nationalisation in the United Kingdom over the post-war period has effectively functioned to restructure unprofitable enterprises so that they could be restored to commercial viability and thereby open, only as a culmination of this process, to privatisation under the Thatcher government.[2]

If our approach eschews the state versus market stance and sees each as heavily and mutually conditioned by the more fundamental exercise of economic interests, it equally recognises that the latter are subject to change. Thus the class forces that are reflected through the state *and* the market are transformed over time, together with the content of the connections between them all.[3]

It follows that the counterposing of the state and market has been made possible not by neglecting the role of class interests but by analytically privileging the presence of the state and the market above class, rather than vice versa. In short, the state and the market exist; how might they be influenced by class or other interests? To consider the other perspective, we can first identify class interests and then examine how the state and market relate to them.

The justification for doing so can be made by highly selective reference to a huge literature on the theory of the state. Drawing upon some of its traditions and neglecting others, the most recent contributions can be divided into two types: the economic school and the political school, although some contributions straddle both. What they each have in common is to proceed as if previous, often influential debates about the role of the state had never existed, especially those that take class interests and structure as decisive and analytically prior. This neglect applies particularly at the expense of the state-derivation school, which, whatever

[2] See Fine and Harris (1985) for a full discussion of UK privatisation from this perspective; also see Fine (1990) and Fine and Poletti (1992) for discussion of the coal, electricity and steel industries.

[3] While it is generally more readily accepted that the state is not neutral relative to class interests, as opposed to the market, the market itself is not class-neutral. Yet the class content of the market is rarely addressed, with the implicit presumption that it is neutral. However, whether we all face the same prices or not, the market is not neutral in so far as access to and through it depends, for example, upon class position. This is not simply a matter of income or credit-worthiness but of such factors as differential provision of infrastructure. Most immediately, physical access to the market according to availability of transport is often crucial, especially in the South African context.

its merits may otherwise be, begins with capital and the economic and political forms that it assumes.[4]

Consider first the economic school. While more longstanding in terms of the theory of market failure as a rationale for state intervention, it has come more to the fore in order to combat the laissez-faire stance. For example, as previously described, literature on the South Korean miracle illustrates that economics has often paid more attention to linkages than to agencies. Accordingly, analysis has too readily been concerned with identifying developmental linkages and then either assuming that an eye for a profit brings forth the private, commercial agency to realise these linkages or that this is the appropriate function of state policy.

This is so for Stewart and Ghani (p. 569), with externalities as a special case of linkages: 'Externalities thus constitute market failures. Their presence means that the unregulated price system does not result in a social optimum and consequently provides a *prima facie* reason for government intervention.' Accordingly, the state should promote winners in the race after comparative advantage:[5] 'What is at stake is *not* for the most part picking winners but *creating winners*...it is a matter of choosing a *few* industries (and *not* promoting all industries) and then creating winners.' (p. 589) Thus, the market may or may not create and choose industrial successes. Where it does not, it is incumbent upon the state to do so.

In this light, the economic school can construct a theory of the state as a corrective mechanism for market imperfections. These need not be confined to the static imperfections associated with standard neoclassical economics but may also be extended to include dynamic economies of scale and other rationales, such as inadequate training, technology, institutions, etc. Both in the new growth theory and new trade theory, in which comparative advantage accrues over time, formal economic models have been employed to justify protection or other forms of industrial policy.[6]

A similar if differently expressed conclusion derived from an alternative theoretical stance is to be found in Jenkins' (1991) examination of the comparative performance of Latin American and East Asian NICs. His is a careful review of the literature, bringing out the main features

---

[4] This literature was popularised by Holloway and Picciotto (eds) (1978) and still prospers. In its early, crude forms, it derived the role of the state from the need, for example, to mediate on behalf of capital as a whole against the interests of individual capitalists or capital against labour. Hence, the state is derived from the capital-relation and varies analytically dependent upon how this is understood. As such, it has tended to address more concrete issues at too abstract a level.

[5] For Wade (1990): 'The governments of Taiwan, Korea and Japan have not so much *picked* winners as *made* them.' (p. 334)

[6] Thus learning-by-doing implies that the overall level of investment is liable to be too low, given that productivity effects of any private investment accrues to all producers.

concerned both with linkages and agencies. Ultimately, his conclusion is that the main explanatory factor in the superior performance of the East Asian NICs is in the agencies involved. Thus: 'The key to the superior industrial performance of the East Asian NICs does not lie in the general superiority of export-oriented industrialization strategies over import substitution or of market-oriented policies over state intervention as some writers have suggested.' (p. 224) Central for him is the fact that the East Asian states have been able to adopt the necessary policies without undue interference by special class interests:

> It is rather the ability of the state to direct the accumulation process in the direction which is required by capitalist development at particular points of time which is crucial. This in turn has to be located in the existence of a developmental state with a high degree of relative autonomy from local classes and class fractions. This paper has high-lighted the ways in which specific historical experience and the inter-national context gave rise to such states in East Asia but not in Latin America in the postwar period. (p. 224)

Consequently, the key is agency and the key agency is the state, given its relatives autonomy. In addition, the direction of the accumulation process displaces orthodox neoclassical models' reliance upon market imperfections as the determinant of the appropriate policies to be adopted by the state. Jenkins goes on further to argue that the capacity of the state to perform this function is directly related to the weakness of the classes from which it is autonomous:

> The degree of relative autonomy of the state is neither invariant within regions nor over time. The degree of state autonomy appears to have been higher in Taiwan than in South Korea and the growing importance of the *chaebols* in Korea and the predominance of small-scale industry in Taiwan have served to intensify this difference...Developments in South Korea in the 1980s suggest that the very success of the state in promoting industrialisation is reducing its relative autonomy. (p. 224)

As a general historical law – the state has the capacity to create large-scale capital only with the effect of undermining itself – this view must be open to question, as it implies for example, that the interests of large-scale capital are best served if it along with other classes is initially weak in its influence over state policy. In effect, Jenkins' view does not advance much beyond that of Stewart and Ghani, the latter identifying a policy role for the state and the former stating that it can be adopted subject to the absence of countervailing class pressures.

In short, within the economic school's theory of the state and from a variety of economic perspectives and theories, an economic path is identified and the state is required to pursue it to the extent that the market does not or is unable to do so. Logically, however, this leaves an empty box: under what circumstances does the state carry out its assigned role? Unfortunately, many economists have been satisfied with simply demonstrating theoretically or historically how important the state can or has been. But with the determinants of the state's actual rather than preferred role unspecified, the laissez-faire position has been able to counter the charge of market failure or imperfections with the equally powerful claim of government imperfection, be it regulatory failure or whatever. It has been argued by the anti-interventionists that there is no reason to presume that government will function any more satisfactorily than the market. Indeed, there are reasons to believe that it will not. Once the state is open to interventionist policies, they will be targeted by interest groups irrespective of their merits, giving rise to inefficient rent-seeking and the costs attached to it. Nor can it be presumed that the state has the superior information with which to override those actions that would be adopted by reliance upon market forces alone. Thus it is argued that as state intervention opens up and distorts the vested interests, it is better to rely on the market forces alone, other than for activities that are essential to it or which command collective, possibly unanimous consent.

In other words, the pursuit of profit-making through the market is seen as beneficial, whereas its pursuit through the state is seen as wasteful, with pejorative overtones of immorality. This explains the use of the term 'rent-seeking' for such activity through the state, whereas it is simply good old profit-seeking when commercial gain is sought through the market. This is despite, and implicitly confirms, the absence of an adequate theoretical distinction between profit and rent in neoclassical theory,[7] as advantage gained through state intervention is made land-like, accruing as a rent. This is true even though, following Alfred Marshall, it has been conventional to dub the abnormal profit realised in the short-run through advantage over competitors as a 'quasi-rent'.

Whatever language might be used, it follows that the pursuit of profitability through the state as opposed to the market is a distinction that cannot in and of itself adjudicate whether one or the other is more beneficial or worthy. As Chang (1994) summarises his own eloquent discussion of these issues:[8]

> The point is *not* that people do not seek rents in markets... However, rent-seeking in markets is regarded as productive because we *assume* that

---

[7] See Fine (1982).

[8] He also argues that the state's interventions may induce organisational innovations that are more productive in minimising rent-seeking costs, whether economic or political, and in handling the informational and other problems that are not and cannot be fully synchronised by the market alone. For similar and other arguments in the same vein, see Streeten (1993).

it creates more resources than it uses up in the process and not because it does not use any resources. ... Political competition is wasteful only because it is implicitly *assumed* that it does not create any value. (p. 44)

Once freed from an individualistic methodology, it only needs to be added that the balance in practice between economic and political forms of rent-seeking is a reflection of the contest between underlying economic and political groups and their interests. It cannot be presumed that a policy of lesser state intervention can succeed, let alone be desirable, without addressing the presence of such interests and how they respond to and/or subvert the intended policies and their effects. If theft of state property by a corrupt oligarchy is the main problem, a policy of privatisation is liable to see them benefit handsomely through subsidised purchases, etc. More generally, there is a complex relationship between rent-seeking through the market and the state and it is illegitimate to presume that it is absent in the market through being dubbed profit and counterproductive when pursued through the state. These matters cannot be analysed in the abstract but must be related to the specific circumstances in which economic and political interests are pursued: 'Interest-group politics may be properly understood only when the particular process of contest for political and economic rights in the society concerned are analysed in detail.'(Chang 1994, p. 22) Chang proposes what he terms a new institutionalist theory of state intervention in which 'the state – along with the market, the firm and other institutions – [is examined] as an important device of coordination.' (p. 53) Thus the economic school becomes a generalised theory of the representation of interests or rent-seeking through the available institutions, of which the state and market are but two.

The political school approaches the theory of the state from the opposite extreme. Unlike the economic school, which starts by identifying a role for the state in promoting economic development, this school leaves this aspect more or less unexamined and focuses upon whether the state is able to adopt that role, whatever it might be. As Kohli (1994) puts it:

Arguments about 'developmental states', whether in Evans's or in other versions, often focus more on explaining a state's capacity to implement goals and less on where these goals come from in the first place. (p. 1287)

Picking up on the terms in which Jenkins has previously been seen to express the problem, the capacity of the state to intervene favourably is related to its 'autonomy'. This usage of the term derives initially from Althusserian structuralism. It has subsequently taken on a number of different meanings in the context of the state, depending upon what is taken to be the latter's source of independence. It can be relative either to specific fractional interests of the dominant class, with the state serving capital as a whole even if at the expense of individual capitals, to all class interests, mediating between conflicting classes without being subordinated to any. Alternatively, the state can, through its own personnel and institutions, develop interests and practices that are separate from those of others or it can be free of the imperatives that govern the economy, such as the pursuit of profitability and what that entails. Finally, autonomy can also be seen as the separation or separate effect of political and ideological factors in which the state is prominent from economic factors.

Initially, the use of autonomy in the context of Marxist structuralism was intended to provide a means by which to avoid excessive determinism while retaining a causal contact based on systemic, class and economic factors. Hence, arises the reference to relative autonomy and to economic determination in the last instance. In the current political school, these ill-specified provisos have been cast aside. The autonomy of the state is taken as an analytical starting point in order to explain why some states can intervene more successfully than others. It is simply a matter of identifying that autonomy and what makes it possible. Thus the political school is the mirror image of the economic school. The latter identifies appropriate economic policies as the analytical priority, thereby leading to the issue of whether the state has the autonomy to adopt them; the former starts with the question of how much autonomy is enjoyed by the state and, consequently, what policy options are open to it.

Thus the current analytical appeal of relying upon the relative autonomy of the state is the product of a number of factors which have entailed the convergence of different schools of thought and disciplines to this way of thinking, whatever their remaining, residual differences. For political theory, this has been stunningly highlighted by Cammack's (1989) critical review of P. Evans *et al.* (eds) (1985). He first shows that they have been able to autonomise the state first of all by structurally setting it aside from the rest of society. This does not render the state free of influence from society's class or other interests, nor from its laws of motion as a mode of production. But it does allow it to intervene according to its own interest or as a selective filter for the interests of others. It becomes an agency with special interests and powers.

Secondly, Cammack finds that theories of the autonomy of the state represent a step away from the previous orthodox functionalist/structuralist accounts of the state but they misrepresent this step by claiming it as consistent with neo-Marxist theories of the state, where these are defined as retaining a causal content dependent upon the class nature of, rather than influence upon, the state. The new theories set aside an emphasis on the class nature of the state and accordingly do themselves break with a fundamental aspect of the Marxist tradition.[9] There is, then, a close relation between autonomising the state from society so that it can intervene within it and from class and other interests so that it can do so with its own interest over and above that of others. Such autonomy no longer requires hypotheses, potentially derived from neo-Marxism, concerning the constraining structures, interests and forces of capitalist society.

Thirdly, Cammack argues that there has been a serious conflation between two propositions concerning the autonomy of the state, one weak and the other strong. The first, more or less unexceptional, is that the state may act autonomously from class interests. From an analytical point of view, much more important than establishing this proposition is to discover the way in which classes and class interests are formed and, in the course of conflict and change, how they are (mis)represented through the state which is heavily constrained by its being rooted within society. This is what is denied by the second, strong and unacceptable proposition that the state always acts autonomously. In practice, these two propositions tend to be run together in empirical analyses so that the complexity of the state's actions are explained by its autonomy where they do not appear to be immediately derived from the direct representation of class interests.

Indeed, the political school can be viewed as having appropriated the concept of relative autonomy from Marxist theory, rendered it absolute by separating the state from society and then used that autonomy and separation to explain the complexities of the state's actions when not immediately reducible to class interests. The analysis has then been driven by empirical imperatives. Starting with instances such as South Korea, theoretical factors are then identified which are perceived to explain the state's capacity to be autonomous and to adopt successful developmental policies. These factors have already been outlined in the previous chapter. However, this then gives rise to empirical anomalies once the theory is projected on to other countries. Some countries with the same characteristics as South Korea are not found to have yielded a developmental state, whereas others have done so on the basis of different characteristics. Consequently, the number of explanatory factors is expanded to resolve the empirical anomalies.

This is true for Zhao and Hall (1994), who appeal to five fundamental factors: geopolitical position; freedom from influence of previous regimes; nationalism for a common purpose; the sequencing of democratisation and national independence; and the degree of cultural unity and governance.[10] In addition, they modify the understanding of

---

[9] See Jessop (1990) for a survey of Marxist theories of the state.

[10] Kohli (1994, p. 1288), drawing on his study of the influence of Japanese colonialism on the South Korean economy, perceptively observes how such analyses tend to be historically

autonomy and argue that it must be 'bounded', that 'states need to be, at one and the same time, autonomous from and yet constrained by their societies'. (p. 211) On this basis, it is transparent that theoretical development has stagnated, with an accumulation of empirical studies being complemented by a corresponding set of conceptual innovations which, not surprisingly, tend merely to put whatever empirical regularities are hypothesised into a more abstract and general terminology; bounded autonomy is a perfect illustration of this. This borders on tautology, especially given the extent of conceptual virtuosity that has emerged across the literature. Thus apart from more long-standing characterisations of the state as democratic or authoritarian, it is variously categorised as soft or hard, predatory or benevolent, weak or strong, centralised or decentralised, and so on. And in the search for conditions that are conducive or not to appropriate state economic intervention, each of these terms can have different meanings according to the set of activities, interests or functions to which it is applied.

This assessment is borne out by the outcome of the research programme that was set in motion by P. Evans *et al.* (eds). With the subsequent gathering of case studies, autonomy is no longer found to be sufficient for state intervention to be favourable and the state is found to be closely integrated with other social relations. This is reflected in the notion of 'embedded autonomy'. It is for P. Evans (1992) essential to ensure that an autonomous state is not classified as developmental if it is based on a self-serving elite simply appropriating whatever surplus is created. Thus:

> The autonomy of the developmental state is, however, of a completely different character from the aimless, absolutist domination of the predatory state. It is not just relative autonomy in the structural Marxist sense of being constrained by the generic requirements of capital accumulation. It is an autonomy embedded in a concrete set of social ties which bind the state to society and provide institutionalised channels for the continual negotiation and renegotiation of goals and policies. (p. 164)

------

limited, not surprising given their attempt to find determinate relations between the developmental state and country characteristics:

A variety of answers have been proposed in recent years as to why some developing countries have better performing economies than others; these vary from sharply market-oriented answers, through more state-focused analyses, all the way to religion and culture as real variables. What many of these efforts in the hands of 'developmentalists' lack, unfortunately, is historical depth.

Note that Kohli continues to pose his analysis in terms of the relationship between the state and capital (and other classes) as though the former was a given, even if changing, entity. Nonetheless, his contribution can be readily interpreted in terms of the state as a product of underlying class forces and interests.

Further, it is now recognised that the role of the state also incorporates a feedback mechanism on the reproduction of the classes whose interests are expressed through the points of contact forged through embedded autonomy: 'Class structure must be seen, at least in part, as the product of the state action.' (p. 179)

The concept of autonomy has now turned full circle. By setting the state up as an independent entity and examining, both theoretically and empirically, the conditions under which it might prove developmental, the analysis increasingly requires the state to be ever more integrated or embedded in the other social relations from which it has initially been torn. Further, the state is also seen to embody a dialectical relationship with the formation and representation of classes. Only the slenderest of threads now sustains the initial analytical starting point of the autonomy of the state. It is readily cut if the state is rejected as an independent entity and reconstructed as a complex product of underlying class relations.

It should also be noted that the political school has now attained a stance that is essentially identical to that of the economic school, as in the case of Jenkins discussed above. Apart from the difference in emphases on the sources and exercise of political autonomy as opposed to the economic policies that need to be adopted, each acknowledges the influence of classes on the state *and* vice versa. The evolving class structure has been endowed with what might itself be termed 'relative autonomy' but it has rarely been subject to substantive analysis. This is hardly surprising and signifies only the token acknowledgement of the influence of the state. For if it were properly incorporated, it could only be done through a full examination of all of the factors determining the class structure with which it necessarily interacts. Once again, this would tend to undermine an analysis that begins by privileging the autonomy of the state and would restore class relations to an even stronger position.

Instead, the literature has focused on the conditions in which the putative autonomy of the state is sufficient to guarantee appropriate economic policies. Necessarily, the position of the state relative to various classes is far from symmetrical, although it must command the capacity to resist 'pork barrel' politics in which it simply reflects the immediate demands of vested interests. This raises the problem of how the state's interests are themselves determined, to the extent that they are independent of other interests, and why they would not override those interests. As Przeworski and Limongi (1993 p. 57) put it: 'What it fails to answer is why an autonomous state would behave in the interests, long- or short-term ones, of anyone else.' The answer has been provided by excluding the conditions necessary for plundering authoritarianism and including embedded, bounded or other more refined forms of autonomy.

The state must also be free from the influence of those classes attached to previous, non-developmental regimes, especially a landed oligarchy, although this could itself be transformed into a burgeoning class of industrialists through its control of the state. Relative to the class of industrialists, the state must be able to resist the demands of individual sectors in order to be able to promote their short and long-term common interests, such as setting the appropriate level of protection. In this way, it is possible to see that the state will also play some role in adjudicating over which capitals survive, since its policies will not be neutral between them; for example, protection for one is a cost increase for another. Finally, the state must be able to resist the immediate, short-term demands of 'populist' pressures in order to meet their goals more effectively in the longer term after developmental goals have been realised; this means containing wage increases and welfare expenditure.[11]

As seen in the debate over South Korea, this almost inevitably leads to the hypothesis that too early democratisation is not necessarily advantageous for economic development, although its absence entails the risk of authoritarian plundering. It may give rise to irresistible pressures through 'militant populism' (usually associated with Latin America) in which excessive wage increases and state expenditure result and lead to macroeconomic instability in the form of hyperinflation. Thus a strong or authoritarian state is essential initially in order to be able to resist, even suppress, popular demands until levels of economic development warrant popular participation. Hence, this is as much about the sequencing of the relationship between economic development and democratic change as it is about what political forms are most appropriate.

Initially an attempt was made with some success to establish a statistical correlation between more authoritarian regimes and economic performance, reminiscent, perhaps, of the cliché that Fascism ensures that the trains run on time. This has subsequently been shown to be a questionable exercise.[12] Apart from the need to disaggregate and specify exactly what are meant by democratic and authoritarian conditions and institutions, the statistical exercise is open to sample selection bias. It is reasonable to suppose that an authoritarian regime is more likely to be overthrown when economic conditions have become disastrous under its tutelage. Then the democratic regime with which it may be replaced is almost certainly to be statistically associated with poor performance over the subsequent period. In short, unless the causes and mechanisms by which political change itself takes place are incorporated, democracy will be systematically discriminated against in statistical analysis, as it tends to be selected by poor economic performance rather than vice versa.

More generally, it can again be suggested that the search for a regular

---

[11] The points in this paragraph are covered in Bardhan (1993).

[12] With a fuller set of arguments, see Haggard and Webb (1993) and Przeworski and Limongi.

and simple relationship between economic development and political change is both futile and misleading. Both are the complex outcome of developments in underlying class relations which are liable to dominate any direct causal or even statistical relations between them. Nonetheless, whether in other more guarded forms in which authoritarianism is to be achieved under the guise of democracy, the idea persists that the representation of the interests of the popular classes must be suppressed in order that their own longer-term interests and a path of economic development can be served.

The South African state and the state of South Africa

Debate over the South African state has traditionally been dominated by the conflict between the liberal and the Marxist revisionist schools. In many ways, this can be viewed as a remarkable anticipation of the more recent theories of the state covered in the previous section. This is because the debate has been concerned with the relationship between capitalism and apartheid, which mirrors the issue of the relationship between the economy and the state.

The liberal school, for example, has understood apartheid as a set of policies adopted by the state that have obstructed the realisation of modernisation and economic progress based on a free labour market and equal access to welfare provision. In this light, it can be seen as belonging to the previously identified political school; apartheid represents a racist form of predatory autonomy in which socio-economic progress is impeded by the self-interest of a diminishing minority of whites and Afrikaner bureaucrats, for it is argued that large-scale capital is increasingly opposed to apartheid as it harms long-run profitability by holding up white wages and restricting the supply of skilled black workers. Interestingly, the demise of apartheid was not only welcomed but also predicted, since apartheid was seen as increasingly dysfunctional as the economy modernised.

The Marxist revisionists have previously argued successfully against the liberal school by showing how apartheid has been capable of generating high levels of profitability through oppressive control of the labour market. It can also be understood as belonging to the political school, but with the accumulation of capital in South Africa being based upon a racist form of authoritarian autonomy. Thus the revisionists emphasise the compatibility of apartheid with capitalism whereas the liberals view apartheid as alien to it. Further, we assign each to the political school since the extent of economic analysis has been remarkably limited for both.

However, each school shares a major difference with the political school. First, the policies and the nature of the state are derived from underlying class relations; mining, agricultural and industrial capital are seen to be crucial, along with the different sections of the workforce. In more sophisticated analyses, such as that of Posel (1991), this never degenerates into a crude economic reductionism but neither does it depend upon an autonomising of the state before consideration of class interests. Even the liberal tradition has tended to discuss the state in terms of control by a coalition of classes made up from the white minority rather than the state having been captured by it.

Our own approach draws upon the revisionist school. In particular, it ultimately identifies a disjuncture between economic and political power within the capitalist class which came to a head in the 1930s with the Afrikaner fraction holding state power and the variously named English, mining or foreign fraction exerting economic control.[13] However, the revisionist analysis then proceeds by searching for the formation of an elite power bloc and reading off the resolution of underlying class conflicts by reference to the policies adopted. In other words, the representation of economic interests are more or less directly reflected through the state.[14]

This leads us to develop, or break with, the revisionist approach in two respects. First, we argue that the formation of economic policies for the inter-war period itself are complex and uneven across different sectors which thus have to be assessed in detail. Therefore the development of a state-owned industry, for example, cannot simply be read off as a policy to create an indigenous, Afrikaner capital. It depends upon how each potential policy is integrated into the rest of the economy, reflecting both economic and political considerations. This discussion forms the focus for Chapter 6, where the revisionist school is considered in greater detail.

The second development over the revisionist school concerns consideration of the shifting class structure on which the apartheid state has been constructed. The revisionists do consider shifting class structure and even the impact of the state upon it, as MacDonald and James reluctantly accepted in the case of O'Meara's (1983) work on Afrikaner capitalists. Even though MacDonald and James emphasise the importance of changes in class structure in understanding the role of the state, they abandon this imperative once they approach more recent times and focus instead upon the ANC as a party of government.[15] By contrast we show in Chapter 7 how state economic policies on behalf of Afrikaner capital in the post-war

---

[13] See especially Davies et al. (1976) and detailed discussion below in Chapter 6.

[14] In this, we reject the assessment of MacDonald and James (1993) that the revisionists are overly economic at the expense of politics, motivated, from their perspective, by an exaggerated emphasis on class. We would point to the underdevelopment of their economic analysis as justification for rejecting their analysis.

[15] A further peculiarity is their neglect of the role of COSATU.

period eventually gave rise to its evolution into large-scale capital integrated with English capital. The path by which this occurred is of considerable importance and the result has been a shifting scope and content of state economic policy itself.

However, the purpose in the remainder of this chapter is not to address past literature on the South African state but to examine how the literature has been transformed with the demise of apartheid. By an accident of timing, the theories of the state previously discussed were emerging just as the apartheid state was suffering what has proved to be its terminal crisis – at least in the political arena. Consequently, it is hardly surprising that the new theories should not have been applied to the apartheid state, although they could have been as part of a renewed historical analysis.

For the liberal school, whose mantle we will consider to have been adopted by N. Nattrass,[16] there has been an astonishing reversal of analytical position. Whereas apartheid is characterised as a state form which obstructs progress through denial of economic and political rights to blacks, and especially to workers, the post-apartheid period is seen as one in which wage increases, state expenditure and economic intervention must be curbed to guard against 'militant populism'. Indeed, drawing heavily upon a selective sample of the new literature on the developmental state, Nattrass essentially concludes that the South African state is incapable of being more than minimally constructive in undertaking economic policy. As it is open to being captured by trade union and other popular pressure groups, business confidence is an essential target of policy, without which there will be inadequate investment. And as business confidence depends upon low wages and minimal state intervention, these must be seen as the central pillars of a social democratic South Africa.

Fine (1995) disputes each of these propositions at length. Of more concern here is to highlight how the political school's approach to the state has been fully adopted. There is an exclusive concern with whether political conditions are conducive to the adoption of the correct, previously determined policies, which are themselves only cursorily examined in terms of wage and public expenditure restraint. The spectre of militant populism, the mirror image of the authoritarian autonomy attached to apartheid, is now perceived as the risk run by a democratic South Africa.

Of course, this view has close affinities with the notion that some sort of authoritarian autonomy is essential, at least in the short term, for the pursuit of appropriate economic policies. However, this is proscribed by

[16] It is probably inappropriate to attach N. Nattrass to the liberal school during the apartheid period but she has best represented their subsequent stance in a series of contributions (1994a–d).

the very conditions in which debate over the South African state must take place. Having only recently won electoral freedom, it can hardly be argued that the state should be able to impose policies against the wishes of the electorate. Consequently, Nattrass seeks a solution to this conundrum in which the restraints of authoritarian autonomy prove accessible to an elected government. She proposes two means to this end. One is to educate the electorate, so that democratic participation is reduced to a programme of persuasion of the virtues of limited wages and welfare. The other is to bind the trade union movement into wage restraint by emulating some form of tri-partheid incorporation with the state and business.

The revisionist school has also experienced a dramatic transformation in its stance on the state; it has tended to assume a position within the economic school, although contributions are few and far between. Far from continuing to examine the class nature of the state, the focus has shifted to identifying the appropriate economic policies in the light of one or another theory of development strategy. Apart from the usual debates around the strategies being peddled by the IMF/World Bank, such as degree of openness, a prominent example of the more passive role played by classes is provided by the analytical framework adopted by the ISP. Informed by a political economy based on the increasing significance of flexible-specialisation, it has attempted to identify appropriate policies sector-by-sector, with attention to the role of either capital or labour classes only as constraints or conduits for those policies, with the state assessed for its capacity to deliver those policies.

In Chapter 10, we include a brief critical assessment of the analytical basis for the ISP project.[17] The purpose here is more to observe to an even greater extent than for the transformed liberal school how the derivation of the state from underlying class relations has withered away. As a corollary, there has necessarily been a neglect of prospective shifts in the South African class structure, with the possible exception of the attention devoted to the prospects for small black business. Paradoxically, the last serious discussion of South Africa's shifting class structure concerned the potential success of a strategy by the apartheid regime to incorporate a buffer layer of middle-class blacks to encourage greater socio-economic and political stability. While that strategy is deemed to have failed, there is no doubt that the character of the post-apartheid state and its policies will reflect what are liable to be fundamental changes in the class structure.

Although our major concern here is not with these prospects, we do examine how the class structure, economic development and the policies of the state have been related to one another. Hopefully, in doing so, we

---

[17] Indeed, much of its detailed sectoral research is inconsistent with the broader ISP framework. The studies are to be published by the University of Cape Town Press.

provide not only some methodological lessons for those who seek to divine the future but also an appropriate starting point for their speculations. As will be seen, the newly emerging literature on the South African state has generally been based upon a limited and false understanding of the apartheid regime's evolving economic and political structure.

Part II. THE MINERALS-ENERGY COMPLEX

4

THE BOUNDARIES OF THE M.E.C.

This chapter demonstrates that the South African economy's current strength lies in what is termed a Minerals-Energy Complex (MEC). This includes the mining and energy sectors and a number of associated sub-sectors of manufacturing, which have constituted and continue to constitute the core site of accumulation in the South African economy. By taking account of the systematic linkages between these different economic activities, the direct and indirect dependence of the entire economy on the MEC is exposed. Contrary to the popular view that there has been a declining role for mining, the economy's dependence on this MEC core has in fact increased.

This discussion first uses a conventional input-output approach to examine the more visible backward linkages between mining and manufacturing sub-sectors, their respective contributions to GDP, exports, employment and their import propensities. It then identifies the specific sub-sectors of manufacturing that constitute the MEC and justifies the MEC concept largely in terms of the material flows between the various sub-sectors. In the process, traditional categories of mining and quarrying and manufacturing are redefined. The role of the MEC in the economy is analysed through macroeconomic indicators, sketching the institutional fabric that supports the MEC, linking it to other economic agencies, such as labour, the state and capital. Finally, this examination moves beyond the notion of the MEC as a core set of activities, as previously examined empirically in the chapter. It goes on to reconstruct the MEC as a system of accumulation, relating the control of the core sectors of the economy to the potential direction that this imparts to the economy as a whole.

Mining and manufacturing in the South African economy

South African statistics normally divide mining into four sub-sectors: gold, coal, diamonds and other mining. Manufacturing covers a range of value adding activities (listed in Appendix A). The traditional view considers mining activities as separate from manufacturing, some outputs

The Minerals-Energy Complex

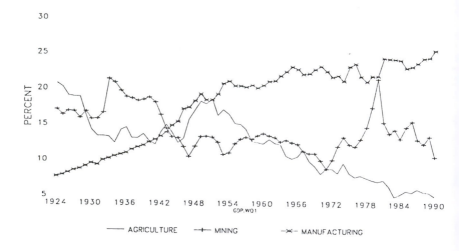

Fig. 4.1. G.D.P. CONTRIBUTION: CONVENTIONAL
PERCEPTIONS, 1924–90

Source: Union Statistics for Fifty Years (1960); *South African Statistics* (1990); IDC (1992).

of mining feeding into manufacturing, and with manufacturing supplying some of mining's requirements for consumable items, such as explosives, drill steels, chemicals and timber roof supports as well as certain capital goods, like earthmoving equipment, mine winders and continuous mining equipment.

The mining industry is widely perceived by policy makers, the business sector and the labour movement to be an industry in decline relative to the manufacturing sector. Mining's role is nevertheless recognised as being important, particularly as a major generator of foreign exchange and as an employer of labour. Particular analyses and policy options flow from the way in which statistics are compiled on the division between mining and manufacturing. Such analyses will be shown to be different from analyses based on recognising the central role of the MEC.

Mining's relative decline is evident in its sectoral contribution to GDP, as low as 12 per cent in 1990. This share has fluctuated between a low of 8 per cent in 1971 and a peak of 22 per cent in 1980 (Fig. 4.1). This is equivalent to about half the contribution of manufacturing and is roughly equal to that of the financial sector and the trade and catering sector

Table 4.1. G.D.P. STATISTICS, 1989

	Million Rand[1]	GDP %
Agriculture, forestry, fishing	11,629	5.6
Mining and quarrying	24,936	12.0
Manufacturing	50,896	24.6
Electricity, gas, water	8,923	4.3
Construction	6,503	3.1
Trade, catering, accommodation services	27,436	13.3
Transport, communication	17,145	8.3
Finance, real estate, business services	28,615	13.8
Community, social, personal services	3,539	1.7
less Imputed financial services	(5,883)	(2.8)
General government	28,285	13.7
Other producers	4,924	2.4
TOTAL	206,948	100.0

1. GDP at factor incomes at current price.

Source: *South African Statistics* (1989).

(Table 4.1). Since 1950, manufacturing's contribution has risen relative to mining.

Since 1970, the mining and quarrying sectors have consistently employed about half the number of workers as manufacturing (Fig. 4.2). Mining employment has fluctuated in a narrow band between 650,000 and 730,000, largely in rhythm with major gold price movements. The crisis in the mining industry in the late 1970s is reflected by a fall in gold's contribution to exports as well as a significant decline in numbers employed. Both sectors have been eclipsed by a steady rise in employment in the social and personal services sectors and in financial, real estate and business services. Since 1986, there has been a steady fall in mining employment, from 763,000 to 707,000 in 1989. About 42,000 or 75 per cent of these jobs were shed in the gold mining industry. Further falls have taken place since 1989.

Compared to mining, manufacturing's share of GDP has risen more consistently in the post-war period (Fig. 4.1). Manufacturing sector employment has grown in the 1970s to more than double that of mining and manufacturing exports have risen faster than mining exports in the 1980s, dovetailing with other historical experiences of growth and development (Fig. 4.2).

The arguments for policies supporting export-oriented manufacturing are rooted in such statistics. Sacob (1990, pp. 45–6), for example, compares South African manufactured exports as a percentage of GDP with similar statistics for developed and developing countries. It then concluded

Fig. 4.2. EMPLOYMENT IN MINING AND MANUFACTURING
Source: South African Labour Statistics (1990).

that South Africa's ratio is among the lowest: 'South Africa is becoming a consistently smaller player in international trade. This is a combination of the effect of sanctions and the lack of an industrial environment
which encourages investment and growth in those industries where the
world's markets are growing the most, namely manufactured products.'

Such policy thrusts, which regard manufacturing as relatively independent from other sectors, are supported by official input-output statistics (Fig. 4.3). These indicate that 7.5 per cent of manufacturing inputs (or
R8.1bn) are sourced from the mining sector. The mining sector on the
other hand seems more dependent on manufacturing which contributed
50 per cent (or R5.5bn) of mining inputs. A high proportion of manufacturing outputs are intermediate ones (of R153.0bn produced, R62.5bn was
intermediate) being fed into other manufacturing sub-sectors. This partly
justifies the focusing of policy on manufacturing, especially for exports
which make up only 10.8 per cent of total manufacturing output (R16.6bn)
(Fig. 4.3), compared to mining exports of 73.6 per cent of total output.[1]

---

[1] Economic activity in both the mining and manufacturing sectors are categorised according
to the International Standard Industrial Classification (ISIC) standards; statistics following

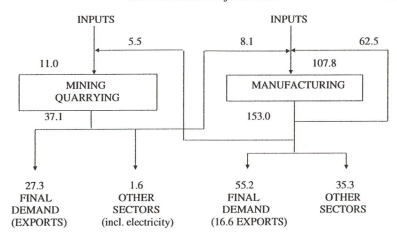

INPUTS   INPUTS

       5.5   8.1   62.5

11.0   107.8

| MINING QUARRYING | MANUFACTURING |

37.1   153.0

| 27.3 FINAL DEMAND (EXPORTS) | 1.6 OTHER SECTORS (incl. electricity) | 55.2 FINAL DEMAND (16.6 EXPORTS) | 35.3 OTHER SECTORS |

Fig. 4.3. MATERIAL FLOWS BETWEEN MINING AND
MANUFACTURING SECTORS (*billion Rand*)

Source: Input-Output Tables (1988).

Manufacturing's importance is illustrated by the scale of its activities, which dwarfs those of the mining industry. In 1988, the mining industry produced ore to the value of R37.1bn, using inputs of R11.0bn (Fig. 4.3). Manufacturing produced goods to the value of R153.0bn, using material inputs worth R107.8bn. An indication of sectoral contribution to GDP is the value added (i.e. the difference between output value and input value). The value added in mining, some 237 per cent of inputs, was almost six times larger than manufacturing's 41.9 per cent of inputs. Nevertheless, the total GDP contribution of manufacturing was about twice that of mining.[2]

South Africa's development trajectory thus appears to be one where mining output provides foreign exchange to pay for imported manufacturing inputs, with the manufacturing sector constituting the engine of growth. In absolute terms, imported mining inputs are one-tenth of the value of manufacturing's imported inputs (Table 4.2). At the aggregate

---

these categorisations are used to determine sectoral contributions to GDP as well as to categorise trade statistics. South African statistics are rather difficult to decipher because much of the production and export of strategic commodities are hidden in catch-all categories like 'classified' or 'mineral products not elsewhere classified'. Approximately half of total reported trade is listed under the 'classified' category. The method used to cull the statistics used in this study is outlined in Appendix B.

[2] See UNIDO (1992) for the use of input-output linkages to chart stages in economic development. We have not compared South Africa to other countries but suspect that it is not typical of the standard if properly disaggregated.

level, economic expansions have required increased imports for manufacturing, which in turn have affected the balance of payments, influenced
monetary and fiscal policy and, finally, have acted to choke off expansion.

The high import propensity of manufacturing is interpreted as arising
from past inward-looking policies of ISI. The apparent shift to more
export-oriented policies in the late 1980s appears to have succeeded in
raising manufacturing exports (Fig. 4.4) and is used to justify the per-
severance with policies which reduce state intervention, are export-
oriented and enhance the capability of the manufacturing sector (IDC
1990).

However, import propensities differ in terms of inputs as a proportion
of outputs. Table 4.2 shows mining's import propensity in terms of share
of inputs is only slightly less than that of manufacturing: 15.1 per cent
compared to 17.8 per cent. However, imports contribute much more to
output in mining. The latter's import propensity as a percentage of output
is 4.7 per cent compared to 12.3 per cent for manufacturing, or more than
three times greater. This is a reflection of the even greater proportion of
value added in mining. Import propensities also differ according to the
diverse activities carried out in mining and manufacturing sub-sectors,
each of which involves different levels of technology, different processes
and linkages and, in particular, specific inputs that are or are not available
locally. This highlights the need for disaggregation of industrial sectors,
particularly when conducting policy studies. Within mining, the coal
sub-sector has the largest propensity to import, with 20.5 per cent of inputs
compared to the mining sector's average of 15.1 per cent. Coal mining,
both underground and open cast, is highly mechanised, requiring a large
quantity of imported equipment.

With this background, we can now move on to show that the conventional view of South Africa's economic development as one of declining
mining and increasing manufacturing activities is misleading, since it is
based on an unduly aggregated notion of manufacturing. Rather, it will
be demonstrated that, apart from their aggregate impact on economic
development, ISI policies are focused on specific sectors and directed at
strengthening and concentrating specific fractions of capital.

The MEC and manufacturing

Although the previous section shows that mining only provides 7.5 per
cent of manufacturing inputs in aggregate terms, these inputs are essential
to several key sectors of manufacturing which in turn support many other
productive activities. At the beginning of 1990, 1,100 mines and quarries
were in operation, producing 80 different minerals. *South African Statistics* (1990, p. 11.16) define the mining sectors as:

Table 4.2. MINING, MANUFACTURING AND M.E.C.
INDUSTRIES – IMPORT INTENSITY (*million Rand*)

	Imported inputs	Total inputs	Import %	Total output	Import %
MEC mining					
Coal	260	1,271	20.5	3,188	8.1
Gold	398	2,924	13.6	11,712	3.4
Diamonds	27	295	9.2	707	3.8
Other mining	269	1,831	14.7	4,888	5.5
Average mining	954	6,321	15.1	20,495	4.7
Total manufacturing					
(incl. MEC)	10,054	56,507	17.8	81,772	12.3
MEC manufacturing					
Fertilisers amd pesticides	193	690	27.9	1,074	17.9
Synthetic resins, plastics	235	1,162	20.2	1,423	16.5
Other chemical products	116	639	18.1	944	12.3
Other basic chemicals	2,061	6,699	30.8	10,380	19.8
Other plastic products	140	1,029	13.6	1,602	8.7
Bricks, tiles, refractories	68	370	18.3	699	9.7
Cement	41	238	17.2	523	7.8
Other non-metallic mining	129	654	19.7	1,090	11.8
Iron and steel	539	3,774	14.3	6,110	8.8
Non-ferrous metals	336	1,581	21.2	2,387	14.1
Electricity	123	2,929	4.2	6,654	1.8
	3,981	19,765	20.1	32,886	12.1
Other manufacturing					
(excl. MEC)	6,073	36,742	16.5	48,886	12.4
Total MEC sectors	4,935	26,086	18.9	53,381	9.2

Source: *Input-Output Tables* (1984).

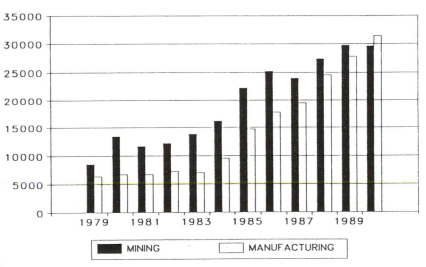

Fig. 4.4. MINING AND MANUFACTURING SECTOR EXPORTS

Source: *South African Statistics* (various years).

Any activities in connection with underground and surface mining, including stone quarries, clay and sand pits, wells (except for water) and salt pans and all supplemental activities for the dressing and beneficiation of ores and other crude materials, such as crushing, screening, grading, milling, flotation, melting, pelleting, topping and other preparations needed to render the material marketable.

Many productive mining activities are integrally linked, often physically integrated, with productive activities within the manufacturing sector. The separation of value added in each usually takes place at the level of national and corporate accounting procedures.

Few mineral-producing countries today export unbeneficiated primary mineral commodities. Many developing countries in recent years have tended to process their minerals at least partially, mainly through smelting, to produce a concentrate of higher value which is then either refined or, more often, shipped to refineries in more developed economies. Jourdan's 1990 study of minerals production in the Southern African region shows that this tendency is fairly advanced: of Zambia's copper production (6 per cent of world supply in 1988), about 98 per cent is exported in the form of pure refined copper cathodes; its cobalt (14 per cent of world supply in 1988) is produced as a by-product of copper smelting; 50 per cent of the region's nickel output is exported as a beneficiated sulphide matte; almost all chromite ore mined in Zimbabwe is smelted and exported as ferrochrome, constituting 7 per cent of world supply in 1988. There are exceptions. Zaire, for example, exports copper blistera (less refined form of copper) to Belgium for refining, even though excess capacity exists in neighbouring Zambian smelters.

Although the smelting and refining of mineral ore is usually integrated with mining operations, with smelters and refineries sited on or close to the mine, the value added is often arbitrarily divided between mining and manufacturing in official statistics. Consider the case of chrome. The mining of this ore underpins the manufacturing activity of smelting the ore, yet the mining activity contributes about one-third less value than the processing of ore. In 1987, the mining of chrome ore contributed about 0.16 per cent to South African GDP, with sales of R242.4m. Smelting the ore produced ferrochrome worth R730.6m and this contributed about 0.48 per cent to the GDP.[3] Smelting is statistically located in the non-ferrous metal basic industry sub-sector of the manufacturing sector, even though there is an almost continuous process involved from mining to ferrochrome production.

The concentrated levels of ownership that characterise the South

[3] Census on Mining (1987, pp. 33, 82–3); GDP data from *South African Statistics* (1990, pp. 21–9).

African economy also have an impact on the allocation of value added. For example, General Mining (Genmin), a subsidiary of Gencor itself formed by the merger of Genmin and Union Corporation in 1980, owns a number of mines through its Cromore (Pty) Ltd holding company. Ore is transported to the nearby smelters of Genmin-owned Tubatse Ferrochrome (Pty) Ltd. The smelting process is operated by a different company within the same conglomerate group for a number of reasons, including the objective of minimising tax and maximising use of specific state policies, such as manufacturing incentives promoting beneficiation and exports. A critical factor is the price at which the raw material is transferred from the 'mining' activity to the 'manufacturing' activity. Often this price is simply an accounting variable which is fixed to maximise group profits. However, the effect of this often exacerbates the artificial difference between mining and manufacturing activities. If the transfer price were lowered due to attractive tax incentives and write-offs in beneficiation, the effect would be to reduce the GDP contribution of mining and, correspondingly, to raise artificially the measured contribution of manufacturing.

The construction and casual interpretation of economic statistics categorised as mining or manufacturing, together with the arbitrary allocation of value added to each, does not adequately and accurately represent the strengths and weaknesses of South Africa's resource-based economy and can therefore be misleading. It is more apposite to recognise productive linkages and to conceptualise them integrally. In this vein, a MEC can be identified which includes as a minimum the following economic sectors:[4]

– coal, gold, diamond and other mining activities;
– electricity;
– non-metallic mineral products;[5]
– iron and steel basic industries;
– non-ferrous metals basic industries;[6] and
– fertilisers, pesticides, synthetic resins, plastics, other chemicals, basic chemicals and petroleum.

The rationale for including these primary and secondary mineral processing activities, together with electricity, within the boundaries of the MEC is developed further below.

---

[4] These are largely related to productive activities downstream of mining. The capital goods and mining supply industries that produce inputs for mining are not dealt with empirically in this chapter. However, it is clear that their inclusion would serve to extend the scope of the MEC.

[5] Includes mica, phosphate concentrate, bricks, tiles, refractories and cement.

[6] Includes platinum group metals, silver and ferrochrome.

While existing statistics categorise 'electricity' as an economic activity separate from mining and quarrying and manufacturing, there are extensive linkages between these.[7] More than 90 per cent of electricity is generated from coal, a mining activity, with the balance sourced from hydro-electric and nuclear stations. The latter also ultimately sources its feed from uranium mining and electricity-intensive enrichment. Some 21.6 per cent of electricity output is consumed in the coal, gold, diamond and other mining sectors. An additional 21.3 per cent of electricity output is consumed in the energy-intensive smelting and refining processes in just three sub-sectors of manufacturing: other non-metallic mineral products, iron and steel basic industries and non-ferrous metal basic industries.[8]

While chemicals and petroleum production activities may seem remote from mining, they are linked largely through the coal mining industry, on which the South African economy is heavily reliant. The production of fertilisers, plastics, chemicals and petroleum depend on energy-intensive processes which consume large quantities of electricity generated from coal. The Sasol II and III plants at Secunda in the eastern Transvaal utilise a large proportion of the output of the nearby 3600MW Kriel power station, which in fact was built specifically for that purpose.[9] Of the 175.6 million tonnes of coal mined in South Africa in 1989, 46.8 million tonnes was exported. From remaining local sales of 128.8 million tonnes, 70.0 million tonnes was used by Escom to produce electricity, 35.0 million tonnes was consumed by the three Sasol plants to produce synthetic fuels and chemicals and 1.1 million tonnes was used by the African Explosives and Chemical Industries (AECI) company to produce ammonia, explosives and methanol at Modderfontein. AECI also produces some chemicals at Umbogintwini from coal feedstock. The AECI/Sentrachem Coalplex plant at Sasolburg produces PVC from coal and, until it was recently mothballed, Sentrachem was producing synthetic rubber at Newcastle from coal at its Karbochem plant. A coal-based industrial gas grid supplies industries in the PWV (Pretoria-Witwatersrand Vereeniging) area from the Sasol plant in Sasolburg.[10]

Non-metallic mineral products such as cement and bricks, the inputs to building and construction industries, are immediate downstream activities from mining. In both cases, mined or quarried products, such as

---

[7] Strictly speaking, this category is defined as electricity, gas and steam although the value of gas and steam generated is low. See *South African Statistics* (1990).

[8] Based on *Input-Output Tables* (1988), after excluding losses in generation and transmission.

[9] 500MW is generated internally and 400MW is bought in. The greatest demand is from the air separation plants.

[10] The PWV triangle contains the heart of South Africa's mining and manufacturing.

limestone and gypsum, are crushed mixed and heated, often using coal as the fuel. These plants are usually located close to the quarries which supply their raw materials.

Iron and steel industries are not as numerous as cement and brick-making plants. They are more capital-intensive and have also been regarded by almost every government in the world as a strategic economic sector. Even today, when state intervention is no longer fashionable and under ideological attack, many of the steel industries in Europe are protected either directly or indirectly. Of the three steel producers in South Africa, the recently privatised Iscor dominates the industry. Iron ore, coal and electricity constitute the major inputs to steel manufacture which is produced in the form of shapes, sections, tubes, wire and castings. Other mineral products, such as chrome and vanadium, are also used to produce alloys and various grades of stainless steels, although at present only one plant, Middleburg Steel and Alloys, produces stainless steel. Some 62.8 per cent of direct inputs to the iron and steel basic industries is sourced from within the MEC while 22 per cent of the iron and steel sector's output is fed back into the MEC.

Chrome, copper, silver, aluminum, platinum and platinum group metals are the major components of the non-ferrous metals category. As with steel, the respective ores are smelted and refined to produce the basic sections, castings or refined mattes that are then either sold on commodity markets or used in subsequent manufacturing activities.

The cohesion of the MEC is illustrated by Table 4.3, which shows that 58.3 per cent of MEC inputs are from the MEC and that 27.7 per cent of MEC output is returned to MEC sectors. Both the above discussion and this table make it clear that it is more useful to distinguish between a non-MEC manufacturing sector and the MEC core, made up of mining and quarrying, the electricity sector and a number of related sub-sectors of manufacturing.

The change in the composition of GDP resulting from focusing upon the central role of the MEC is illustrated in Fig. 4.5. Since 1960, non-MEC manufacturing has stagnated within a narrow band of 15–17 per cent of GDP. The MEC's relative contribution to GDP fell in the 1960s from 22 per cent to about 17 per cent but rose to a high of 32 per cent in 1980; it then settled within a band of 25–27 per cent. The impact of the most recent decline in the gold price is partly shown by the dip in the MEC's contribution to GDP from 27.5 per cent in 1989 to 25 per cent in 1990. But unlike mining alone, the MEC is not only affected by the gold price. Escom power generation, Sasol's petrochemicals complex and the rise in minerals processing have underpinned its integrated dominance of the economy. The largest growth in the MEC's GDP contribution seems to have taken place in the capital-intensive minerals processing and chemical

Table 4.3. THE INTERDEPENDENCE OF THE M.E.C.–
INPUT/OUTPUT LINKAGES

MEC value added as % of output	52.6
MEC inputs as % of total inputs	58.3
MEC outputs as % of total outputs	27.7

MEC sub-sector	Inputs from MEC	Inputs from other sectors	Value added labour profit taxes	Output to MEC	Output to other sectors
Coal	653	1,484	2,988	1,952	3,172
Gold	1,843	3,228	16,706	0	21,776
Diamonds	197	734	1,081	0	2,012
Other mining	963	1,920	5,319	6,709	1,492
Fertilisers and pesticides	755	315	267	181	1,155
Synthetic resins, plastics	1,964	417	697	1,726	1,352
Other chemicals	692	470	525	1,016	672
Other basic chemicals, petroleum	6,477	2,918	6,674	4,831	11,237
Other plastic products	1,437	602	916	300	2,654
Bricks, tiles, refractories	397	264	511	94	1,079
Cement	212	162	497	202	669
Other non-metal mineral products	691	441	699	284	1,547
Iron and steel basic industries	4,899	2,897	4,096	1,725	10,167
Non-ferrous metal basic industries	2,057	1,166	1,879	1,123	3,980
Electricity	3,269	1,939	7,279	6,364	6,122
Total	26,506	18,957	50,134	26,507	69,086

Source: Input-Output Tables (1988).

(largely Sasol) industries in the 1980s, whereas it was the electricity industry that grew in the 1970s (Fig. 4.6).

What particularly stands out is that the growth of the MEC has been accompanied by stagnation of the non-MEC manufacturing sector since 1960. The latter's contribution to GDP has not risen above its 18 per cent level of 1981 and has declined to 15 per cent in 1989. Non-MEC manufacturing also exhibits weak forward and backward linkages with the MEC (Fig. 4.7). However, forward linkages between the MEC and non-MEC manufacturing are stronger than between mining and manufacturing. Some 22.1 per cent of non-MEC manufacturing inputs are drawn from the MEC, mainly from the iron and steel, basic chemicals and petroleum, synthetic resin and plastic and non-ferrous metal sub-sectors. However, MEC backward linkages are relatively weak, almost de-linked from manufacturing. Only 13.4 per cent of MEC inputs were drawn from manufacturing. This contrasts with the more conventional analysis of mining versus manufacturing, where 50 per cent of mining inputs are drawn from the manufacturing sector.

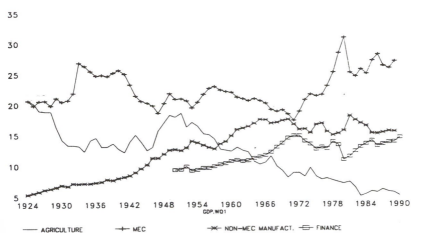

Fig. 4.5. G.D.P. CONTRIBUTION OF THE M.E.C., 1924–90

Source: Union Statistics for Fifty Years (1960); South African Statistics (1990); IDC (1992).

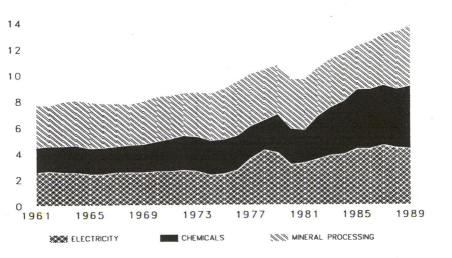

Fig. 4.6. G.D.P. CONTRIBUTION OF MINERAL PROCESSING,
CHEMICALS AND ELECTRICITY

Source: South African Statistics (1990).

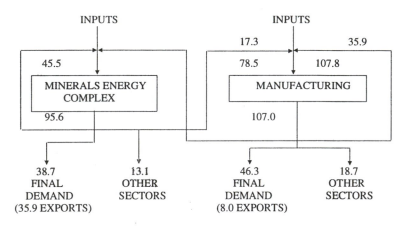

Fig. 4.7. MATERIAL FLOWS BETWEEN M.E.C. AND
MANUFACTURING (*billion Rand*)

Source: Input-Output Tables (1988).

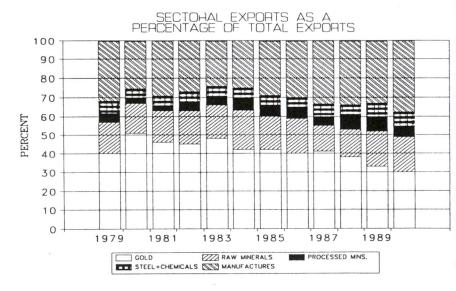

Fig. 4.8. SECTORAL EXPORTS AS % OF TOTAL EXPORTS

Source: South African Statistics (various years); South Africa's Mineral Industry Yearbook (various
years).

The impression drawn from Fig. 4.4 that manufacturing exports are rapidly surpassing those of mining is misleading. While mining as a percentage of total exports have gradually declined during the 1980s, the economy has remained dependent on exports from the more broadly defined MEC. Dependence on foreign exchange from gold exports has shifted to dependence on exports of other raw minerals, processed minerals, steel and chemicals (Fig. 4.8). Thus, in the same period that gold's share fell from 51 per cent to 31 per cent of exports, total MEC exports as a percentage of all other exports fell from 75 per cent to only 63 per cent, emphasising the centrality and resilience of the MEC within the South African economy, even if the absolute export volume has not always grown or ever been sustained. The apparent relative rise in exports of non-MEC manufactures is partly due to declining commodity prices, including that of gold.[11] One-third of manufacturing exports consist of processed minerals, steel and chemicals.

What is also apparent is the classic vulnerability of a developing economy to fluctuating mineral commodity prices, both raw and beneficiated. Fig. 4.9 illustrates cyclical movement in the share of gold exports. Non-gold raw mineral exports as a percentage of total exports have fluctuated between 17 per cent and 21 per cent during the 1980s, with the exception of 1987 and 1988 when they fell to 14 per cent (Fig. 4.10). Processed minerals (mainly ferro-alloys and vanadium) have swung between 3 per cent and 8 per cent of total exports between 1979 and 1990, falling back to 5 per cent in 1990 due to plummeting commodity prices (Fig. 4.11). Exports of beneficiated minerals, such as steel and chemicals, which are both part of the MEC, rose from 5 per cent of total exports to 9 per cent between 1980 and 1990.

The import propensity of the MEC is higher than that of non-MEC manufacturing in terms of inputs (18.9 per cent versus 17.8 per cent) and slightly lower in relation to output (9.2 per cent compared to 12.3 per cent). Despite the highly capital-intensive nature of MEC sectors and their acknowledged reliance on imported capital goods, imports of intermediate consumables are also included in aggregated statistics of import propensity. A major reason for the high import propensity of the MEC is the continuing dependence of the other basic chemicals sub-sector on imported crude oil. Roughly 20 per cent of all 1984 manufacturing sector imports were related to crude oil imports. Of course, this might have reduced since 1984, the year on which these statistics were based.

Shifting MEC activities out of manufacturing reveals a more even pattern of employment between the MEC and manufacturing (Fig. 4.12). Employment in manufacturing outside the MEC grew from 0.81 million

---

[11] Commodity Export Price Indices (CEPI) have declined in real rand terms since 1983. Refer to Minerals Bureau (1988; 1991).

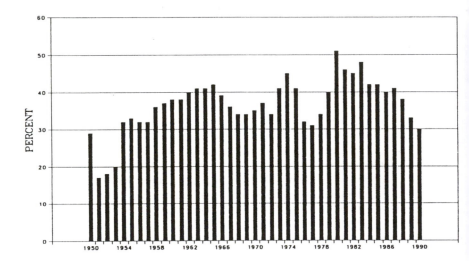

Fig. 4.9. GOLD EXPORTS AS % OF TOTAL EXPORTS

Source: *South African Statistics* (various years).

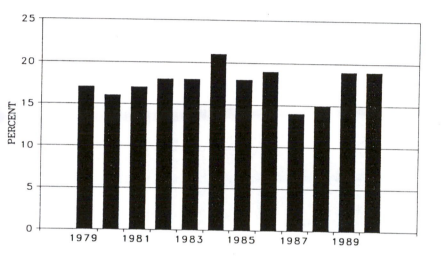

Fig. 4.10. NON-GOLD RAW MINERAL EXPORTS
AS % OF TOTAL EXPORTS

Source: *South African Statistics* (various years), South Africa's Mineral Industry Yearbook (various
years).

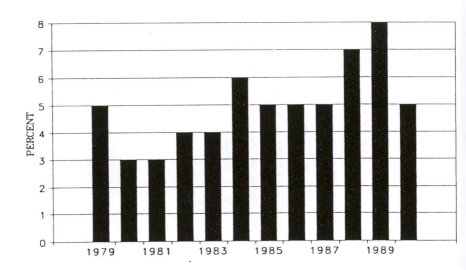

Fig. 4.11. PROCESSED MINERAL EXPORTS AS % TOTAL EXPORTS

Source: *South African Statistics* (various years), South Africa's Mineral Industry Yearbook (various years).

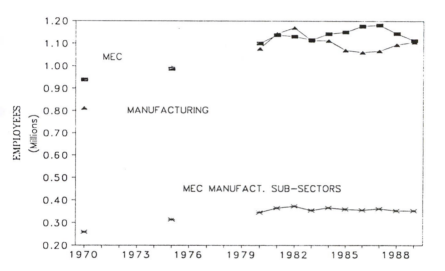

Fig. 4.12. EMPLOYMENT IN THE M.E.C.

Source: *South African Labour Statistics* (various years).

in 1970 to a peak of 1.12 million in 1982, falling to about 1.06 million in 1986 but subsequently rising again. MEC employment has been falling since 1986, largely due to the declining gold mining industry. Sub-sectors of manufacturing that have fallen within the MEC have employed a fairly static number of workers in the 1980s (about 350,000). In part, this reflects the capital-intensity of MEC manufacturing sectors. The downturn in the gold mining industry has had a severe impact on many other sectors of the economy. Frost (1990) shows that it also led to attempts to increase the mechanisation of gold mining, although this met with limited success. The mechanisation of mining has been a continuous process, driven by material factors such as ore grades and depths as well as by the exploitative relationships between labour and capital. Mechanisation has been increasingly energy-intensive, particularly through electricity use.

The liberal-modernist view of capitalism's progressive impact on apartheid[12] is thrown into doubt empirically by recognition of the MEC. Apartheid and in particular the system of supplying cheap labour are said to have favoured mining but not some of the more sophisticated capital-intensive continuous manufacturing processes. This stance suggests a tension between these manufacturing interests and those of mining. However, the evidence of increasing mechanisation in mining sectors such as coal, platinum and diamonds imply that the above dichotomy between mining and manufacturing in this respect is not so stark. In addition, mechanisation is lower in the case of gold mining largely due to technical factors rather than the low level of wages. For huge quantities of capital have been expended by gold mining houses through the Chamber of Mines Research Organisation (COMRO) in searching for ways to raise productivity in gold mining.[13] Contrary to assertions that the manufacturing sector is the greatest creator of wealth, value added is actually higher in the mining sector (Table 4.4); it is on average R35,282/employee, compared to manufacturing's R31,236/employee in 1988.[14] This is likely to rise with increasing mining mechanisation. Low wages are not relevant here since value added is defined as wages, taxes and profits. Mining is clearly as important a site of national accumulation as manufacturing. Moreover, as has been demonstrated above, mining is the starting point for much downstream MEC and other economic activity.

---

[12] See, for example, Lipton (1986).

[13] Interestingly, Edwards (1991) has shown that R&D spending in the mining and mineral processing industries is highest when commodity prices are high, with it falling with the fall in prices. Thus there has recently been a drastic curtailment in R&D spending by the Chamber of Mines, suggesting a tightening budget constraint in times of economic recession.

[14] Based on *Input-Output Tables* (1988), with aggregate figures for revenue minus costs relative to employment, given by mining at (R37bn-R11bn)/732522 and manufacturing at (R153bn-R108bn)/1448500.

Table 4.4. VALUE ADDED IN MINING AND MANUFACTURING

	Wages	Gross profits	Indirect taxes	Employees[1]	Value added per employee
Coal	1,209	1,709	69	93,767	31,855
Gold	7,005	9,554	146	531,640	31,422
Diamonds	356	689	36	14,497	74,567
Other mining	1,679	3,421	219	99,619	53,393
Total mining	10,249	15,373	470	739,523	35,282
Manufacturing	23,771	20,476	998	1,448,500	31,236

Source: Input-Output Tables (1988).
1. 1987 figures, *South African Statistics* (1990).

The MEC as a system of accumulation

The MEC thus far has been referred to as and has been demonstrated to be *a core set of industrial sectors* which exhibit very strong linkages between each other and relatively weaker linkages with other sectors listed in input-output tables. In short, the MEC has primarily been identified descriptively. However, subsequent chapters also refer to the MEC as *a system of accumulation*. An explanation of the difference in the uses of the term minerals-energy complex is necessary at this point for two reasons: first to avoid confusion; secondly, to outline the methodological position occupied by a concept which can be applied to interpret and explain the process of industrialisation in the specific context of South Africa. There is no presumption that the MEC is applicable to other countries since it has been analytically developed to suit the South African case. As a system of accumulation, the MEC addresses the process by which the core set of industries outlined above have developed historically and have influenced how other sectors have developed.

Thus the next chapter outlines the important political and economic counterparts to the strength and cohesiveness of the core, namely the form of ownership and control of the core sectors. Here it is shown that, while conglomerate ownership dominates the MEC core industries, control extends to other sectors also. In the specific South African context, conglomerate power over the economy, reinforced through simultaneous control of the financial sector, is shown potentially to extend to *all* activities and sub-sectors within mining, manufacturing and financial activities. This is specific, possibly unique, to South Africa.

The MEC is also used to refer to the process by which accumulation is carried out within the broader economy, not just within the MEC core. This arises in part because, in South Africa, conglomerate control across all productive sectors means that even though strong linkages have evolved within MEC core sectors, the process of accumulation has often encompassed other sectors with varying intensities at different points in time and with different outcomes. This complex history is outlined in Part II. It is also shown how relationships between various arms of the state and private capital as well as the role of the financial sector have led to the particular structure and location of the sectors defined as lying inside or/and outside the MEC core. The way these relationships have manifested themselves in the process of industrialisation is referred to as the MEC as a system of accumulation. Sectorally, this system encompasses those sectors outside the MEC core industries but this does not contradict the simultaneous understanding of the MEC as comprising a core set of industrial sectors. Instead, the analysis of the system of accumulation is tailored to unravelling the specific process of South African industrial development. It analyses the internal dynamics and empirical outcomes of industrialisation in the context of a particular evolution of economic and political power.

As a system of accumulation, then, the MEC potentially incorporates all economic sectors, since these have necessarily been associated with each other through ownership and control, through relationships between state and capital or through the imperatives of apartheid. Some ambiguity necessarily arises over the boundaries between MEC (core) and non-MEC sectors since multiple criteria of (non)-membership arise: by core sector or not, by political, economic and functional forms of control, by the linkages in input and output tables, etc. Thus the arbitrary boundary drawn in this chapter around the MEC core has not been extended to the engineering industry (in part in the form of capital goods), although the latter has long been associated with MEC core sectors.

There are a number of reasons for this. First, although closely linked to MEC core sectors, engineering sector activity in the South African instance is shown to have been subordinate to these sectors in the sense of its having exhibited limited momentum of its own in diversifying from serving the core sectors. Secondly, the purpose of singling out engineering is to demonstrate how the MEC as a system of accumulation has followed a limited and narrow pattern of industrial development and that the reasons for this lie outside the fact that close *linkages* existed between the MEC core and engineering. It is precisely because much of engineering has been closely linked to the MEC core that it has been limited in scope as a reflection of the evolution of the MEC as a system of accumulation. Ownership may have been extended from the core to the engineering subsectors but many of the input-output linkages (itself a separate criterion) have remained weak.

Appendix A
I.S.I.C.* MANUFACTURING CATEGORIES

Food
Beverages
Tobacco and tobacco products
Textiles
Wearing apparel (footwear)
Leather, products of leather and leather substitutes
Footwear
Wood
Wood and cork products (excl. furniture)
Furniture and fixtures
Paper and paper products
Printing, publishing and allied industries
Industrial chemicals
Other chemical products
Rubber products
Plastic products (not elsewhere classified)
Pottery, china and other earthenware
Glass and glass products
Other non-metallic mineral products
Iron and steel basic industries
Non-ferrous metal basic industries
Fabricated metal products (excl. machinery and equipment)
Machinery (excl. electrical)
Electrical machinery, apparatus, appliances and supplies
Motor vehicles, parts and accessories
Transport equipment (excl. motor vehicles parts and accessories)
Professional and scientific, measuring and controlling equipment
Photographic and optical goods
Other industries

---

* International Standard Industrial Classification.

Appendix B

NOTES ON STATISTICAL SOURCES

The major sources of mineral production statistics have been:
1. Minerals Bureau – used to determine the extent of raw and processed minerals production and exports.
2. National Accounting/Foreign Trade Statistics – the basis of input-output tables; used to determine forward and backward linkages between mining activities and the rest of the economy as well as the contributions of the various economic sectors to gross domestic product.

Minerals Bureau: raw minerals

Total annual raw minerals production and exports (tonnage and value) are published in South Africa's Mineral Industry Yearbook's, *Minerals Bureau*. These statistics are reproduced by the Department of Mineral and Energy Affairs in their *Annual Report*. Categories of minerals are divided as follows:

Precious: diamonds, gold, platinum group metals, silver
Metallic minerals: antimony, beryllium, chrome ore, cobalt, copper, iron ore, lead, manganese ore, monazite, nickel, tantallite/colombite, tin, titanium minerals, uranium oxide, zinc, zirconium minerals
Non-Metallic minerals: andalusite, asbestos, barytes, coal, corundum, feldspar, fluorspar, gypsum, kieselguhr, limestone and dolomite, magnesite, mica, mineral pigments, nephaline syemite, perlite, phosphate concentrate, pyrophyllite, salt, semiprecious stones, silcrete, silica, sillimanite, sodium sulphate, sulphur, talc, vermiculite
Dimension and building stone: granite, marble, quartzite, schist, shale, siltstone, slate
Clay: attapulgite, bentonite, fire clay, flint, kaolin, brickmaking
Aggregate and sand
Miscellaneous: Includes several of the above minerals for which individual production statistics are classified as secret: precious diamonds, platinum group metals, metallic antimony, cobalt, monazite, tin, titanium minerals, uranium oxide, zirconium minerals, non-metallic mica, phosphate concentrate

Minerals Bureau: Processed Minerals

Ferro-alloys: chromium alloys, manganese alloys, ferromanganese, ferrosilicomanganese, ferrosilicon, silicon metal
Aluminium
Vanadium
Other: titanium slag, manganese dioxide, low manganese (ductile) iron, antimony, trioxide
Iron and steel

Foreign trade statistics

These are published by the Commissioner for Customs and Excise under two classification systems:

Harmonised system – statistics published at the 8-digit level
ISIC – statistics published at the 4-digit level

National accounts

These classify industrial activity according to the Standard Industrial Classification (SIC) and divides mining and MEC manufacturing activities as follows:

MINING AND QUARRYING

Coal (SIC 2100)
Gold (SIC 2400)
Diamonds (SIC 2700)
Other mining (SIC 2200, 2300, 2800, 2900).

MANUFACTURING

Iron and steel basic industries (SIC 371): basic iron and steel, steel pipe, tube mills
Non-ferrous metal basic industries (SIC 372): primary non-ferrous metal products (including platinum)
Other non-metallic mineral products (SIC 361, 369): bricks, tiles, refractories, cement etc.
Fertilisers, pesticides, synthetic resins, plastics, other chemicals, basic chemicals, petroleum (SIC 351–4)

5

CORPORATE STRUCTURE

The South African economy has been dominated by six conglomerates which, because of their simultaneous control of the mining, manufacturing and financial sectors, are more usefully viewed as 'axes' of capital. The historical process by which this particular corporate form has evolved in South Africa is discussed in other chapters and represents the operation of the MEC as a system of accumulation.

Section one analyses the extent of concentrated ownership by economic sector. Starting with the mining industry, the economy's dependence on gold is shown to have shifted to a broader range of minerals, in which the production of each is controlled by one or more of the six axes. Conglomerate control extends into the manufacturing sector. In the first instance, it covers the activities immediately downstream of mining, including mineral processing and chemical production. Secondly, the industries that produce the key inputs for these sectors, particularly the engineering industries, are also characterised by conglomerate domination. Thirdly, all other sub-sectors of manufacturing exhibit considerable ownership concentration. The financial sector is also shown to lie within the sphere of control of six axes of capital; this has served to reproduce and further extend conglomerate control of other productive sectors. Acknowledgement of conglomerate control of the South African economy is not novel. The corporate structure that is outlined here is typical of modern capitalism, although the degree of concentration in South Africa is more acute than in other developing and industrialised economies. In recent debates, concentration is acknowledged and usually interpreted in terms of the way it has adversely affected industrial performance.[1]

The South African economy is also a 'mixed' economy, in that there is both state and private ownership of productive sectors (agriculture, mining, manufacturing) and the financial sector. The extent of state ownership is outlined in the second section of this chapter, where it is shown that, while state ownership of the productive sector is not large in com-

[1] See, for example, Lewis (1993).

parison with private ownership, it is concentrated in sectors associated with the MEC. The historical relationship between state and private capital in the industrialisation process is dealt with elsewhere in this book but what is demonstrated in particular here is that the state-owned sectors have fulfilled a particularly important function in lubricating both the growth of MEC core sectors and the ascendance of large-scale private capital. In addition to its creation of industries in and around the MEC, the state in its regulatory role is shown to have supported the emergence of large-scale capital which, as demonstrated in Chapter 4, has concentrated its activity within the MEC core. This is discussed in the final section of this chapter.

To a large extent, coordination of private capital has been through its own corporate structures, as detailed in this chapter, and through the century-old Chamber of Mines at the historical core of the MEC. Within mining as a whole, the six main producers – forming the so-called group system – have dominated the Chamber of Mines with each of the six producers allowed two representatives on the Chamber's governing council and one each on its executive, which has been charged with day-to-day policy. In the 1980s, the Chamber had an annual budget of over R300m., dealing with a range of matters for the mining industries as a whole, including negotiation of wages and conditions, the running of migrant recruitment, and the marketing of Krugerrand etc.

The relations between private and public corporations and the coordination of policy have also been institutionally formalised, most explicitly with the formation of the Department of Mineral and Energy Affairs (DMEA). This was initially created in 1980 by bringing together previously separated departments covering energy and minerals (DMEA 1980, p. 71):

> For the first time in the history of the public administration system in South Africa all energy related functions are not only housed in one and the same department, but are housed in a department which is responsible for both the energy and the mineral policy of the country.

The concentration of power involved is explicitly detailed as follows – noting that the Energy Policy Committee, formed in 1974, has been responsible for making policy recommendations to Cabinet:

> The energy function of the former Department of Environmental Planning and Energy was incorporated into the newly formed Department of Mineral and Energy Affairs on 1st March 1980. This transfer of function included the transfer of the Energy Policy Committee. The Electricity Control Board, Escom (Electricity Supply Commission) and Sasol (S.A. Coal, Oil an Gas Corporation Ltd) were transferred from the former Department of Industries to the Department of Mineral

and Energy Affairs on 1 June 1980 as were several other institutions and functions concerned with liquid fuels. Energy functions of the former Department of Commerce and Consumer Affairs relating to coal and liquid fuels were taken over on 7 October 1980 so that all energy functions in the Public Service, with the exception, at present, of the energy-related aspects of coal research, are now vested in the Department of Mineral and Energy Affairs. (p.71)

The Energy Policy Committee has itself been made up from all of the leading public sector figures in energy (including transport, finance, commerce and industry) together, in 1981 for example, with two private sector representatives – from Gypsum Industries Limited and Sentrachem Limited, for example, both heavy energy users within the MEC and subject to major corporate affiliate control (DMEA 1981, p. 60).

This is a brief outline of the institutional relations between the state and corporate capital at the core of the MEC. We begin here, however, with the structure of private corporate capital.

Corporate Structure and the MEC

Corporate structure has evolved around the MEC core. The origins of the MEC lie in mining. After exhaustion of surface gold deposits, it was the enormous economies of scale required by deep mining conditions which led to early concentration of ownership: 'Out of the 576 gold mining companies floated on the Rand during the period 1887–1932... only 57 remained in existence in 1932... The 57 goldmining companies in existence in 1932 were, with some minor exceptions, controlled by six finance houses or groups.' (Davies 1979 p. 50 quoting Frankel 1938)

The conglomerate forms that have developed since then are extensions of this oligopoly, whose power is in part rooted in the control of the financial sector (discussed below). The economy has gravitated away from a dependence on gold and diamond mining to a range of other raw and processed minerals (Table 5.1). This has largely occurred during and after the 1960s, particularly with the growth of coal, ferro-chrome, platinum, vanadium and copper mining. The smelting and refining activities of many of these are measured under the manufacturing sector.

Table 5.2 illustrates the extent of oligopoly in the production of the most valuable minerals. The subsidiaries of six large mining houses, namely the Anglo American Corporation (AAC), General Mining Corporation, Anglo Transvaal (Anglovaal), Rand Mines (itself a subsidiary of SA Mutual, the Life Assurance Company), Genmin, Sanlam (the life assurance company), Gold Fields of South Africa (GFSA) and Johannesburg Consolidated Investment (JCI, a subsidiary of AAC) dominate the production and marketing of all individual mineral markets. With the exception of iron ore, the six conglomerates mine more than 70 per cent of all major minerals in South Africa. Bain (1951) has suggested that significant monopoly or oligopoly power is indicated if the eight largest firms (C8 ratio) control more than 70 per cent of the market. Alcorto argues that such ratios are largely a matter of degree but that a C4 ratio of 75 per cent can be regarded as significant (Table 5.3). Even if Alcorto's more conservative indicators are used, the production of most minerals fall into the highly concentrated category. In any case, the purpose here is less to highlight individual *market* dominance and more to illustrate the pattern of evolving economic dominance by large-scale capital.

Table 5.1. MINERAL PRODUCTION, 1988

	Tonnes	Estimated value (million Rand)	% share of total mineral value[2]
Gold	612	19,687	54
Coal	180,182,000	5,761	16
Diamonds	n.a.	n.a.	n.a.
Ferro-chrome[1]	1,190,000	3,551	10
Platinum[1]	2,580	3,092	9
Vanadium[1]	29,545	1,249	3
Copper	168,000	932	3
Iron ore	25,029,000	560	1
Manganese ore	3,447,000	354	1
Lime/limestone	15,721,000	320	1
Chromite ore	3,401,000	316	1
Nickel	n.a.	n.a.	n.a.
Uranium	4,590	n.a.	n.a.
Zircon sand	135,000	176	<1
Titanium	n.a.	n.a.	n.a.
Asbestos	109	n.a.	n.a.
Fluorspar	358,000	84	<1
Silver	182	81	<1
Salt	794,000	59	<1
Antimony	8,838	46	<1
		36,268	100

1. Item statistically recorded under the manufacturing sector. We have included it here since secondary processing is often carried out by subsidiaries of the major holding companies.

2. This represents only the totals listed and thus should be regarded solely as indicative.

Source: Central Statistical Service, (1990).

Table 5.2. MINERAL PRODUCTION, 1988: MARKET CONCENTRATION
OF THE SIX MAJOR MINING HOUSES (%)

	Anglo American (AAC)[1]	Rand Mines (SA Mutual)	Gencor (Sanlam)	JCI (AAC)	Anglo Vaal (family)	GFSA (family)	% of total market
Gold[2]	39	8	14	6	6	18	91
Coal[3]	23	20	21	3	–	4	71
Diamonds	100	–	–	–	–	–	100
Ferro-chrome	–	27	42	13	8	–	90
Platinum	49	1	39	2	–	–	91
Vanadium	77	–	–	–	–	–	77
Copper	69	–	–	–	29	2	100
Iron ore[4]	?	–	–	–	?	–	30
Chromite ore	3	30	42	–	9	–	84
Antimony	–	–	–	100	–	–	100

1. Ultimate controlling shareholder in brackets. *Source*: McGregor (1990).

2. 1989 statistics used for market share.

3. 1984 statistics used for market share.

4. Information not available. Iscor is the largest consumer of iron ore, owning most of its mines. Since privatisation, no clear ownership control of Iscor has emerged, but AAC, SA Mutual and the IDC hold significant stakes.

Source: Rustomjee (1990).

Table 5.3. MEASURES OF INDUSTRY CONCENTRATION

	C4 concentration %[1]
Highly concentrated	>75
Concentrated	50–75
Mildly concentrated	25–50
Not concentrated	<25

1. C4 represents the cumulative market share of the four largest firms.

Source: Alcorto.

The MEC core has expanded out of mining into downstream mineral processing activities carried out by subsidiary companies of the conglomerates. Such statistics are measured within the manufacturing sector, which itself exhibits an oligopolistic pattern of market control and a concentration of ownership among the same conglomerates that control the mining sector.[2] About 37 per cent of the manufacturing sector's output is from MEC sectors, including the steel, chemical and mineral processing industries, each of which is dominated by one or other conglomerate. Each

[2] See Dollery (1983), Du Plessis (1978), Fourie and Smit (1989), and Tregenna-Piggott (1976; 1979; 1980).

of these sectors is highly concentrated, with the C5 per cent index (i.e. the cumulative market share of the dominant 5 per cent of firms) above 75 per cent (Table 5.4).[3] Engineering sectors exhibit slightly lower C5 per

Table 5.4. MANUFACTURING FACTOR CONCENTRATION
INDEX: MARKET SHARE OF TOP 5% OF FIRMS

	Value of sales 1988[1]	*1972 % market share*[2]	*1982 % market share*[2]
MEC industries			
Industrial chemicals	7.3	55.2	77.0
Other chemicals	15.3	51.7	76.0
Rubber	1.8	n.a.	n.a.
Plastic	2.2	37.2	55.8
Non-metallic minerals	3.5	67.4	77.1
Iron and steel	10.8	71.3	78.3
Non-ferrous metals	3.2	46.7	51.3
	44.1		
Engineering industries			
Fabricated metal	7.1	57.2	64.5
Machinery	5.4	51.5	62.4
Electrical machinery	6.0	59.0	66.5
Motor vehicles	12.2	79.0	82.4
Transport equipment	1.2	69.3	73.8
Professional and scientific	0.4	52.4	60.6
	32.3		
Non-MEC industries			
Food	17.4	56.4	66.4
Beverages	5.2	74.3	60.6
Tobacco	1.3	n.a.	n.a.
Textiles	4.6	44.9	55.1
Wearing apparel	2.6	46.3	48.3
Leather	0.7	34.1	48.2
Footwear	1.3	40.2	42.2
Wood and cork	1.9	43.1	58.2
Furniture	1.0	49.6	50.0
Paper	5.8	45.5	64.0
Printing and publishing	2.5	61.2	61.9
	44.3		
Total (all sectors)	120.7		

1, *Source*: Central Statistical Service (1990).

2. *Source*: Fourie and Smit (1989).

[3] Fourie and Smit (1989) have also demonstrated this tendency using the Gini Coefficient and provide a discussion of the pros and cons of these widely accepted indicators. Leach (1992) questions whether concentration has increased in South Africa by using alternative measures of absolute and relative concentration. However, concentration is high whatever the niceties of measurement and Leach tends to neglect control exercised through interlocking ownership, etc.

cent concentration ratios. The engineering industries have been historically linked to the development of the MEC core both in ownership terms
and in providing a large proportion of MEC inputs. Non-MEC industries
exhibit similar, highly concentrated ownership structures and demonstrate
that oligopoly in South Africa is not only confined to industries requiring
large economies of scale (Table 5.4). This is confirmed in table 5.7 by the
example of SA Mutual's subsidiaries dominance in the food industries.

Du Plessis (1977; 1978; 1979) demonstrates that the South African
manufacturing sector exhibits higher levels of concentration than France,
West Germany, the United Kingdom and Italy. Although one would
expect South Africa, with its relatively smaller economy, to have greater
levels of concentration, the trend in concentration has actually been
increasing. As early as 1972, 63.5 per cent of manufacturing industries
classified under the SIC were regarded as highly oligopolistic (Table 5.5).
More recent data are not available but since mergers and acquisitions
accelerated in the 1970s and 1980s, it is reasonable to assume that this
trend has increased.[4]

Table 5.5. MANUFACTURING SECTOR:
MEASURES OF OLIGOPOLY (1972)

	No. of firms with >80% industry's turnover	*Cumulative % of industry*
Monopolistic	1	6.6
Duopolistic	2	15.4
High-oligopolistic	3–10	63.5
Moderate-oligopolistic	11–15	74.6
Low-oligopolistic	16–20	77.9
Unconcentrated	21–40	90.6
Competitive	41+	100.0

Source: Du Plessis (1978).

Ownership of manufacturing firms can be traced in two ways to the six
large conglomerates that dominate mining (see list below). First, it is
reasonable to consider ownership on the JSE as indicative of the ownership
structure of manufacturing, since the magnitude of ownership by the state,
by domestic or by transnational corporations outside of the JSE is small
in comparison. In 1988, 82.5 per cent of the entire JSE was controlled by
the six conglomerates (Table 5.6), three of which were dominant. The
changes between 1985 and 1988 were due to changing corporate structures
through mergers and acquisitions as well as changing stock valuations.
For example, the relative predominance of gold shares in AAC's portfolio
has contributed to the relative decline in its share since October 1987.

---

[4] Du Plessis (1977; 1978) had access to unpublished official data.

Table 5.6. SHARE OWNERSHIP ON THE
JOHANNESBURG STOCK EXCHANGE (%)

	1985	1988
AAC	53.60	49.5
Sanlam	12.20	10.8
SA Mutual	10.60	9.8
Rembrandt	3.80	7.6
Anglovaal	2.10	2.2
Liberty Life	2.00	2.6
	84.30	82.5

Source: Rustomjee (1990) using McGregor.

Secondly, the conglomerates exercise control over these industries through pyramid or holding companies without a significant outlay of capital. An examination of the distribution of the largest 100 listed companies by asset size reveals extensive use of the holding company as a vehicle of conglomeration and a corresponding concentration of ownership of these companies (Table 5.7). More recently, conglomerate ownership has been extended to the financial sector. An important role of the financial sector in any economy is to collect, store and distribute national savings. Major institutions within the South African financial sector include commercial banks, merchant banks, pension funds, mining finance houses and, until recently, building societies. Banks have traditionally made loans and bonds to both state and private sectors and have specialised in financing trade through merchant banking interests. Building societies have traditionally operated in the long-term financing of property, although with deregulation in the early 1980s, their position has changed (see below). Insurance and pension funds have traditionally made loans to the state and public sector and have channelled the balance of their large cash inflows onto the JSE, which itself is an important institution within South Africa's capital market.

The distribution of financial sector assets is illustrated in Table 5.8. The actual occurrence of concentrated ownership of the financial sector is less important than the sector's organic, facilitating and lubricating role in financing and linking the various mining, manufacturing and other productive sectors in a dynamic manner along a particular growth path. Oligopolistic control of the financial sector has not only contributed to the process of concentration and centralisation but has also shaped the pattern of industrialisation itself around the MEC core. In 1988 commercial banks and long-term insurers deployed 59 per cent of the financial sector's assets, the balance being spread between general and merchant banks and building societies. Tables 5.9 and 5.10 show that conglomerates dominate each of these specialised financial activities.

Table 5.7. OWNERSHIP OF LARGEST LISTED
INDUSTRIAL COMPANIES, 1988

	Turnover (million Rand)	Parent company
Holding companies		
Barlow Rand	21,115	SA Mutual
CG Smith	10,064	SA Mutual
Malbak	5,234	Sanlam
Anglovaal	3,712	Hersov/Menel family
Amic	3,546	AAC
Murray and Roberts	3,039	Sanlam
Fedvolks	2,864	Sanlam
Safren	2,799	SA Mutual
Plate Glass	2,324	SA Mutual/Lib.Life
South Atlantic	1,120	Anglovaal
W & A	706	ESI Directors
Hunts	539	ESI Directors
Pichold	488	Pickard Family
Cullinan	415	SA Mutual
BTR Dunlop	411	BTR plc
SA Bias	n.a.	Seabrooke Family
Darling and Hodgson	397	Sanlam
FSI	284	FSI Directors
Grincor	275	Directors
Food sector		
CGS Foods	6,863	SA Mutual
Tiger Oats	4,395	SA Mutual
Premier Group	3,204	AAC
ICS	1,666	SA Mutual
Fedfood	1,010	Sanlam
I & J	890	Anglovaal
Kanhym	801	Sanlam
Gants	220	Directors
Chemical/oils sector		
Sasol	3,615	State
AECI	3,276	AAC
Semtrachem	1,254	Sanlam
Trek	785	Sanlam
SA Drug	675	Sanlam
Adcock	335	SA Mutual
OM Hold	181	Directors

Source: Rustomjee (1990) using *Financial Mail*, Top Companies Supplement, 19 May 1989, and McGregor.

Table 5.8. ASSETS OF THE FINANCIAL SECTOR, 1988

	Billion Rand	% of sector
Private sector		
Commercial banks	82.7	30.7
General banks	28.1	10.4
Merchant banks	6.5	2.4
Building societies	36.0	13.3
Long-term insurers	77.6	28.8
Pension/provident funds	38.9	14.4
	269.8	100.0
State sector		
Official funds[1]	31.3	45.8
PIC[2]	27.8	40.7
Land bank	9.2	13.5
	68.3	100.0

1. Administered by SATS and Department of National Health and Population Development.

2. The Public Investment Commission (PIC) administers public sector pension funds.

Source: South African Reserve Bank, *Quarterly Bulletin*, March 1990.

Direct control over financial sector assets in 1988 were as follows: SA Mutual R52.9bn; AAC R41.0bn; Sanlam R38bn; and Liberty Life R21bn (Table 5.9 for major holdings). Indirect or joint control increases this significantly, reinforcing the contention that the financial sector is under oligopolistic control. This does not mean absence of competition between finance houses. Rather, the basis of competition is a narrow one characterised by capital-intensity (South Africa has one of the highest ratios of automated teller machines in the world, higher than the United Kingdom and the former West Germany),[5] speculative activity like the channelling of funds onto the stock market causing it to boom during recessions, and other activities that attempt to circumvent capital controls.

Liberalisation policies pursued by the state between 1980 and 1983 lifted controls over interest rates, exchange rates and on activities of various sectors within the financial system. Traditionally, building societies competed ineffectively with banks for individual savings accounts. But their capacity to compete was enhanced in the short term by deregulation through a new Building Societies Act. This allowed them to convert themselves from mutual organisations, owned by their depositors, to companies which could raise funds through such products as share issues. However, this has in the longer term paradoxically encouraged the tendency to concentration by allowing existing monopolies to buy up the building society competitors. Those societies that converted after 1988,

---

[5] For further details on automated banking see *Weekly Mail*, 1 June 1990.

Table 5.9. OWNERSHIP OF FINANCIAL SECTOR ASSETS, 1988:
COMMERCIAL AND GENERAL BANKS

	Billion Rand	Ultimate controlling shareholder	% holdings
Commercial banks			
First National	24.9	AAC	
Standard	19.9	Liberty Life	30
		SA Mutual	23
		Rembrandt	13
Trust Bank	12.8	Sanlam	
Volkskas	10.3	Rembrandt	30
		UBS Holdings	30
Nedbank	8.9	SA Mutual	
	76.8		
General banks			
Santambank	5.7	Sanlam	
Stannic	5.2	As per Standard above	
First Western	4.4	AAC	
Boland Bank	2.2	Rembrandt	10
		Volkskas	10
		Lifegro	9
		Sanlam	7
Allied Bank	2.1	Minority shareholders	
		Rembrandt	10
		Rembrandt	4
First Industrial	1.9	AAC	
Nedfin	1.7	SA Mutual	
French Bank	0.8	n.a.	
Volkskas Industrial	0.7	Rembrandt directors	
Syfrets Bank	0.5	SA Mutual	
United Bank	0.5	Minority shareholders	
	25.7		

Source: Rustomjee (1990) using *Financial Mail*, Top Companies Supplement, 19 May 1989, and McGregor.

namely United Building Society (UBS), Allied and Saambou have all fallen within the orbit of the major conglomerates while the Perm, which is the only society to remain a mutual, is now a division of Nedbank and thereby controlled by SA Mutual. One result of this is the recent emergence of the Amalgamated Banks of South Africa (ABSA) as the largest banking group, representing the merging of Volkskas, United, Allied, Bankorp and Trust Bank, historically Afrikaner-oriented institutions.

In conclusion, the structure of private corporate capital in South Africa is represented by six broad-based, organically linked axes of capital, each

Table 5.10. OWNERSHIP OF FINANCIAL SECTOR ASSETS (1988):
MERCHANT BANKS, BUILDING SOCIETIES, INSURERS
AND PENSION FUNDS

	Billion Rand	Ultimate controlling shareholder	%holdings
Merchant banks			
Senbank	1.5	Sanlam	
Standard Merchant Bank	1.1	As per Standard in Table 5.9	
First Corporate	0.8	AAC	
UAL Merchant Bank	1.1	SA Mutual	
Volkskas Merchant Bank	1.1	Rembrandt/directors	26
Rand Merchant Bank	0.9	Rembrandt	13
		Allied	
Finansbank	0.7	SA Mutual	
Investec	0.8	Directors/staff	
Corbank	0.5	Directors	25
		Sanlam	16
		SA Mutual	13
	8.5		
Building societies			
Perm	6.8	SA Mutual	
UBS	10.0	Minority shareholders	
		Volkskas	10
NBS	3.1	Minority shareholders	
Allied	6.1	Minority shareholders	
		Rembrandt	10
		Rembrandt	4
Saambou	2.0	Minority shareholders	
		Volkskas	9
		Sanlam	8
	28.0		
Long-term insurers			
SA Mutual	33.2	Unlisted	
Sanlam	18.4	Unlisted	
Liberty Life	14.8	Standard Bank/Donald Gordon	
Southern Life	9.0	AAC	
Lifegro	3.9	Rembrandt	30
		Volkskas	30
Federated Life	2.7	Volkskas	
	82.0		
Pension/provident/funds	38.5		
Total financial sector	264.7		

Source: Rustomjee (1990) using *Financial Mail*, Top Companies Supplement, 19 May 1989, and McGregor.

with varying interests in mining, manufacturing and the financial sector. Three of these (SA Mutual, Sanlam and AAC) control a long-term insurance group, a commercial, general or merchant bank, and/or a building society, an industrial holding company and a mining holding company. The Liberty/Standard and Rembrandt/Volkskas axes are more active in the financial sector while Anglovaal is more concerned with direct investments in manufacturing and mining industries. The six capital axes are as follows:

SA Mutual: SA Mutual, Nedbank, UAL/Finance Bank, Perm Building Society, Barlow Rand, Rand Mines.

Sanlam: Sanlam, Trust/Santam Bank, Senbank (no building society), Gencor, Malbak

AAC: Southern Life, First National Bank, First Corporate Bank (no building society), AMIC, Amgold/Amcoal/De Beers/JCI

Liberty/Standard: Liberty Life, Standard Bank, Standard Merchant Bank (no building society; no direct mining/industrial arms).

Rembrandt/Volkskas: Lifegro/Federated Life, Volkskas/Boland, Rand Merchant Bank, United Building Society, Remgro, GFSA

Anglovaal: Operates with relative independence of financing with some Sanlam and SA Mutual influence in their mining and industrial holding companies.

State and private ownership and the MEC

South Africa's mixed economy has evolved through close inter-relationships between the state and English and Afrikaner fractions of capital. This is particularly so with respect to MEC. The extent of state involvement is reflected in its share of national fixed assets (Table 5.11). In the post-war period, the bulk of national fixed capital stock in industrial sectors has been privately owned, mainly by conglomerates. Private ownership of national fixed capital stock fluctuated between 50 and 56 per cent between 1946 and 1960 before falling to 42 per cent in 1980. State sector investment has been of two sorts. It has been concentrated in specific large-scale MEC core industries such as steel, chemicals, processed minerals and energy (liquid fuels and electricity). Public corporations' share of fixed capital stock grew from 5 per cent in 1955 to 7 per cent by 1970. Thereafter, it accelerated to 15 per cent in 1985, reflecting state-led direct investment in synthetic fuel, chemicals, steel, energy and armaments. This declined in the 1980s, falling to 10 per cent by 1990, as state-led investment fell[6] and as state corporations like Iscor

---

[6] The South African Reserve Bank's *Quarterly Bulletins* show that total gross domestic fixed investment (GDFI) at 1975 prices rose from R5.6bn in 1970 to R7.2bn in 1979, reached

and Sasol were privatised. Private capital's share correspondingly rose with the privatisation from 43 per cent to 47 per cent between 1985 and 1990, reflecting the continuing process of its growth by acquisition rather than by new investment. The second form of state investment has been indirect support to the MEC core through its provision of railway, harbour, fuel pipeline and telecommunication facilities (public authority business enterprises). The share of such infrastructure has remained fairly steady between 22 per cent and 18 per cent of investment in the post-war period.

Table 5.11.OWNERSHIP OF FIXED CAPITAL STOCK (%)

	Public authorities[1]	*Public authority business enterprises*[2]	*Public corporations*[3]	*Private business enterprises*
1949	44	–	3	53
1950	41	–	4	55
1955	39	–	5	56
1960	20	22	5	53
1965	22	22	5	51
1970	24	21	7	49
1975	24	20	9	46
1980	24	20	14	42
1985	23	19	15	43
1990	25	18	10	47

1. Public Authorities: central authorities, provincial administration and local authorities.

2. Public Authority Business Enterprises: South African Transport Services (now Transnet and Portnet), Posts and Telecommunications, South African Mint, National Supplies Procurement Fund, Community Development Fund. Public authority statistics were only disaggregated after 1960.

3. Public Corporations: Escom, Iscor, IDC, Rand Water Board, Sasol, Uranium Enrichment Corporation (Ucor), Armscor, Atomic Energy Corporation (AEC), Corporation for Economic Development.

Source: South African Reserve Bank, *Quarterly Bulletins*.

Table 5.12 reveals a concentration of state assets in a handful of large corporations or organisations, several of which have either been or are in the process of being privatised. Of the R80bn worth of major public fixed assets, R63.5bn was either directly or indirectly associated with the MEC.

The historical process of state involvement with private capital around the MEC is outlined in subsequent chapters. However, state-created industries have tended to provide the means by which the MEC core could be expanded. This began with the creation of the primary steel industry in the 1920s and continued through the nationalisation and subsequent

a peak of R9.6bn in 1981 before falling to R7.1bn in 1988. Private sector percentage share of expenditure was as follows: 1970, 57; 1979, 47; 1981, 51; 1988, 67.

Table 5.12. FIXED ASSETS OF MAJOR PUBLIC ENTERPRISES, 1986

Direct and indirect MEC Industries	*Million Rand*
Escom	35,664
Sats	18,614
Iscor	3,894
IDC	3,058
Armscor	1,706
Alusaf	500
Foskor	126
Total	63,562
Other	
Post Office	8,297
Land Bank	7,939
Total	16,236
Grand total	79,798

Source: McGregor (ed.) (1987).

investment in the under-capitalised electricity industry in 1948. Electricity has continued to provide a key impetus to the trajectory of industrialisation.[7] The Sasol I plant was the first large-scale support to be given by the state to the chemicals sector, extending the links between coal mining and the manufacturing sector. One of the characteristics of state-ownership has been that it has often been accompanied by joint ventures with domestic and international private capital.

To summarise, the extent of state ownership of fixed assets in the productive sectors of the economy is relatively small compared to the private sector. But state investment is focused in and supportive of MEC core sectors. Furthermore, the control of investable surpluses is firmly in the hands of private capital. Before the privatisations after 1988, the state had direct control of only R68bn of financial sector assets, whereas the private sector controlled some R270bn (Table 5.8).

Mergers and acquisitions have characterised the growth of the conglomerates since the early 1960s, when the Sharpeville massacre (1960) prompted a flight of foreign capital. Acquisitions increased dramatically in the 1970s; this was accompanied in the 1980s by increasing interpenetration of ownership, particularly between English and Afrikaner capital. In subsequent chapters, the empowerment of large-scale Afrikaner capital is shown to have been a major political and economic objective of the apartheid state. Aided and abetted by English capital, it contributed to the emergence and interpenetration of large-scale capital as embodied by the 'axes'. This took place at different times across the

---

[7] The IDC managing director, Van der Merwe (1992), argued that the decision to spend some R12bn on an aluminum smelter and a stainless steel plant in 1992 was partly justified on the grounds of utilising the estimated 40 per cent excess electricity generating capacity.

various sectors. Table 5.13 illustrates the ultimate controlling interest in each of the mining houses and the cross-holdings between them. AAC's interest in GFSA and JCI is significant, as is Sanlam's interest in Anglovaal.

Table 5.13. MINING HOUSE CROSS-HOLDINGS, 1988
(% owned by parent/controlling interest)

Ultimate controlling interest	Parent	AAC	Rand Mines	Gencor	JCI	Anglovaal	GFSA
AAC	AAC	–		5.5	50.0		21.8
SA Mutual	Barlow Rand			10.3	10.3	<10.0	
Sanlam	Gencor			–		26.7	
AAC	JCI				–		
Hersov/Menel family	Anglovaal				2.3	–	
Rembrandt	GFSA						–

(–) denotes a controlling interest

Source: McGregor.

Extensive cross-holdings are evident in the financial sector. Within the AAC stable, First National Bank (FNB) owns a large percentage of Southern Life which in turn has a large stake in FNB. Standard Bank, owned largely by Liberty Life, SA Mutual and Rembrandt, in turn owns 50 per cent of Liberty's controlling company. UBS Holdings (listed) controls UBS and, together with Volkskas, controls United Bank.

Large-scale capital and anti-monopoly regulation

One of the ways by which large-scale capital was empowered was through the support of the state in regulating capital in general. Direct regulatory policy on monopoly and competition has existed in South Africa since 1955 in the form of the Regulation of Monopolistic Conditions Act no. 24 of 1955. This was governed by the BTI under discretionary control of the then Minister of Economic Affairs, who had powers to initiate and terminate investigations and negotiations. This was superseded by the Maintenance and Promotion of Competition Act no. 96 of 1979 and modified by Act no. 5 of 1986. This latter Act effectively increased the scope and power of the Competition Board (CB). Legislation in July 1990 appears to have further strengthened the powers of the board.[8]

However, such legislation has never challenged large-scale capital. In

[8] 'Sharper Bite for Board', *Sunday Times* (Johannesburg), business section, 29 July 1990, p. 3.

the 1950s, the consolidation of Afrikaner capital and its deployment into large-scale mining and industrial activities was promoted. In the 1960s, both Afrikaner and English large-scale capital acquired footholds in a wide range of industries as foreign capital disinvested following the Sharpeville massacre. In the 1970s, the state promoted a wide range of industrial activity in expanding MEC core sectors, further enhancing joint-venture activity between English and Afrikaner capital under state co-ordination. With the fall in commodity prices and the growing crisis of apartheid in the 1980s, co-ordinated policies, including those concerning ownership and control, weakened as policy-makers increasingly embraced policies of deregulation and privatisation.

The National Party (NP) used its control of the state apparatus after 1948 not only to provide jobs for Afrikaners who had been economically and politically disadvantaged among whites in the preceding period, but also to consolidate and build an Afrikaner economic base. Manufacturing at this time was controlled by a mixture of firms of domestic and foreign origin while mining capital was more monopolised, dominated by domestic or foreign firms without Afrikaner connections. Commerce and finance were controlled by foreign firms, although there was a significant and growing domestic presence.

The passing of the 1955 Act should be viewed in the context of the NP's diverse constituency, for subsequent NP policy aimed not to break up existing monopolies but rather to force them to admit large-scale Afrikaner capital. Lipton (p. 286) quotes Verwoerd, leading ideologue of apartheid and prime minister in 1958-66: 'The encouragement of local capital formation was one of the guiding principles of our financial policies during this past decade.'

The entry of Afrikaner capital was effected by favourable treatment by the state through its institutional position and in its role as a major consumer in the market through such activities as shifting state bank accounts to Afrikaner financial institutions and awarding lucrative coal supply contracts for power stations to Afrikaner-owned mines (see Chapter 8). The rise of Afrikaner capital was a slow process; the breakthrough into gold mining only occurred with the takeover of Genmin by the Fedvolks mining subsidiary Federale Mynbou in 1964 through the assistance of AAC seeking to secure its political position with government. The government's objective of empowering large-scale Afrikaner capital contradicted any commitment to the promotion of competition under the 1995 Monopolistic Conditions Act. Evidence of investigations under this act indicates that monopoly was justified if it contributed to overall national productive efficiency. However, what constituted the 'public' interest was never clearly defined.[9]

[9] See Tregenna-Piggott (1980, p. 29).

The rapid concentration of ownership that took place in the 1960s and early 1970s and the uneven effects that both gold and oil price rises had on the economy, particularly the manner in which cash-rich sectors of capital like AAC and GFSA threatened the takeover of assets of other sectors of capital that had little interest in gold mining, led to the appointment of a Commission of Inquiry into the 1955 Act. The Commission gathered considerable evidence of concentration in sector after sector, showing extensive oligopolistic conditions. Oligopoly was found to have been exacerbated by protectionist barriers, small market size, distance between geographical centres and historical factors which had influenced the pattern of industrialisation. The Commission recommended that changes were required to speed up the process of investigation which conflicted with other BTI activities and priorities. Apparently, proper investigation under the Act in order to determine whether a merger was in the public interest, for example, was hampered by the lack of qualified staff and resources.[10] A major criticism was that the Act applied only after abuse had occurred and since it was not pre-emptive, it was unable to deal effectively with the rising spate of mergers.

The Commission's report led to the 1955 Act being superseded by the Maintenance and Promotion of Competition Act no. 96 (1979), under which CB was set up and empowered to investigate and advise the Minister of Industry, Commerce and Tourism on the existence of restrictive practices, on proposed or completed acquisitions and to interpret whether such practices were or were not in the 'public interest'.[11]

If monopolistic conditions were found to be against the public interest, the Board had the power to negotiate with the infringing parties to resolve the specific problem. If the latter did not comply, legislation could be enacted to prohibit the practice. In addition the CB had specific responsibilities to monitor ownership concentration, enabling it to guide investigations into acquisitions or mergers and to publish guidelines on acquisitions policy. These guidelines encouraged consultation with the Board before making acquisitions through the granting of immunity against any subsequent dissolution through legislation. Maximum penalties for contravention of clauses issued under the Act were R100,000 and/or five years' imprisonment. No such penalties have so far been imposed.

The most important aspect of the 1979 legislation is that, like its predecessor, it was an enabling measure. It did not contain any prohibitions, could not be contravened and merely established guidelines for assessing monopoly issues. The objectives of the 1979 Act were clearly stated: 'This is not anti-monopolistic legislation. It is just a bill to regulate

[10] Competition Board, *Annual Report* (1980).

[11] See Competition Board *Annual Report* (1981, p. 3) for a detailed definition of restrictive practices. See Competition Board (1981, pp. 7–26) regarding acquisitions.

monopolistic conditions and it appears very clearly from this that even though a monopoly exists and even though combines exist, they can still be justified in South Africa if they do not have a deleterious effect on the public.' [12]

The Act did not address the extent of concentration of ownership nor market share as an issue. Monopoly was not regarded as a problem in itself; it was of concern only when it affected the 'public's interest' as interpreted by the CB and finally judged to be so by the minister. Where mergers were concerned, the focus was to inhibit future mergers to prevent concentration, while dismemberment of existing concentrations was regarded as retarding growth and as too drastic or difficult a task. [13]

In practice, however, the Board's investigations have focused on relatively minor sectors as Table 5.14 shows below; furthermore, no concept of linkage between economic sectors appears to have been considered until after 1986. The case of alcoholic beverages provides a good example of this. The board appeared to avoid confronting South African Breweries (SAB), which had consolidated total control over the beer market by taking over its rival Intercontinental Breweries under an industry restructuring directive given by the BTI in 1979:[14] 'SAB's acquisition...constituted a restriction on competition in the beer industry but...little could be done to restore the slight degree of competition that had existed.' In another sector of the industry, a minority report criticised the Board's neglect and its decision instead to condemn the wine industry, 85 per cent of which was controlled by a company jointly-owned by Rembrandt and the KWV vine growers co-operative.

In the case of explosives, restrictive practices were found and the CB was instructed by the minister to negotiate rectification. This decision assisted Sasol's entry into the explosives market. As for coal, the Board regarded the excessive regulations governing the industry to be contrary to the public interest. However, coal production, distribution and export continued to be monopolised by conglomerate subsidiaries.

Between 1980 and 1986, political and economic crises deepened. Large capital outflows and a collapsing currency forced the South African state to declare a moratorium on debt repayments in 1985. The embracing of deregulation and privatisation policies prompted the CB to shift its attention to investigations in these areas after 1986 (Table 5.14). [15]

---

[12] Minister of Economic Affairs, when introducing the Draft Bill of the 1977 Act. *Hansard*, 28 February 1977, p. 1824, quoted in Tregenna-Piggott (1980).

[13] See Fourie (1987).

[14] Competition Board, *Annual Report* (1982).

[15] Deregulation also had the effect of empowering capital. Under the Temporary Removal of Restriction on Economic Activity Act No. 87f (1986),the State President could exempt entrepreneurs from a host of national and local ordinances including safety requirements 'if it unduly impedes economic development or competition or the creation of job opportunities". Competition Board, *Annual Report* (1987, p. 11).

Table 5.14. COMPETITION BOARD ACTIVITIES, 1980–90

Industry investigated	Report no., date	Investigation type*
Pharmaceutical products	BTI 1884(M), 1980	
Motor vehicle parts	BTI 1929(M), 1980	
Building industry (sanitary/hardware)	1, 1980	RP
Poultry industry	2, 1981	RP
Fertiliser	3, 1981	SD
Discrimination in pricing and conditions of sale	4, 1981	D
Association of SA Travel Agents	5, 1982	Act
Electrical Contractors Association	6, 1981	Act
Interflora	7, 1982	RP
Soft drinks industry	8, 1982	RP
Supply and distribution of explosives	9, 1982	RP
Supply and distribution of alcoholic beverages	10, 1982	RP
Supply and distribution of ferrous scrap metal	11, 1983	RP
Supply and distribution of coal	12, 1983	RP
Supply and distribution of anthracite	13, 1983	RP
Acquisitions by Scaw Metals	14, 1983	Acq
Collusion on prices and conditions	15, 1985	
Acquisition by Argus	16, 1986	Acq
Real Estate Multi-Listing Services (Pty) Ltd	17, 1987	RP
Acquisition by Nedbank Group	18, 1987	Acq
Economic concentration in sawmilling	19, 1987	Act
Possible acquisition of GFSA by AAC	20, 1989	Acq
Acquisitions in the baking industry	21, 1989	Acq
Acquisitions in the animal feed industry	23, 1989	Acq
Acquisitions in the stationery industry	24, 1989	Acq

Post-1986 deregulation activities
Trade regulation: licencing and trading hours
Taxi licencing
Legislation affecting black traders
Food handling regulation
Deregulation of industrial parks
Professional associations
Regulation at local government level

* Investigation Type: RP = Restrictive Practice; Act = Activities; Acq = Acquisition; D = Discrimination; SD = Supply and distribution.

Source: Competition Board, *Annual Reports*, 1980–90; *Published Investigations*, nos 1–24, 1980–90.

In 1986, an amendment to the 1979 Act was passed (Act No. 5 of 1986) which had the following implications:

(1) It extended CB powers to take action against an 'existing concentration of economic power'. Previously, it could only act against new concentrations.

(2) Powers were extended to cover financial institutions; these powers previously had been limited by Section 16 of the Act.

(3) It removed exemptions covering agricultural co-operatives and control boards (Section 2 (i) (c)). Up until 1990, no action had been taken in these sectors, although an investigation into the Eastern Transvaal Co-operative (OTK) was instituted in July 1989.

(4) It formally introduced issues of deregulation and privatisation into the activities of the Board, which subsequently played on increasing advisory role in formulating state policy in this regard.

(5) The Board's composition was increased through South African Reserve Bank (SARB) and Agricultural Ministry appointees to include expertise on agricultural and financial matters.

A changing relationship between capital and the state is reflected in the extension of the scope of the CB to cover existing concentrations of private power. The financial crisis at the time was overriding; perhaps it was for this reason that the CB was instructed in 1986 by the minister to abandon their investigation into structural linkages between businesses through interlocking directorates and cross-holdings and focus instead on the concentration in the financial sector. The Board justified this investigation as follows:

> Because of the close links which financial institutions in particular had with the major conglomerates in the country the issue of economic concentration had to be addressed on a broader basis. In this respect the investigation proved to be very fruitful and has provided the Board with a sound overall picture of the considerable diversity and extent of conglomerate activity in South Africa. (Competition Board *Annual Report*, 1988, p. 90)

Here the result of previous complacency is clearly apparent, perhaps arising from the consensual approach that the Board had taken since 1979. It is a reflection on the activities and role of the CB, its predecessors and other state agencies that between 1955 and 1988, such an important study had never been carried out. Ovendon and Cole (1989) have pointed out that at the time of the declaration of the debt moratorium, the extent of debt exposure was not known. Capital flight played an important part in the decision to focus on the financial sector. They report:

In...December 1988 a working group was set up at the request of the Minister of Finance to examine various completed foreign exchange transactions in response to information had had come to light suggesting new methods of avoidance...the South African Reserve Bank...was taking a number of measures to improve exchange control methods of enforcement (by) a Senior Deputy Governor of the bank...(assuming)...specific responsibility of co-ordinating the exchange control and banking supervision departments of the bank...The exchange control department was to take outside advice from accountants and other government departments in the search for methods for detecting and preventing over-invoicing of imports and other fraudulent methods of avoiding exchange control of capital exports. (pp. 123-4)

Since 1986, there appears to be a new thrust in the approach of the CB. First, the focus on agricultural co-operatives also served a political purpose in responding to the increased threat that the Conservative Party and other splinter groups posed to the NP. Secondly, the support for privatisation, while falling within the ideology of neo-liberalism and minimum state involvement, echoes the perspectives of the conglomerates who are the beneficiaries of privatisation and deregulation policies.

In summary, although anti-monopoly legislation has been in existence since 1955, it has never been exercised to the detriment of large-scale capital. Rather, it was initially used as a lever to force, or assist, the then dominant English capital fractions to accommodate Afrikaner enterprises. By the mid-1970s, growing interpenetration between English and Afrikaner capital led to a review of competition policy but the emergence of the CB did not have any effect on the process of ownership concentration around the MEC core. Since 1986, the crisis of the NP appears to have shifted the position of the Board towards a less interventionist posture, reflecting the virtues of privatisation and deregulation. However, there is a continuity in the Board's own interventions, or lack of them, with its failure to address the high levels of concentration across and between all the sectors of the economy described in this chapter.

To sum up, six axes of private capital dominate the South African economy. Control has initially been extended as an articulation of mining activities into MEC core sectors. This, in turn, has broadened to cover all other productive sectors as well as the financial sector, the control of which serves to reinforce conglomerate power.

The growth of the MEC core sectors and the increasing interpenetration between sectors of large-scale capital, formerly characterised as English or Afrikaner capital, have been heavily dependent on the state's direct role in ownership of sections of the productive sector. State investments have largely contributed directly and indirectly to enlarging the MEC core. In regulating the process of oligopolisation of the economy, the MEC as a system of accumulation has been lubricated through such factors as the effect that this regulation has had on the empowering of Afrikaner capital. The overall impact on broader industrial development will be explored below. At this stage, however, we warn against any simplistic correlation between high levels of conglomeration and concentration of capital, close involvement between the state and large-scale private capital, the blunting of market or competitive forces and the weakening of economic performance. We are not suggesting that economic performance would have been superior if only there had been more competition and the six conglomerates had been forced to unbundle their constituent affiliates and interlocking forms of ownership and control. Such is the stance of much of the analysis that informs current anti-monopoly policy: that competition will improve economic performance by increasing, even if only marginally, the number of firms in a sector.

However, there is neither empirical nor theoretical evidence to support this view and comparative evidence raises doubts about the efficacy of anti-monopoly policy in this form. Corporations have, more often than not, proved themselves able to circumvent such forms of regulating competition and they often prove difficult to sustain through the necessary political and administrative obstacles. It must also be recognised that conglomeration is often used successfully as a form of industrial policy in order to accrue economies of scale and scope, although the counterpart can be the featherbedding of inefficient monopolies and cartels.[16]

In other words, there cannot be a presumption that anti-monopoly policy in and of itself is advantageous. Whether monopoly leads to classic increases in prices and restrictions on output or dynamic accrual of scale economies and technological change is both industry-specific and contingent upon other, otherwise unspecified, determinants of industrial performance. In a sense, this is always acknowledged in anti-monopoly legislation and South Africa is no exception; there is inevitably reference to meeting the public interest which gives rise to extreme lassitude both in principle and practice, especially as large-scale corporations have the power to obstruct and to contest decisions through the legal system. Indeed, anti-monopoly policy is notable for its failure to be constructive; it forbids corporations, however often and with whatever ultimate impact, from doing what they want to do. The resources devoted to coming to and policing decisions of this type might be better employed and sufficient for the alternative purpose of defining industrial policy more constructively: what should be done within and between sectors. That this has been notably absent in South Africa is the subject of Part III.

---

[16] This is discussed at length in the context of the British coal industry in Fine (1990).

Part III. THE SOUTH AFRICAN FORM OF INDUSTRIALISATION

6

THE POLITICAL ECONOMY OF
THE INTER-WAR PERIOD

As will be seen later, debate over the inter-war years has previously been based on an analytical and policy milieu of dependency theory and import-substituting industrialisation. Accordingly, the main focus for a developing and potentially industrialising economy has tended to fall on the issues of markets and protection at the policy level and on the issue of class interests over these at the analytical level. In the light of the success of the Asian NICs, it has now been found that the range of policies involved in industrialisation (and hence the role of the state) is much broader, with trade policy as such not necessarily foremost. Nor is industrialisation simply a matter of discovering the right policies and adopting them. The capacity of, and pressures upon, the state to do so depend upon the state's relations to class interests and economic structures as discussed in Part II.

In this light, the analytical position adopted here is straightforward and far from original, although its implications are possibly stretched further than before. It accepts that mining and other closely related capitalists held and continue to hold economic power in South Africa. However, the exercise of this economic power politically was limited in the inter-war period as the attempt was made by the state to support and create Afrikaner-based capital with the corresponding advantage of prompting political support from the Afrikaner working class. However, success in the goal of creating Afrikaner-based capital was dependent on collaboration as well conflict with mining capital, given the surplus generated by the latter. As a contemporary put it: 'It therefore seems likely that secondary industry will be in a better position to meet the fluctuations of trade, provided always that no sudden set-back to gold-mining, on which so much of our prosperity depends, should occur.' (Pearsall 1937, p. 422)[1]

---

[1] See also Busschau (1945, pp. 220–1):
   The fact that the output of 'Manufacturing' is more valuable and has probably increased more rapidly in volume than the outputs for 'Mining' and 'Agriculture' also does not prove that 'Manufacturing' is the prime generator of income, since, as already explained, much

The more surplus that could be generated by mining, the more capital was potentially available for subsidising national capital. Consequently the inter-war development of South African capital is best seen as one in which the strength of mining capital dictated the boundaries within which national capital could be economically, and hence politically, supported. There were then limits on the economic policies of the state, whatever its politically derived objectives, because of its own and the economy's dependence on mining capital. By this same token, the possible accumulation strategies of mining capital were circumscribed by its relation to the exercise of state power.

These issues will be explored further here by reference to the debate over hegemony in the inter-war period. It is suggested that this debate is limited by its being too much oriented around zero-sum pay-offs, seeking to read off the exercise of political power by reference to the redistributional advantages bestowed by the state's economic policies. Instead, it is necessary to look more closely at the complex relation between economic and political power at a greater level of detail and according to the particular issues concerned.

This closer investigation is then undertaken by reference to the development of the inter-war economy, examining broad economic aggregates as well as specific industrial sub-sectors. A focus is placed on trade policy and the role of state enterprises. It is less concerned with exploring the motives, consequences and beneficiaries of such interventions than in revealing the limited extent to which they were attached to coherent industrial policy. This reflected the uneasy relation between mining capital and the state, which essentially foreclosed the emergence of industrialisation strategy based on diversification out of the economic base provided by mining.

Hegemony or conflict and compromise

Central to debate over the inter-war South African economy is the contribution of Davies *et al.* (1976). !2 Methodologically they adopted the approach of Poulantzas, in which there is a structured tier in the exercise of power where the various fractions of the exploiting classes (identified

---

of the output of both manufacturing and agriculture depends on the needs of the chief consumer, the mining industry...one cannot escape the conclusion that the primary impulse towards a greater national income in the immediate past has come, and in the future will have to come, from increased mining activity, particularly that of gold mining.

[2]   This article constitutes a synthesis of the four authors' Ph.D. theses: Davies (1979) on the white working class; D. Kaplan (1977) on class fractions and the economic policies of the state; Morris (1979) on the development of capitalist agriculture; and O'Meara (1983) on the Afrikaner bourgeoisie.

at the economic level) jockey for advantage politically through the formation of a power bloc to control the state. Thus there can be shifts in the relative economic positions of different sections of capital as well as in their political influence. Necessarily these structures and their associated dynamics are dialectically related to one another and to intra- and inter-class conflict.[3]

For Davies *et al.* the primary division is between national and imperial capital, with a secondary division within the former between agriculture and manufacturing, both of which are closely identified with Afrikaners. Imperial, foreign or English capital is primarily identified with mining. The election of the Pact government in 1924, an alliance of the white Labour Party and the Nationalist Party, signalled for them the loss of hegemony by imperial capital to national capital. Consequently, despite the formation of the Fusion government in 1933, economic policy in the inter-war years is seen as representative of the interests of national capital, particularly in its support of agriculture by a variety of measures, its protection of domestic industry and agriculture, the creation of state corporations, especially in steel (Iscor) and electricity (Escom), and the heavy reliance upon taxation of gold mining to fund these policies. As a corollary, political support depended upon incorporation of the white working class, partly by more or less temporary schemes of employment relief for poor whites and partly by job reservation more generally. However, this is seen as secondary and contingent upon the level of white working class economic and political pressure.

This approach and the specific stance within it has been the subject of much criticism. Methodologically, however well it is an application of Poulantzas' theory,[4] the net result is simply to couch interest group analysis at the economic and political levels in the more obscure language of hegemony, power bloc etc., in which changes of government and/or policy are read off in accordance with a corresponding judgement of who wins and who loses. There is a notable absence of the analysis of dynamics and contradiction in practice. In particular, there is a peculiar inversion of Marx's method, in which the economy is read off through the policies of the state, although this is always a danger within the Poulantzas method of relative autonomy, displaced contradictions and the formation and hegemony of power blocs. As Freund (1989, pp. 94–5) succinctly puts it, the problem lies 'in trying to understand material change by an unwandering gaze on the state rather than the actual economy'.

There are also criticisms to be made of the detail. First, support for

---

[3] For a sympathetic account of Poulantzas, see Jessop (1985).

[4] Bozzoli (1978), Clarke (1978) and Innes and Plaut (1978) all point to the treatment of hegemony in Davies *et al.* primarily as a relationship within the capitalist class rather than as one of dominance over the exploited classes. For a response, see D. Kaplan (1979).

agriculture was not initiated in the inter-war period; it reflected a continuity of policy even if it became increasingly favourable to white farmers. As Horwitz (1967) reports: 'Between 1910 and 1935, eighty-seven bills relating to the land were executed ... in a Parliament in which farmer-members were a high proportion in all political parties.' (p. 129)

Secondly, there are complex issues concerning the boundaries of the various fractions of capital, with foreign capital involved in many non-mining activities, including agriculture and manufacturing.[5] Freund (p. 81) refers to diversification from mining into repair and maintenance and other engineering. This contrasts with the Cape garment industry which did not generate much by way of indigenous spin-off engineering. This suggests a lack of homogeneity in secondary industry whether sectorally, politically or regionally.

Thirdly, some, most notably Yudelman (1983), would take 1933 and not 1924 as a turning point in policy, either because they reject the view that the Pact government represented a victory for white miners or because the later date witnessed a stimulus to manufacturing out of the revenue and demand generated by the gold industry as the gold price rose in the thirties. This debate, however, is less to deny or to exaggerate the significance of political change as to situate it in a fuller and more complex analysis of economic interests and relations of dependence as much as of conflict.

Fourthly and relatedly, the approach of Davies *et al.* may be considered too historically delimited. It has primarily been motivated by a wish to anticipate and explain the subsequent period of classical apartheid. Consequently, continuities with the past concerning the conflict and compromise between fractions of capital are implicitly reduced to the presumption that the second Boer War (1899–1902) implied an unambiguous hegemony for foreign capital before its overthrow in the inter-war period. Yet, as Marks and Trapido (1979) so clearly demonstrate, even the reconstruction period after the war involved continuing compromise between the interests of different capitals, even if the primary objective of the state was to guarantee conditions favourable to the pursuance of mining, which it never subsequently threatened.[6] Finally, the taxation of

---

[5] See Bienefeld and Innes (1976), Bozzoli (1978; 1981), Fransman and Davies (1977) and Kubicek (1991).

[6] For the same approach to a somewhat later development, Gelb's (1989) analysis of the creation of the South African Reserve Bank in 1921 is obscured rather than illuminated by the idea that it simply forms part of the shift in power from foreign to indigenous capital. Nevertheless, he is sufficiently sensitive to the empirical details of what occurred to qualify, possibly to undermine, the historiography involved: 'This contradiction (over the control of monetary policy), it would seem, is indicative of *the complexity and the duration* of the transition in South Africa during the inter-war period from imperialist domination to peripheral national capitalism.' (p. 65, present author's emphasis)

For analysis of the preceding period, where emphasis is placed on the shifting realities of

gold mining, whether directly or indirectly through differentially disadvantageous railway charges and protection, is indicative of dependence on and not dominance over mining, especially after the rise in gold prices when heavy profits were to be made and in which the state would surely be expected to share.[7] As D. Kaplan's (1977, p. 157) own account of the excess profits tax on the gold mines in the 1930s reveals, there was give-and-take in the amount appropriated by the state. In response to Chamber of Mines and other protests: 'Duncan, as Acting Minister of Finance, granted a number of concessions. The most important of these were to place definite limits on the tax yields for the next five years – £6 million in the first year, £7.4 million in the second year, and for the three subsequent years a maximum of 50 per cent of the excess profits.'

With limited exceptions, it is not the intention here to pass judgement on these issues. To a large degree they suffer from being situated in too simple an approach in which the various interests involved, capitalists and white labourers, gain or lose at one another's expense. The analysis is primarily redistributional, with a greater or lesser weight being given to the motives of, pressures upon and power of government. Given its political complexion, this discussion essentially can be reduced to the extent to which the exercise of political power on behalf of national capital (and possibly white labour) is both genuine and able to overcome the economic power of foreign, mining capital.

Such a general framework for assessing policy is necessarily insensitive to the differences in the material organisation and development of particular economic sectors and these differences will determine the scope for policy interventions by government. To give an extreme example from finance, the policy of remaining on the gold standard, as an act of independence from Britain after it had abandoned gold in 1931, proved so disastrous that it had to be dropped even though this boosted gold mining profitability in particular. Indeed, with the presence of the pay limit system to ensure the full working of poorer ores when the gold price was higher, it can be argued that policy was directed to prolonging mining capital rather than allowing the maximisation of immediate returns, because of its continuing importance in sustaining other government objectives. Government policy cannot be read off from political power irrespective of the specific economic conditions involved.

---

the world financial system, within which mining capital and the City do not represent a homogeneous foreign capital, see Ally (1990; 1991). More generally, the history of the MEC can be traced back further than the period covered here. See, for example, the debate over mining capital at the end of the nineteenth century and its relationship to the Boer War, as reviewed in Phimister (1993).

[7] See Fransman and Davies (1977).

This all takes us to the point of recognising that the various fractions of capital were highly interdependent and not just in conflict, not least because the surplus to be obtained from mining was essential to the support of other indigenous economic activity. One of the results of focusing on the politics of power blocs is that differences between fractions of capital tend to be exaggerated at the expense of recognising a common interest in relation to the exploited classes which, of necessity, sets the structural limits within which capitalists can compete.[8] However, to move beyond this analytical observation and uncover the relationship between economic and political factors requires specific studies. These have been notably absent in the literature, especially for manufacturing. For all the discussion of hegemony of manufacturing and agriculture over mining in the inter-war period, industry has hardly been investigated. When it has, this has usually been as background for some other purpose such as the history of a trade union.

Perhaps the one area of 'economic' policy in which most analytical and empirical advance has been made and for which many of the above criticisms are less applicable is for labour control not least because it has been explored both in terms of the practical needs of different sections of capital as well as politically and ideologically. Consequently, a much more complex and complete picture has emerged in which the conflicts of interest between different actors over access to black labour have been set against a common interest. Thus Lacey (1981) describes the situation as:[9]

> How the Hertzog regime handled the issues between 1924 and 1932, and how finally the dominant classes in the rival capitalist sectors determined to sink their differences and hammer out a policy which enabled them to tackle the one overriding issue: how best to super-exploit all African workers in the interest of capitalist profitability and the national economy as a whole. (pp. 3-4)

Starting with the gold-maize alliance of the turn of the century, a com-promise was reached in the inter-war period which privileged

---

[8] Clarke (1978, p. 55) makes a similar point when both oversimplifying and constructing too sharp a dichotomy between state and capital:

'Normally the relations between capitals, and so between departments, are regulated by competition and the ability of the state to intervene in these relations without disrupting accumulation is limited. There are normally severe limits on the ability of the state to intervene to redirect surplus value. These limits are not given, as the fractionalists (Davies *et al.*) would have us believe, by the total available surplus value and the relative political strength of the various parties involved in political conflict. They are rather given by the role of surplus value in the expanded reproduction of the capitalist mode of production.

[9] Following Wolpe (1972), the labour control issue has been treated with increasing sophistication, recognising differentiation within the black workforce, as in Hindson (1987). See also Dubow (1989) and Posel's (1991) discussion of the inter-war period.

agriculture's access to domestic supplies of black labour by simultaneously promoting the mines' access to foreign migrant labour.[10]

What follows is a small step for other areas of application in matching the progress made in the study of labour control. It seeks less to identify the conflicts between various fractions of capital than to explore how their mutual interactions determined the policy options that were or were not available. More specifically, the narrative below is intended to illustrate a number of overlapping themes: the policy preference for Afrikaner economic interests over those that dominated the economy and on which they were dependent, particularly because of the weight of mining in the economy as a source of revenue and as a structural determinant for industrialisation; the need to disaggregate economic activity to unravel the interplay of economic and political forces; and the underlying failure to develop coherent and comprehensive industrial policies because of the separate location of or disjuncture between economic and political power, leading to a corresponding fragmentation of policy making.

Industrial intervention

The inter-war years are acknowledged as the period when industrial policy was first overtly and extensively implemented. It appears to have met with some success in bringing about industrialisation. However, it is important to clarify what 'industrialisation' is perceived to be. At an aggregate level, commentators have interpreted industrialisation in terms of the relative shifts between manufacturing, agriculture and mining activities.

Private manufacturing grew from contributing 9.8 per cent to national income in 1918 to 17.7 per cent in 1939. Mining fluctuated between the low of 15.2 per cent in 1922 and the high of 23.8 per cent in 1933 after the gold standard was abandoned. Agriculture clearly declined in relative importance; its contribution to national income fell from 20.2 per cent in 1918 to 12.2 per cent by 1939.

However, it is important not to read off the rhythm of economic and political power and the impact of policy choices from such aggregate data. It is also necessary to recognise what policy options were not adopted. The purpose of this section is to highlight the absence of coherent state policy both for broad aggregate sectors of the economy and for certain sub-sectors of manufacturing. It supports the conclusion that the disjuncture between economic and political power in the inter-war period gave

---

[10] On the gold–maize alliance, see Trapido (1971); see Morrell (1988) for its dissolution in the inter-war period. See Crush *et al.* (1991) for discussion of the mines' foreign migrant labour empire. It is important, however, to recognise the heterogeneity of Afrikaner farmer interests. See Bradford (1987 and 1994) and Schirmer (1994), for example.

rise to different outcomes according to the incidence of compromise and conflict sector-by-sector.

In the case of agriculture, the central authority of the state was unable to provide a clear lead through its own policy; it resorted to devolving responsibility and decision-making powers to the various agricultural control boards that were set up at this time. This reveals another deficiency in the literature on the economy of the inter-war period, namely that regional differences and class differentiation within the ruling party in government have not been adequately addressed; the state is often interpreted as a relatively monolithic central authority, more plausibly for its relations to mining, less so for Afrikaner capital.

Although agriculture was protected, state support was neither fully centrally controlled nor implemented on behalf of a readily identifiable and uniform agricultural interest. The process of agricultural policy formulation is described by Richards (1935) as follows:

1. The passing of an enabling act. This permits the Minister to make regulations for the control of a particular agricultural industry or product.
2. In pursuance of this policy, the Minister sets up boards of control composed largely of representatives of the particular agricultural industry whose interests it is desired to protect, with wide and arbitrary powers affecting all phases of the industry, and incidentally the interests of the consumer.
3. There is a third method whereby the Minister delegates his powers to existing organisations but with increased jurisdiction, e.g. in the case of the central Co-operative for Maize in 1933, and the KWV for the Wine Industry. (p. 397)

Protection after 1925 has often been seen as favourable to agriculture and manufacturing at the expense of mining capital that had to foot the bill in terms of higher input prices. The impact of protection, however, is not quite so simple; along with other factors in play, *effective* rates of protection and their ultimate incidence do not appear to have been assessed, either in policy-making or in retrospect. Not least among these factors is the issue of whether conditions were conducive to promoting infant industries or to feather-bedding inefficiencies or whether policy was more likely to lead to one or the other.

Specifically, manufacturing sectors dependent upon agricultural inputs faced higher costs, reflecting the absence of a strategy favouring the development of linkages between agriculture and manufacturing.[11] The opposite appears to have been the case, as the BTI acknowledged:[12]

[11] For details from a political perspective, see O'Meara.
[12] Horwitz (pp. 248–9), citing BTI Report No. 282.

'Confectionery manufacturers must buy highly protected sugar, glucose made from maize and milk powder at relatively high prices and that agricultural protection must be followed by industrial protection, if local factories are to use South African raw materials.' Horwitz points to a further factor undermining the development of food processing industries: 'What the Board of Trade and Industries did not elaborate was that the dumping of many of these agricultural raw materials under forced-export policies enabled foreign manufacturers to obtain *their* raw materials at below cost to the even further disadvantage of their South African competitors.'

Another example of the lack of coherent policy towards agriculture and industry is presented by Alexander (1935). He refutes the arguments of the day excusing the failure to penetrate dairy export markets. Citing the cases of New Zealand and Denmark, which had successfully over-come similar debilities, such as soil infertility, uncertain rainfall, vast travelling distances, product quality and lack of monetary incentives to dairy farms, Alexander observes that: 'The reasons for the comparative failure of agriculture in the Union...is not the natural conditions of the country which are so largely to blame as the incompetence of past governments, ever since Union, and, largely arising from this, the ineffi-cient methods of the majority of farmers.' (p. 359)

While most observers have recognised that the thrust of inter-war state policy was to favour domestic industry and the agricultural sector, the resources allocated to the latter appear to outweigh the commitment to developing the former. For example, the cost of agricultural subsidies in 1933 alone are estimated at £7.5m.,[13] more than twice the £3.5m. that was spent on Iscor between 1929 and 1933. If the establishment of a domestic iron and steel industry proved possible with such support, surely much more could have been done for food processing? As Richards observes, that it was not reflects the devolution of responsibility to fragmented interests. The state's representation of small-scale Afrikaner capital, whether agricultural or industrial, did not preclude a concerted policy for the development of food processing and marketing but it could not be pushed through by the state centrally. Consequently, the relative absence of direct political representation of mining interests weakened industrial policy through its inability to diversify from mining. In addition, even where mining capital had no direct role to play other than in paying taxes to support subsidies etc., the state's room for manoeuvre in the policies that it could adopt were contingent upon the economic and political structures of indigenous Afrikaner capital; more so because of the political weakness of the economically dominant form of capital.[14]

---

[13] Richards (1935, p. 365). It is evident that other forms of subsidy, such as transport rates, also favoured agriculture relatively.

[14] Consequently, the economic and social histories of the food and other consumer goods

Despite this disjuncture between economic and political power, the history of the wine industry illustrates how, through the devolving of price-fixing power in 1924 to regionally, particularly Cape, based interests, it was possible for small-scale Afrikaner capital to be accumulated through the concentration and centralisation of the resources of a relatively small sector of the economy. The strength of its political lobby is evident in that, despite the numerous Commissions of Inquiry and BTI reports from as early as 1934 consistently recommending the economic disempowerment of the vintners represented by the KWV, these recommendations were never implemented (Fridjon *et al.* 1986). It was precisely from these and other similar roots that the Rembrandt, Sanlam and Old Mutual conglomerates grew into economic rivals to the offshoots of imperial capital. As Fridjon *et al.* observe:

> All groupings of farmers in South Africa are politically powerful, but the most powerful of all are the 6,000 grape farmers. There are many reasons for their power. They...have always supported the Nationalist Party with votes, money and...are heavily represented in Parliament as Cape Nationalists...are extremely well and cohesively organised, and, not least, they enjoy a statutory framework that is extraordinarily helpful to their interests. (p. 62)

From a critical, free market perspective, Fridjon *et al.* argue that the industry was held back from greater efficiency and dynamism. By the criterion of creating relatively large-scale Afrikaner capital, however, the KWV can be considered a success in forging a linkage between agriculture and food processing. Experience across the food and beverage industry more generally is much more mixed. As a sector, it stands out during the inter-war period, accounting for 37.6 per cent of manufacturing's gross output in 1924. By 1939 this had declined to 26.6 per cent. J. Nattrass (1988) attempts to explain this decline in part as an outcome of the operation of Engel's Law, that a diminishing proportion of mainly white incomes would be expected to be spent on food. But such demand-side explanations, essentially tautologous in nature, are insensitive to differences across sub-sectors and to the potential availability of export markets.

R. Smith (1945) has addressed the supply-side, pointing to the significant degree of concentration within the food and beverage sector of manufacturing. By 1940–2, 3.5 per cent of all firms within this sector produced more than 50 per cent of total sector output. Consider the crushing and processing of sugar cane, for example. By 1933, sugar

---

industries are different from one another, each depending upon regional specificities and their associated political and economic factors, e.g. Cape wine as opposed to Natal sugar, the maize triangle, etc.

processing accounted for about 20 per cent of the food sector's output. Its growth during the inter-war period was dramatic, from 82,000 tonnes in 1919 to 500,000 tonnes in 1939; it also had a disproportionate impact on the spatial pattern of development in South Africa. Most of its associated activities were concentrated in Natal, a province dominated by a mixture of imperial and domestic English capital. Sugar was not cultivated in the Eastern Transvaal until much later, and that development was associated more with the growth of the Rembrandt Afrikaner conglomerate.

Table 6.1. PRODUCTION CONCENTRATION IN MANUFACTURING, 1940–42

	% firms producing 50% of total output
Food and drink	3.5
Vehicles	0.4
Metal and engineering	5.0
Clothing and textiles	3.9
Building	6.4
Stone and clay	3.1
Paper and printing	5.0
Wood	6.4
Furniture	8.0
Leather	6.0
Chemicals	4.8
Heat, light and power	3.5
Surgical instruments and jewellery	4.8
Raw materials[1]	6.5
Other	3.3

1. Raw materials include tallow rendering, bone milling, fellmongering, wool scouring, chaff cutting, corn crushing, cotton ginning, and wattle bark grinding.

Source: R. Smith (1945).

Sugar processing is just one of several activities within food processing in South Africa (Table 6.2). A further 30 per cent of food output in 1933 consisted of the production of tobacco, bread, biscuits, cake, wheat and maize milling activities (Pearsall). With the exception of maize and breadmaking in the Transvaal, the other activities were mainly Cape-based. Tobacco and cigarette manufacture has long been the preserve of a single company, Rembrandt, whose origins lie in the Voorbrand Tobacco Corporation. Its products were distributed through Afrikaner Broederbond meetings in the early 1930s, and the company subsequently grew to control the international cigarette company Rothmans, along with other diverse activities.[15] Maize milling, on the other hand, was geographically

[15] 'We were asked to smoke and cough for Volk and Vaderland', recounted an old Bond member. Cited in Wilkins and Strydom (1978, p. 425).

located in the Transvaal near its main markets provided by the mines. Ownership was less concentrated, though some early ownership linkages existed between mining houses and millers. In 1896 Premier Milling was linked to the Corner House Group (the forerunner to Rand Mines). M. Kaplan (1986) observes that this activity, like most of manufacturing in South Africa, was gradually concentrated through a series of mergers.

Table 6.2. FOOD AND BEVERAGE INDUSTRY: DISTRIBUTION OF ESTABLISHMENTS, 1937–38

	% of total establishments
Flour and grain mills	43.1
Bakeries	18.4
Aerated water works	7.8
Butter and cheese factories	6.4
Fruit factories	3.5
Salt factories	2.5
Tobacco works	2.5
Ice works	2.2
Distilleries	1.8
Coffee works	1.4
Malt works	1.3
Sugar mills	1.1
Tea and fruit packers	1.1
Fish canneries	1.0
Other establishments	5.9
Total	100.0

Source: R. Smith (1945).

Such a cursory overview provides some evidence of disparate developments across the food industries, in part as a consequence of the absence of coherent industrial policy. Further detailed study is urgently needed. But the apparently separate experiences of the wine and dairy industries, for example, follows from differences in their economic and political leverage. Even so these are in part mutually dependent upon absence of central direction.

There were two major industrial policy instruments utilised in the inter-war period: tariff protection and the creation of a state sector around heavy industry. The latter's initially stated objectives were, among others, to cheapen industrial inputs and strengthen linkages between mining and manufacturing.

A major focus of debate has been over the reasons for protecting manufacturing. D. Kaplan (1974, p. 90) in particular insists that protection was primarily designed to serve the interests of manufacturing. 'Where the two objectives of 'civilised labour' and industrial development conflicted...the government came down firmly on the side of local industrial development.' This is opposed to the view of those scholars who see it as part of civilised labour policy, meeting the needs of poor white workers.[16] Some, such as Innes and Plaut (p. 57), combine the two motives. Martin (1990a; 1990b) takes a broader view of the goals of indigenous industrialisation through protection, incorporating the construction of South African manufacturing hegemony in the Southern African region as a whole. He views this as representing a break in policy from 1925, in part to reduce dependence on gold mining, although this was tempered in the 1930s following increases in the gold price. For Norval (1962, Chapter 5), tariff policy combined a mix of motives: providing for poor white employment, raising government revenue, protection for existing or soon to be established industries, safeguards against dumping, and avoidance of unduly harming the interests of agriculture, mining and the availability of capital goods and raw materials.[17]

These different perceptions of the role of protection derive more or less directly from the correspondingly identified economic interests, these varying both between authors and their analytical prejudices as well as over time. If the belief is that the Pact government represented a swing towards the interests of national capital and/or white labour, so it is argued that protection was introduced on their behalf etc.

More recently a sharp interchange between Christie (1991a; 1991b) and Martin (1990b; 1991) has centred on the relative efficacy of the dual policy instruments of protection through tariffs and the creation of state-owned heavy industry. Christie emphasises the importance of underlying infrastructure provided by state agencies such as the railways, Escom and Iscor and, consequently, the role of individuals such as Smuts, Hoy and van der Bijl. Although much is made today of providing the economy, particularly manufacturing, with a 'kick-start', for Christie, most of the 1930s economy enjoyed the benefits of an 'electric start'. As such, the benefits were available to all capitals and did not necessarily favour domestic capital. Indeed, mining inevitably enjoyed disproportionate

---

[16] In a retrospective and official account of the development of industry in the context of the role of the IDC, Rosenthal (1960, p. 8) sees providing employment for the 'poor white' class as important. For Horwitz:

> The empirical examination has shown however that the polity accepted and applied a protectionist policy only because it promised increased, improved employment of Whites, otherwise described as 'civilized labour'. That this was the *raison d'etre* of industrialization, if needs be under the encouragement of protection, is brought out unequivocally by the Customs Tariff Commission of 1934 as well as by the launching of a state-controlled iron and steel industry by the Pact Government. (p. 251)

On the issue of white labour, see Davies (1979), Gool (1983), Johnstone (1976) and Yudelman. On poor whites, see especially Abedian and Standish (1985).

[17] For a broad discussion of the policy and empirical issues involved in inter-war protection, see Archer (1981).

benefits, raising doubts over the potential role of such state ventures to promote indigenous capital at its own expense.

On the other hand, Martin (1991, p. 610), attributes the degree of inter-war industrialisation to 'the emergence for the first time in South Africa of a definite policy of industrial development and, as an essential and integral part of this, protective tariffs'. However, he reads this off as part of a global structure in which South Africa's position as a semi- peripheral country was bound to condemn attempts at industrialisation to failure:

> For primary producers and especially mining capital, profits and continued expansion seemed best assured by the reproduction of a peripheral position in the global division of labour. To break these globally and regionally constructed relationships threatened not simply tariff-induced higher costs, lower profits, and the loss of easy access to overseas and regional markets, but the very structure of dominant class alliances across Southern Africa and core areas of the world-economy. As the relatively autonomous Pact government moved in this direction by reshaping tariffs, state intervention, and regional and international foreign relations, and so on it accordingly came into conflict with mining and commercial capital, much of agricultural capital, and the dense web of academics, policy-makers, and ideologues who maintained that South Africa's proper destiny was to from a primary planet circulating the bright if declining sun of Britain. (p. 616)

The heavy emphasis on tariffs is contested by Christie, who points out they they were low in contrast to other colonial countries. Martin replies by arguing that aggregate tariff levels are irrelevant since they were designed to target particular industrial sectors.[18]

However the dispute over the advantages, disadvantages, strengths and impact of protection is resolved, it is much more important to recognise the implicit assumption that tariffs, together with the promotion of state-owned industries such as Escom and Iscor, are considered to be the core of industrial policy. But what stands out is not the greater or lesser role of protection as much as the failure to adopt an additional range of industrial policies, promoting manufacturing through provision of skills, technology, finance, intersectoral linkages and marketing. Even the taxation system seems to have discriminated against such diversification. According to D. Kaplan (1977): 'Companies whose principal business was gold

---

[18] Martin's approach is based on the idea that protection is doomed to fail as a policy to develop indigenous capital in the periphery. Ironically, this view of the inevitable subordination to the needs of metropolitan capital might be better supported by Christie's analysis than by his own, since the former suggests that state corporations were more wedded to the interests of mining (metropolitan) capital.

mining were taxed at 4/- in the pound on all profits earned on non-mining activities. This compared with 2/6d in the pound taxation rate on all other companies.' (p. 270) Although he reports this as not being too significant an impediment to diversification into industry, it did prove so for AAC and attracted the opposition of the Chamber of Mines.

Such a broader range of industrial policies could only have been effectively and significantly based upon support for diversification out of mining. The extent to which this had already taken place prior to the inter-war period has not always been acknowledged, not least because the concept of industrialisation has been primarily dealt with in aggregate quantitative terms. The empirical analyses found in most of the literature on the inter-war period tend not to differentiate economic activity across the diverse sub-sectors within manufacturing and thus are insensitive to both detail and timing.

A useful starting point is to consider the development of the steel industry, which falls within the metal and engineering sub-sector of manufacturing. Christie (1991a) makes the following observation on plans for Iscor:

> [They] were personally initiated by Smuts as a state sponsored project, in 1922. Smuts went to great lengths in 1922 to persuade Lionel Phillips, Solly Joel, the Albus, Ernest Oppenheimer, and other goldmine owners to invest in an iron and steel industry that would be partly state supported...Smuts passed a scheme through Parliament in 1922 whereby the state would pay bounties to any large-scale iron and steel producer in South Africa...This bounties scheme was taken over by the Pact as late as 1926. Only once the scheme was clearly a failure did the Pact create Iscor... In short, the Pact created Iscor but it could only do so because of Smuts' extensive previous work. (p. 604)

In interpreting this critical period, it is crucial to appreciate the extent to which a privately-owned domestic steel industry, based on recycling scrap steel, already existed in the early 1920s and, more important, the extent to which there was competition over plans to expand by shifting to the primary smelting of ore. In 1924, nine years before Iscor began production, the sector already contributed 18.8 per cent of the manufacturing sector's gross output. Simply because of the capital requirements and economies of scale associated with steelmaking, the bounty system could only realistically be extended to one producer and the contest for this concession was played out between the Union Steel Corporation (Usko), who wished to expand its Newcastle (Natal) smelting works based on scrap steel, and the Pretoria Iron Mines (PIM), supported by the Pretoria lobby.

It would be inaccurate to categorise the Usko at that time as imperial capital when compared to the Belgian, German and British companies that supplied most of the steel used in the Union. Even if Usko were to be regarded as representing imperial capital, close relations necessarily existed with the state. The viability of Usko and other companies such as Stott and Company and Dunswart were dependent on the close co-operation of the state, mainly through the railways, who provided scrap for smelting and who were also major consumers.[19]

PIM was very definitely aligned to Afrikaner interests but while Usko's initial capital was subscribed in England, the company was controlled by Lewis and Marks, the latter having had a long association with Boer Republics (Mendelsohn 1991).[20] Even so, M. Kaplan records that C.F. Delfos, the owner of PIM, had unsuccessfully attempted to raise capital in Britain as early as 1924 for expansion:

> [He] approached the board of the Gotehoffnungshotte 'to prepare a report on the possibility of establishing an iron and steel industry'. In 1924, also, the Pact government came into power, not only keen on promoting South African industry, but more in sympathy with Delfos's own political views than the Smuts government which preceded it. (p. 98)

The evidence points to a municipal/regional lobby, with Pretoria's strongly underpinned by Afrikaner nationalism. Within this melee, Delfos' lobbying for a state-owned enterprise is interpreted by M. Kaplan as his last resort to raise capital to compete with Usko (although Kaplan elsewhere suggests anti-semitism as a motive):

> During the recess of 1925, Delfos made his first approaches to Pretoria Members of Parliament and began campaigning for a public utility company similar to that of Escom...Delfos, unable to obtain sufficient capital to expand his own business, was inspired by the foundation of Escom in 1923, and then determined to compete with Usco one way if he could not do it in another. He was obsessive about it. (p. 98)

To assert that Iscor was created by an act of the state in support of national capital against imperial capital is superficial and misleading. Clark (1987b, p. 122) observes: 'The state corporations did not so much challenge private capital nor work as a "tool" of private enterprise, but rather they provided a growing link between the state and the private sector.'

The tensions inherent in its conception persisted, deepened and

---

[19] Much of what follows draws upon Richards (1940).

[20] Many economic analyses proceed as if there were no differences among Afrikaner 'interests'; O'Meara (1983) for example, has clearly illustrated that there are, by sector and by location. How are Lewis and Marks to be classified, given their English origins and yet close collaboration with governments in both the Transvaal and the Orange Free State where they held a wide portfolio of businesses?

broadened as it grew. After Iscor began producing, it was forced into joint ventures with finished steel companies, 'agents' of imperial capital, in order to guarantee its markets. Ultimately it had to come to an accommodation with European producers, joining their international cartel in 1935, reserving just one-third of the domestic market for itself and the other local producers but raising prices for all.

The Pact government's decision did not simply favour the interests of domestic over imperial capital. Within the state itself, the railways had to pay higher costs for steel[21] while Customs and Excise raised higher revenues from tariffs and the steel parastatal made huge profits. Imperial capital, as represented by the mine owners, did have to pay higher costs for their steel inputs but steel producers in Europe and the United States benefited from higher prices arranged for their exports. Of greater importance to the development or rather the stunting of domestic industry, many domestic users of steel, such as the fabrication shops, engineering sector, etc., suffered under the burden of higher costs of steel.

In fact, the impact of Iscor's output on the economy is not accurately reflected within the metal sector alone, for the company reported its activities under four categories: iron and steel; gas, coal, coke and tar; electric light and power; and lime works. Nevertheless, it is important to note that at the aggregate level, the £3.5m capital expenditure on Iscor between 1929 and 1933 represented only 4 per cent of total manufacturing fixed capital. This is not to dismiss the importance of Iscor in the economy but to highlight how misleading it is to read too much from the interplay of interests within a single sub-sector of manufacturing, even if these have been correctly read in the first place.

The policy instrument of creating state industries cannot simply nor even primarily be interpreted as support for domestic capital. Nor was industrialisation necessarily guaranteed as a result of such industries. In the case of the creation of Escom through the 1922 Electricity Act, it is important to note that throughout the inter-war period, Escom remained in a subordinate position to the privately-owned Victoria Falls and Transvaal Power Company (VFTPC) which served the lucrative mining contracts, partially by the delivery of power generated by Escom.[22]

Thus state enterprises certainly reflected the economic and political disjunctures of the inter-war years but in ways that substantially differed according to the resolution of compromises and conflicts. Dependence of power and metal on markets provided by mining, for example, endowed

---

[21] Of the total primary and secondary iron and steel consumption in South Africa, the railways consumed 17.2 per cent and the mines 41 per cent between 1932 and 1937.

[22] The VFTPC was ultimately bought by Escom after the Second World War with finance provided by the Anglo American Corporation. See Clark (1987a, p. 268), a thesis published in amended form as Clark (1994), and also Christie (1984).

that fraction of capital with much greater leverage than for the railways which served as a preferred policy instrument for Afrikaner capital. In such a situation, it was difficult for state enterprises to serve as the commanding heights for a coherent policy of industrialisation. Furthermore, neither Afrikaner nor mining capital could reasonably command such a vision, other than ideologically, given the weakness of Afrikaner-based economic interests.

We now turn to the chemical sector. Fig. 6.1 for sectoral composition of manufacturing indicates that the chemicals industry was relatively

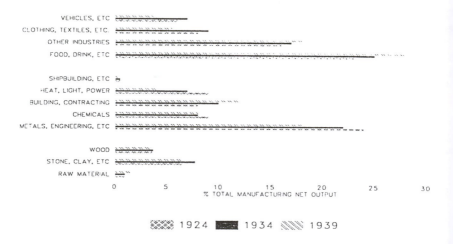

Fig. 6.1. INTER-WAR SECTORAL ECONOMIC ACTIVITY

Source: Union Statistics for Fifty Years (1960, S-2).

well-developed by 1924, contributing 8.3 per cent to industrial output, which was at least as much as the heat, light and power sector. This sector highlights two important features of industrialisation in South Africa. First, it has frequently taken place around and in support of mining activities. Secondly, despite the phenomenal achievements of such industries, they have often failed to develop and diversify.

For example, AECI's Modderfontein factory, built in 1895 by the Nobel explosive monopoly, was the largest dynamite factory in the world and the largest single industrial plant in South Africa at the time. Expansion of this industry was driven largely by its proximity to the mining industry, by economies of scale and by conflict between various fractions of imperial capital.

Striving to reduce costs, imperial mining interests built their own dynamite plant in the Cape in 1898 to challenge the Nobel monopoly and set up an explosives supply system through the Transvaal Chamber of Mines that survives to the present day. A third imperial competitor, Kynoch, set up a plant in Natal in 1903 after the Boer War, and competition between these three producers led to the beginnings of diversification. This was initially limited to backward integration through such undertakings as the production in 1911 of a key input, glycerine, from whale oil.

The early development of the chemicals sector was governed by corruption and collusion between various organs of the South African state and various fractions of imperial capital. The collusive arrangements particularly centred around arms manufacture, which were viewed as strategic; such considerations have influenced many subsequent decisions on industrialisation in South Africa.

It is partly due to the lack of an industrial strategy both before and after the Pact Government that the potential for diversification was not fully realised. By 1911, long before the Pact government which supposedly favoured industrialisation, the chemicals industry (mainly explosives) was the largest sub-sector of manufacturing, capitalised at £2m and employing 3,000 workers. It was the largest single importer of raw materials into South Africa, the largest single source of revenue to Natal Railways and a very large source of revenue for Cape Railways (Cartwright 1964, p. 119).

Some further progress was made. De Beers' Cape Explosives plant at Somerset West even purchased a ship and began exporting explosives to Australia on the eve of the First World War. A detonator plant was built between 1917 and 1920. Paint manufacture had begun in 1918 by virtue of an accident of a British paint manufacturer. Its agent had mistakenly ordered five years of normal supply; after delivery, the parent company had to ship a second-hand paint mill to reprocess the paint to avoid deterioration. Yet these diverse forays were not sustained.

Mergers between explosive companies in Europe in 1924 were followed by the same in South Africa in 1925 and allowed the introduction of the revolutionary ammonia synthesis process from coal in 1930, dispensing with imports of Chilean nitrates. Foreign exchange outflows on Chilean nitrate imports were replaced by a royalty payment to Imperial Chemical Industries (ICI) of between £2 and £4 per tonne of ammonia produced. Furthermore, as Cartwright observes:

> This was an ICI project from start to finish. ICI engineers designed the plant, manufactured a great deal of the equipment and supervised the erection, which was carried out by the factory staff. Wade and Dorman

of Johannesburg were responsible for the structural steel work, and Stuart of Germiston built the foundations. (p. 191)

The merger also facilitated diversification into fertilisers. However, it was limited, not least because of a lack of support on the part of the state. The superphosphate plant at the De Beers Somerset West factory shut down in 1921 after operating for only a few months due to Dutch dumping and the refusal of the government to raise local prices through tariffs. It feared 'losing ground in the country districts [and] was anxious not to antagonise the farmers by imposing a duty that would increase the price of fertiliser.'(Cartwright, p. 163)

Thus one can best interpret Pact policy in regard to explosives and fertiliser manufacture within the chemicals industry as a whole through the prevailing disjuncture between economic and political power. While it was acceptable to subsidise food manufacturing industries whose inputs were based on subsidised agriculture, the government was seemingly not prepared to subsidise agricultural inputs, particularly since the industries producing them were under imperial control. After the merger in 1925, the domestic explosives and fertiliser industry was jointly owned by De Beers and ICI; both of these were regarded as imperial capital.

Other sectors of the chemicals industry exhibited similar patterns. They were usually based around the mining industry. Rand Carbide, for example, began carbide production in 1926 using lime and coke in electric furnaces. By 1930 it was the VTFPC power utility's largest bulk industrial customer with the exception of a few of the gold mines. The major demand for carbide was from the mines but the factory apparently became a major exporter for a while (Christie 1984, p. 93). Similarly, the pulp and paper industry was only set up on any scale in 1936 by the Union Corporation, a major mining house with headquarters in London (Hocking 1987).

Liquid fuel production in the inter-war period was centred around the mining and retorting of torbanite. The first torbanite plant was set up by the Natal Mineral Oil Company in 1895 to extract paraffin from shale. This was followed by the establishment of the Oil Shale Development Company in 1913, with oil shale mines in Natal, Transvaal and Swaziland. In 1934, the first South African oil refinery was set up in Boksburg by an Anglovaal subsidiary, South African Torbanite Mining and Refining Company (Satmar). It processed imported crude and shale oil, retorted at its Ermelo shale mine. There were two factors underpinning the success of the plant in the 1930s. First, there was the natural protection of the inland market through railway freight rates, tariff protection for local manufacture and, during the war years, the irregular imports of crude oil. Secondly, a large proportion of the inland market was supplied by this plant.

The history of Anglovaal itself illustrates the centrality of mining to industrialisation and its importance as a source of finance and surplus:[23]

> The only big businesses by world standards were the mining companies...To be a big mining house you need lots of mines and to have lots of mines you had to be prepared to spend tens of thousands of pounds on holes in the ground looking for them – and that's money written off the moment it's spent. So they decided very soon that they needed to diversify so that they could start businesses based upon local raw materials, satisfying local needs, and raising money for those needs on a booming stock market – which boom wouldn't go on for ever. So within three years of inception we were into petroleum refining, cement and bricks and tiles. (We got out of the bricks and tiles two years later. I think we burned our fingers.) And so from the very start, the premise was that we would start those industries, then in a period of years move them up so that they would throw off cash, some of which we would spend on holes in the ground to find mines which, in their turn, would throw off cash, some of which we would use to build more industries – and lever our way forward on a diversified base on the basis that matters don't go wrong all at once...We were diversified from inception, unlike many mining houses who grew rich and made their fortunes on mines and only at a time that they had these riches did they look for other opportunities – and diversified then.

Anglovaal, a corporation with indigenous roots in both ownership and finance, appears to have been able to challenge imperial capital through a judicious and explicitly diverse investment strategy. This possibility of domestic equity financing seems to have been completely missed by Norval (p. 96), who justifies the establishment of the IDC by arguing that:

> The industries which developed under the stimulus of the customs tariff protection inaugurated in 1925, found very little if any organised financial backing on which to rely. Financial institutions such as the industrial banks in the older countries, for instance the four D. banks in Germany...the banques d'affaires in France, the organised industrial share and capital market and in particular the investment trusts in Great Britain and the United States of America were wholly absent in South Africa. The larger industrial concerns such as AECI, Stewarts and Lloyds, Lever Brothers, Price's Candles, Cadbury-Fry, Nestlé, the motor assembly plants, the tyre factories and many others, all South African branches of overseas concerns were, in the main, initially financed by their parent companies, which thereafter...ploughed back

---

[23] Interview with Clive Menell, deputy chair and joint owner of Anglovaal, by M. Kaplan (p. 110).

their profits to finance further developments and expansions...many other concerns in the industrial field in South Africa developed on the strength of financial reserves built up from within and with such other resources as could be obtained from friends or from the commercial banks by the way of overdrafts or other forms of trade credit.

As a generality, the example of Anglovaal shows this to be false. Highly capital-intensive industries were developed in the inter-war period by national firms, largely originating within mining. More importantly, this took place in the absence of any clear state industrial strategy save for tariff protection. What Anglovaal achieved could have been dwarfed by the results of diversification from the large mining companies, if they had been secure in economic and political support.[24]

The uneasy relationship between state and capital is sharply illustrated by the diamond industry. It shows how mining capital could frustrate the state's economic goals of sustaining economic activity located within South Africa. One of the early acts of the Pact government was to introduce the Diamond Control Bill in July 1925. Newbury (1989) describes it thus:

> The government now had an instrument which it could use to determine quantities produced, set minimum prices, and call for returns of production. All sales agreements required ministerial approval. A 'Diamond Control Bill' might be established to buy and sell, issue advances, and fund monopoly sales through its own officials. (p. 258)

But he concludes: 'Very little of these Draconian powers was ever brought to bear on the industry; but the threat was there, unless the merchants and companies set their house in order.'

What the state required as a minimum, as indeed did the industry itself, was a cartel to limit the output finding its way onto the world market in order to sustain prices; the state would also benefit from this in view of its allocated share of revenue. From its earliest days, the industry had struggled to attain a collusive monopoly over marketing on a world scale, its arrangements always subject to erosion by the emergence of new sources of supply.[25] Despite the weight of South Africa in world diamond

---

[24] Ehrensaft (1985, p. 81) uses the term 'flywheel effect' to describe the potential use of gold as a source of state-promoted industrialisation. For the view that secondary industrialisation depended upon the foreign exchange earnings of the gold industry but was not integrated with it, see Lumby (1976; 1977). For the latter:

> Thus, rather than assisting the secondary sector to develop as a substitute for the gold mines, *the local printing industry remained dependent upon the foreign exchange earnings of the gold mines for its continued existence* (p. 143, the present author's emphasis).

[25] For the early history of the industry, see Newbury, Turrell (1987) and Worger (1987). See also Fine (1994).

production, cartels had always been organised by international capital located in London. This meant that the South African government could only be an influence on, not a determinant of, marketing arrangements. Thus state control of the diamond industry was at most negative in the sense that it could have disrupted attempts to cartelise by raising and marketing its own output but this would be at the expense of the market as a whole and its own revenue as prices collapsed. This situation is illustrated by developments over the inter-war years. In the 1920s, Ernest Oppenheimer gained control over the industry on behalf of Anglo American through De Beers, thereby cementing together an international cartel that has survived to the present day. One issue within South Africa concerned alluvial diggings which had provided a source of employment for independent small-scale white mining. Gregory (1962, p. 171) reports of the Precious Stones Act of 1927: 'The main principle underlying this measure', said the Minister [of Mines], 'is that alluvial diggings, subject to the interests of the State, and a fair participation of the State where necessary and desirable, should remain the reserve and preserve of the small man.' Gregory wryly observes: 'The principle of reserving alluvial digging for the "small man", whether justifiable or not as a measure of social and economic justice, did not in itself meet the essential needs of the situation as it was in 1927, namely, the control of output which was, however, *also* provided for in section 115 of the Act.' By 1929 the independent diggers had all but disappeared and by 1931 De Beers had control over all major diamond production in South Africa.

The 1930s presented rather different problems, even if derived from the same imperative of limiting supply, although it was now in the context of collapsed demand on a world scale. Other than buying up and stock-piling excessive quantities of gems, how were diminished overall levels of demand to be allocated between the different sources of supply? For the South African state, this became a matter of sustaining both its revenue and white employment on the mines. De Beers, however, sought to keep the diamond cartel together by adjusting its own South African output. For Newbury[26]

> The clash between diamond capitalists and the Pact politicians centred on the crisis of overproduction and not on the politics of 'Afrikanerisation' or job protection at the work place. The tensions were real enough, however, and lasted from 1924 till about 1933, beginning with a breakdown in contractual monopoly and ending in accommodation between merchants, producers, and government during reconstruction...In effect, the industry climbed out of the crisis of the 1930s because South African diamond production was used as

---

[26] See also pp. 375 and 369.

the regulator for a measure of control by the Diamond Corporation over total diamond purchases inside and outside the Union. Mines were closed and purchases were held back from resale in the late 1930s, while outside minimum sales contracts and the risk of bulk diamond sales favoured West and Central African producers. (pp. 364-5)

Conflict focused on the closure of the Premier Mine in March 1932, for which the government did not give permission nor did De Beers give adequate notice as required by agreement.[27] As market conditions improved thereafter, the government was reconciled to its subordinate role: 'The South African government then became a partner in the corporation which rationalized its functions to deal with production at home and overseas, and market gem and industrial goods through the London channel.' (Newbury, p. 371)

In short, policy around the diamond industry cannot be seen as a simple conflict between imperial and domestic capital and white labour. The exercise of the government's political power was severely constrained in particular ways by the economic structure of the industry on an international scale, just as it was for steel and its rather different arrangements for a global cartel.

Nevertheless, the extent to which industrial diversification was possible even in the absence of a cohesive industrial strategy is illustrated by the emergence from South African diamond mining of one of the country's most successful industrial corporations, Boart International.[28] The fall in international demand in the 1930s, despite De Beers' global monopoly, precipitated the development of uses for boart, which was then essentially a by-product of the mining of gem diamonds. Beginning from researching and developing a composite diamond impregnated drill bit in Johannesburg in 1936, what is now Boart International has diversified into a range of activities utilising diamonds, including cutting, abrasives and contract drilling. At its peak in the early 1980s, Boart International controlled 100 companies and employed 17,000 people in twenty-eight countries.

In looking back at the inter-war period and considering the literature that has confronted it, a number of conclusions and questions emerge. First, the correctly recognised disjuncture between economic and political power has been too simplistically examined. This is reflected in an overemphasis upon the class *agencies* involved without due attention

---

[27] See also Gregory's (pp. 246–7) discussion.
[28] What follows is from a variety of sources, such as corporation annual reports, newspapers and the financial press.

being paid to actual and potential economic *linkages*. The strategy of developing national capital was heavily circumscribed by the extent of the political acceptability of its being primarily based upon diversification out of the economy's strength in and around mining. This factor was, however, uneven across different sectors of the economy and policy instruments themselves.

Secondly, a further aspect of the overly simplistic view of the disjuncture between economic and political power has been the failure to recognise its heterogeneity. Afrikaner, indigenous and national capital are lumped together in one corner and endowed with political power by way of compensation for their lack of economic strength. Imperial, foreign and English capital are lumped together in the opposing corner with the mirror-image characteristics. This is, of course, analytically convenient in formulating common economic interests within these separate fractions and reading off constrained government policy as reflecting economic or political power according to who is favoured. But there are other differences across these economic interests: they belong to different sectors of the economy, can be of different scale, and are linked to and governed by a variety of diverse factors, such as access to markets, finance, and labour markets, etc. It also follows that the criteria by which the two putative broad fractions of capital are specified are not necessarily consistent with one another. Ownership, origins, markets served etc may not unambiguously be identifiable either with Afrikaner or English.

In this light we will retain the terminology that has been employed in the literature, albeit with some reluctance. For it not only imposes an inappropriate uniformity in referring to the economic and political structure, it also places the legitimacy of the division itself into question. In some cases, for much if not all agriculture and for large-scale mining for example, the stereotypical characterisations might apply to a large extent. For other sectors of the economy, this has yet to be proven empirically on a sectoral basis. Some evidence of the limited extent of Afrikaner-based capital by the beginning of the post-war period is provided at the beginning of the next chapter. But this does not imply that all other capitals were politically powerless or potentially undermined by government policy. In addition, it is the burden of our account that the economic and political structure of South African business has been both heterogeneous and shifting unevenly over time, even if towards an erosion of the significance of differences between Afrikaner and English interests over the post-war period.

Thirdly, then, the one-sided emphasis on class agencies in the literature is also symbolised both by the relative absence of industrial studies and by the continuing ambiguity over the term 'industrialisation' itself. The South African economy has gone through secondary industrialisation so many times in the scholarly and popular literature – around the turn of the century, when stimulated by the wars, in the 1930s and in the 1950s and 1960s – that it comes as a surprise to find that it is now once again suffering from a crushingly uncompetitive and inadequate industrial sector.

Finally, how is the story to be brought forward from the inter-war period? In retrospect it is now known that Afrikaner capital has been built up, not perhaps to be on a par with English capital, but with sufficient strength, interpenetration and co-operation with it that their common interests are and have been closely co-ordinated and served by the state. This is the subject of the following chapters.

7

POST-WAR INDUSTRIALISATION

The position of the MEC during the inter-war period was determined by the disjuncture between Afrikaner political and English economic power which impeded industrial diversification out of the core activities of the MEC. The post-war period has witnessed the erosion of the disjuncture between the two fractions of capital. While uneven across separate components of the economic and political formation, the route by which this was accomplished and its content and consequences have followed a definite periodisation. Afrikaner finance capital first emerges to prominence in the 1950s under state tutelage prior to its integration with the previously exclusive stronghold of English mining capital. But the latter did not stand idly by; the evolution of the MEC up to the 1960s is traced in the first part of this chapter. This is followed by a discussion of large-scale Afrikaner finance capital's interpenetration into mining and other activities in the 1960s. This was supported in particular by the implementation of industrial policy through state-owned corporations in steel, chemicals, fuels and energy.

The resulting commitment to public and private investment in sectors related to energy, mining and mineral processing after the gold and energy price rises in the 1970s was the first signal, possibly further stimulated by international sanctions, that large-scale capital had been integrated economically and politically and was thereby open to coherent and extensive industrial policy. This strengthening of the MEC is discussed in the third section of this chapter. But the costs of this integration were to be felt in the failure to develop a coherent commitment to industrialisation much beyond the immediate concerns of core mining and energy activities. As presented in the chapter's final section, it was this lack of commitment as much as the impediments imposed by apartheid policies as such that led to the continuing structural weakness and paradoxes of the South African economy.

Eroding disjunctures – The development of Afrikaner capital

The disjuncture between English and Afrikaner capital which constrained industrial diversification out of the MEC during the inter-war period was also apparent in the 1950s. While varying in rhythm and extent across sectors, its erosion was evident in the relations of conflict and compromise between English capital on the one hand and Afrikaner capital and state institutions on the other. In the 1940s and 1950s, the latter grew in strength by the promotion of Afrikaner interests in general but more particularly through the promotion of Afrikaner finance capital and its deployment in productive activities which were largely the preserve of English capital in the inter-war period.

The process of accumulation around the MEC in the 1950s included the expansion of gold mining, electricity, coal and chemical sectors as well as the financing of these activities. In the financial sector, compromise with mining capital was evident in the creation of a long-term capital market, necessitated by the collective demands of productive activities within the MEC. Conflict resulted from state patronage of Afrikaner financial interests and similar dichotomies emerged within the electricity, coal and chemical industries.

Afrikaner capital in the 1950s

There is no doubt that, upon assuming power, the Nationalist government supported Afrikaner economic and social advance. One of the best accounts of this is to be found in Lazar (1987) as it is his concern to trace the evolution of Afrikaner politics and ideology in response to changing economic stratification. Our contribution is to locate Nationalist support for Afrikaner capital in the context of the MEC.

To begin with, Lazar (p. 38) states that apart from a purge of government jobs to make way for Afrikaners, 'Afrikaner farmers, financial capitalists, small traders, and workers all received massive direct and indirect hand-outs from the government in the decade after 1948.' Following the development of secondary industry in the war based on the growth of both public and private investment, Lazar finds that Afrikaners already owned 3,385 factories but only employed 14,450 white workers (little more than four per enterprise) out of a total of 170,959; further, they controlled 6 per cent of industrial turnover by 1948. Yet 86 per cent of the unskilled workers in industry in South Africa's principal cities, 79 per cent of mine workers, 74 per cent of rail workers and 63 per cent of factory workers were white males. Only 5 per cent of directors of companies and 15 per cent of professional workers were Afrikaners. Per capita income of English-speaking whites was twice that of Afrikaners.

Lazar points to three trends associated with the promotion of

Afrikaners: the growth of white collar employment; the polarisation of Afrikaner agriculture; and the rapid expansion of major Afrikaner corporations, of which financial enterprises were most prominent. For farming, support through the state to the sector that was and remained dominated by Afrikaners gave rise to rapid development of large-scale mechanised production alongside an often marginal and precarious small-scale sector:

> By 1960, a relatively small number of powerful farmers and 'land capitalists' controlled a sizeable proportion of South African agriculture. Undoubtedly, some smaller farmers also benefited from the huge government input into this sector of the economy. But a growing number of poor farmers forsook the land for the towns; the livelihood of those who remained behind on over-divided uneconomic tracts was only guaranteed by government aid. While the *grootboers* [large-farmer] grew richer from the fruits of a lucrative decade (1950s), the *kleinboer* [small farmer] seems to have become poorer, or given up altogether. (Lazar, pp. 108–9)

Only 16 per cent of all economically active Afrikaners were employed in agricultural occupations by 1960, compared with more than 30 per cent in 1946 and 23 per cent in 1954–5 (p. 97). They had migrated to the towns in search of the higher rewards to be found in waged labour. Much of this was within the public sector which employed 30 per cent of whites by 1960, many of them white-collar employees who had benefited from enhanced levels of educational provision. Income differentials remained to the advantage of the English-speaking but had narrowed considerably. Nonetheless, there was only a limited advance in the numbers of Afrikaner owners, managers and directors, as they constituted only 26 per cent of the total in 1960.[1]

Afrikaner capital in the 1950s, the main beneficiary of this process, was represented by four important groups, three of which (Volskas, Sanlam, Rembrandt) were large and centralised, and involved themselves in a number of diverse and also overlapping activities. The fourth group consisted of a large number of small-scale commercial and industrial enterprises, geographically concentrated in the rural areas of the Transvaal and the Orange Free State (OFS).

The Afrikaner economic movement initiated in 1934 and shaped at the first Economiese Volkskongres (People's Economic Congress) in 1939

---

[1] To some extent, this casts doubt on the commitment to the promotion of small-scale Afrikaner industrial capital by the Nationalists. This is what Phimister (1991, p. 441) argues against D. Kaplan (1977) in regard to the 1948 Customs Agreement between Southern Rhodesia and South Africa, as this favoured small-scale business in the former at the expense of the latter.

had effectively consolidated Afrikaner capital's structure by 1950 but had not significantly raised its share of national economic activity. Although the share of total funds controlled by Afrikaner institutions in the financial sector rose from 5 per cent in 1939 to 6.16 per cent in 1950, what was important was that these funds had been centralised and concentrated in the hands of two or three institutions (O'Meara, p. 205). Manufacturing enterprises were very closely linked to the processing of agricultural produce through co-operatives, with 80 per cent of the firms located in rural areas. They were small-scale in nature, 85 per cent being single-person enterprises. Afrikaner capital was virtually absent in mining activities but a significant presence had been established in commerce, although many of the enterprises concerned were small. 75 per cent were single-person and most progress had been at the expense of Indian traders evicted in the Transvaal.

Table 7.1. GROWTH OF AFRIKANER CAPITAL, 1939–49

| | £m. turnover | | % Afrikaner | |
	1939	1949	1939	1949
Commerce	28.0	203.7	8	25
Manufacturing	6.0	43.6	3	6
Finance	27.0	74.4	5	6
Mining	1.0	1.0	1	1
Total	61.0	322.7	5	11

Source: O'Meara (p. 182).

With the exception of the financial institutions, most of these small-scale enterprises could not compete with established 'English' competitors. Politically, however, they could not be ignored, although their influence on the economic discourse of Afrikaner capital waned during the 1950s. According to O'Meara, the Afrikaner economic movement had been

> ...initiated as a result of a wary cooperation of the driving forces behind each of the two companies – on the one hand the young financiers around W.A. Hofmeyr [Sanlam], led by M.S. Louw, and on the other hand the theoreticians and Bond activists who sat on the Board of Volkskas. Sanlam and Volkskas were without any question the prime beneficiaries of the centralisation of capital aimed at by the economic movement. The 1940s thus gave rise to two powerful Afrikaner financial groups, each based in one of the two most important centres, the Cape and the Transvaal, and each directly linked to a different faction within the nationalist movement – Sanlam to the Cape National Party

[NP] and Volkskas to the Bond, which dominated northern Afrikaner nationalism. (p. 200)

Successful competition with English capital could only be achieved on the basis of scale; recognising this, the second Economiese Volkskongres laid out the course of events for the 1950s:

> A strategy of accumulation based on small undertakings was doomed. Led by the managing director of Sanlam and Bonuskor [a Sanlam subsidiary], all the major theoreticians declared that now the volk would have to reserve its assistance exclusively for well-established, large institutions, and in particular those with centralised capital for investment...no capital would be forthcoming to help develop existing small undertakings. Large-scale Afrikaner commercial undertakings could now only be established on the initiative of, and under the supervision and control of, the investment companies dominated by Sanlam... With the growing differentiation of urban Afrikaners, and particularly with the emergence of two distinct classes out of the economic movement – a small group of financial capitalists and a large, restive, petty bourgeoisie – strong differences over the meaning of the economic movement and what constituted the interests of the 'volk' grew more acute. This was to find its reflection in the nationalist politics of the 1950s and 1960s. (O'Meara, pp. 18–9)

This approach of focusing on large-scale investments was reflected in policies towards industrial development, particularly in the actions of the IDC, and resulted in a strengthening of the MEC. While less relevant to core MEC activities, there were important divisions between the three dominant Afrikaner institutions. Volkskas confined its activities almost exclusively to banking in the 1940s:

> During this period [1940s] Volkskas' activities were almost entirely limited to banking. Unlike Sanlam it did not yet enjoy a wide network of financial and industrial interests. While its role in centralising capital was vital, this archly conservative bank was not itself in the business of directly investing in industry. (O'Meara, p. 200)

Up until 1960, banking was dominated by the Barclays and Standard Banks. Their dominance in mobilising national savings was eroded in the 1950s by: the growth of the National Finance Corporation (NFC) and, subsequently, by private merchant banks; competition from Volkskas, Nedbank and Trustbank; and competition from building societies and life assurers.

Table 7.2. STRUCTURE OF THE FINANCIAL SECTOR

	Commercial bank deposits (£m.)	Building society deposits (£m.)	Life assurer assets (£m.)
1948	156.1	187.8	162.4
1960	376.6	(1959) 531.9	(1957) 365.4

Source: Jones and Muller (1992).

The phenomenal growth of Volkskas, initially founded in 1934 as a 'people's savings bank on a co-operative basis' (Verhoef 1992) is illustrated by the rise in deposits relative to other commercial bank competitors: from 2.8 per cent in 1947 to 18.6 per cent by 1967. Most of the growth in deposits came after the election of the NP in 1948 and resulted from the transfer of the banking accounts of central government, municipalities and state corporations like Iscor, Escom, SA Post Office, SA Railways, Sasol and others.

Table 7.3. DEPOSIT SHARE OF COMMERCIAL BANKS

	Standard (%)	Barclays (%)	Volkskas (%)
1947	47.2	46.2	2.8
1957			9.9
1960	38.0	43.3	
1967			18.6
1977			19.0
1981			18.8

Source: Volkskas data from Verhoef; Standard and Barclays data from Jones and Muller.

However, Volkskas did not venture significantly into financing industrial development until the 1960s, focusing instead on serving small-scale agricultural interests. In 1965, 83 per cent of its branches were in the platteland (rural Transvaal and the OFS); this fell to 75 per cent in 1981 when its business 'was divided fairly equally between its urban and rural customers' (Verhoef 1992).

On the other hand, by 1950 the life assurance company Sanlam was in a position to increase its involvement in mining, manufacturing and commerce. Through its industrial arm Federale Volksbeleggings, it had interests in fishing and canning (Laaiplek Visserye and Marine Production Corporation), agricultural implements (SA Farm Implements Manufacturers), chemicals and pharmaceuticals (Agricultura Laboratoria and Klipfontein Organic Products), coal mining (Klipfontein and Klippoortjie mines) and publishing (Nationale Pers).

As a life assurer or mutual institution, Sanlam was legally restricted in the extent to which it could deploy the revenue derived from life assurance in production. To overcome this, it separated the bonuses accrued to its policy holders and used the newly created Bonuskor (1946) as an additional industrial investment arm. Bonuskor followed a similar pattern to Fedvolks and by 1950, it had invested the bulk of available funds in manufacturing (57 per cent), mining (4 per cent), commerce (21 per cent) and finance (18 per cent). The process of consolidation and concentration continued in the 1950s with a shift of emphasis to mining. In 1953, Fedvolks and Bonuskor merged their mining interests into Federale Mynbou, the forerunner of today's Gencor. By 1957, 23 per cent of Bonuskor's investments were in mining.

The passing of the Regulation of Monopolistic Competition Act of 1955 reflected the tensions between small and large-scale at the time, although it is widely acknowledged that the legislation was ineffective in practice. However, divisions within and competition between fractions of Afrikaner capital also mirrored the tensions between the Cape and Transvaal branches of the NP, with these surfacing from time to time. For example, Trustbank was set up by Sanlam in 1955 in competition to Volkskas. After the election of Verwoerd, Sanlam and the Cape NP became a focus for opposition to the leadership of the NP. The significance of these divisions was not lost on the AAC, as will be discussed later.

But not all fractions of Afrikaner capital grew through the financial sector. Rembrandt's growth in the 1950s was sectorally specific, in tobacco, cigarettes and, later, alcohol spirit. Rembrandt initially sprang from within the Transvaal Broederbond faction. Financed by both Sanlam and Volkskas, Rembrandt bought the Rothmans cigarette mail order company in 1953 and expanded rapidly thereafter. Rembrandt and its founder, Anton Rupert, became associated with Cape financial power. Its position as large-scale capital was articulated more clearly and openly than any other fraction of Afrikaner capital. Together with AAC, it set up the South African Foundation business lobby in the post-Sharpeville period. After the 1976 Soweto uprising it created, again with AAC, the Urban Foundation, a trust committed to promoting 'black advancement'.[2]

The promotion of Afrikaner finance capital in the late 1940s and 1950s overlapped with the creation of a range of institutions around gold mining, then the central activity of the MEC, and challenged the dominance of British commercial banks in mobilising national capital for industrialisation. The process involved significant interaction between state agencies, 'Afrikaner' and 'English' capitals. It had three principal components: the accommodation of Afrikaner banking institutions by the dominant Standard and Barclays Banks (discussed above); the strengthening of Afrikaner institutions through state patronage; and the creation of a long-term capital market.

---

[2] For more details, see Gerber (1973).

The development of a long-term capital market

When the National Party created the NFC in 1949 short-term funds taken in by commercial banks in South Africa were being re-deposited in London. The NFC provided a local market, investing its deposits in treasury bills, thus providing an 'instrument for channelling short-term funds into the hands of government bodies'. (Jones and Muller, p. 210) Despite drawing in considerable funds, Jones (1992) argues that the NFC did not provide the basis for a successful domestic money market because the demand for short-term loans was rather limited. Unfortunately, Jones' descriptive account overlooks the central role of the MEC.

Events in the financial sphere in the post-war period up to 1955 were heavily conditioned by the development of the Orange Free State Goldfields (FSG) from 1950 onwards. Mining and quarrying capital expenditure exceeded R1bn (constant 1985 terms) for four consecutive years after 1950 and more than 80 per cent of this was related to gold mining (Figure 7.1).

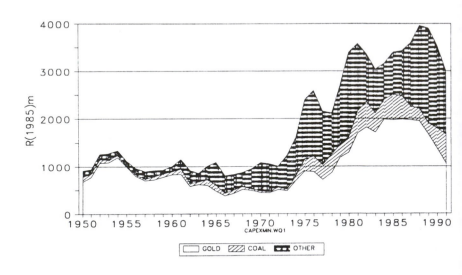

Fig. 7.1. MINING CAPITAL EXPENDITURE

Source: Union Statistics for Fifty Years; *South Africa Statistics*; IDC (1992).

The scale of this project cannot be over-emphasised. The recent AAC decision to develop the Moab gold mine, the announcement of the Columbus stainless steel project and the Alusaf II smelter investments, currently welcomed in the 1990s as desperately needed signs of confidence in the economy, all pale into insignificance compared to the FSG development of twelve individual gold mines in a part of the country where supporting infrastructure was virtually non-existent. De Kock (1951) imparts a striking impression of an interplay between state and corporate planning right down to the last compound for mine workers. The sheer scale of the project was even impressive to the chair of the IBRD (now known as the World Bank) and its £50m loan to the Union Government in 1953 for electrification, railways and infrastructure can be taken as a sign of their confidence. The state utilities overcame huge technical problems; water was pumped 40 miles from the Vaal River and while electricity from the Vaal power station was used initially, Vierfontein station was specially built by state-owned Escom at a cost of £17m in addition to the £370m spent on the twelve mines themselves.

The NFC did not simply subscribe to government bonds but also subscribed heavily to mining house debentures. In many respects, the NFC was a financial intermediary, channelling profits made from AAC-owned De Beers diamond sales into AAC's FSG project. Of the NFC's deposits of £58m in 1958, £21m had been deposited by De Beers (Innes 1984, pp. 148–9), heralding a shift away from private sources of finance to the use of institutional ones. By investing through the NFC, a mining house was able to spread the high risk associated with mining, hedging its liabilities with the purchase of gilt-edged securities. With the NFC bearing the risks, financing investment in mine development followed a well-lubricated path.

Such funding of the development of the FSG was important for the erosion of the disjunctures between economic and political power, despite the prevailing political animosities following the 1948 election of the NP and its re-election in 1952. The benefits of the interplay of interests were overwhelming. Through the NFC, the state profited on the 'spread' between deposits and investment. According to Palmer (1958), NFC turnover rose from £70m in 1949 to £1,045m in 1953. Secondly, direct and indirect state revenues from leasing, royalties and company and employee tax were estimated at around 40 per cent of the goldfields' profits. Thirdly, the project transformed the OFS economically and politically. Economically, it promoted a form of regional decentralisation, developing what had previously been a relatively unpopulated NP stronghold. By 1960, there were 93,000 workers in the OFS, about 20 per cent of the 456,000 employed in the entire gold mining industry. It also raised the white voting population of the OFS thirtyfold over fifteen years from

5,500 whites in 1950 to an estimated 146,000 in 1966, thereby increasing the number of parliamentary seats and strengthening the NP.

In 1955, the AAC founded Union Acceptances Ltd (UAL), its in-house merchant bank. It did so with the support of Barclays, one of two dominant commercial banks. Innes (p. 182) argues that this was the second stage in its strategy whereby:[3] 'First, the state was prevailed upon to make the early running through the NFC (as it were, to test out the market) and only when that venture had proved successful did the Group itself enter the field through UAL.'

Although UAL dominated the merchant banking market, four other merchant banks had been formed by 1961 including the Sanlam-controlled Central Finance and Acceptance Corporation and the IDC-controlled Accepting Bank for Industry. With deposits of £69m, the NFC had been overtaken by private sector institutions, with the latter collectively holding £71m.

The growth in the financial sector's contribution to GDP from 9.5 per cent to 10.7 per cent between 1950 and 1960 is illustrated in Figure 4.6 (p. 109). However, the assertion by Innes (p. 182) that the development of capital markets during the 1950s represented 'the clearest form yet of the merging together of bank capital and productive capital – that is, of the emergence of the phase of finance capital', proves a premature and inappropriate dating.[4] For while Afrikaner capital had grown significantly through the financial sector, it had not acquired a firm and sustainable base within mining or manufacturing industries. The FSG development had been a joint venture between AAC and three other mining houses, none of which was associated with Afrikaner capital.[5] Indeed, the sig-

[3] Innes (p. 135) cites Hagart (1967, p. 110), who asserts that Ernest Oppenheimer was actively involved in the formation of the NFC.

[4] Innes refers to King (1962, p. 163), who suggests that the UAL was to be modelled along the lines of the UK financial system. This is inappropriate as an empirical illustration of Hilferding's concept, given the UK's limited integration of banking with long-term productive investment. Innes seems motivated by the wish to impose concepts such as finance capital on the South African economy. These are borrowed from the analysis of advanced capitalism which, however valid for that purpose, is inappropriate in this case. Here the term 'finance capital' will be used for descriptive purposes only, merely signifying the activity associated with financial institutions.

[5] Innes (p. 256) provides the following record of the distribution of ownership of the OFS gold fields in the early 1960s:

AAC Mines	Western Holdings, Free State Geduld, Welkom, President Brand, President Steyn, Lorraine and Jeannette
Anglovaal Mines	Virginia and Merriespruit
Union Corporation	St Helena
JCI	Freddies Cons
Consolidated Goldfields	Free State Saaiplaas
Central Mining	Harmony
General Mining	Riebeeck

nificant developments in the financial sector were not yet followed by any significant diversification out of the MEC.

Eroding disjunctures in electricity, coal mining, chemical and fuel industries. MEC growth dominated industrial development in the 1950s as the political and economic disjuncture in its component productive sectors gradually eroded. There were two identifiable state industrial strategies which emerged during this process; the nationalisation of the electricity industry and a corresponding power station construction programme; and the creation of a state-owned fuel-chemical industry. Both of these policies were implemented through a mixture of collusion and competition with English capital. While state provision of energy and transport infrastructure was essential for mining, the process of provision implicitly included state patronage for Afrikaner industrial concerns which, supported by burgeoning Afrikaner finance capital, were propelled into several key industries around the MEC.

The role of the energy component of the MEC was most prominent in the 1950s through its impact on other sectors. The electricity industry had been set up in the nineteenth century by the mining industry and was taken over by the state in 1948, with the AAC assisting with financing. At the time, about 59 per cent of generated power was consumed in the gold mines (Christie 1984, p. 218). Uncertain of their future before state takeover, the private power generators did not invest in new capacity and the demand from the OFS goldfields together with increasing post-war industrialisation in the early 1950s led to periodic power shortages. The lack of sufficient railway trucks and locomotives during that period constrained the movement of goods, particularly bulk coal from mines to urban power stations and urban consumers. Coal exports were also constrained by the lack of transport.

Coal mining at the time was dominated by the major 'English' mining houses represented by the Transvaal Coal Owners Association (TCOA), a cartel that effectively controlled access to the domestic market. Controls on the pithead price of coal, in existence in the post-1948 period, encouraged exports at the expense of the local market: 'The average cost of coal at the pit's mouth [was] 7s 4d per short ton, compared with 45s in Britain, France and Germany, 65s in Belgium, 34s in the US, 36s in Canada and 17s per short ton in Australia.' (Christie 1984, p. 151)

An indication of the lucrative nature of exports at the time is that while only 7.5 per cent of total mined coal was being exported, it contributed 46 per cent of coal mine profits. Frustrated by the 'closed shop' of the TCOA, the coal mines owned by Sanlam found other means to further their interests by influencing the Department of Commerce and Industry to allocate scarce rail trucks and export licenses independently of the TCOA cartel. This strategy was fuelled by the ideological debates of the period, with the 'English' TCOA being publicly blamed for the coal shortages, the slightly misleading argument being that they were making excessive profits from export coal which could be made available on the domestic market.

Coal rationing was introduced in 1952, with the TCOA giving first claim on supplies to state railways, the central state, municipal and mine power stations and gold mines. With these priorities, black consumers suffered most from fuel shortages. With its re-election in 1952, the NP ensured continuing support to Afrikaner capital, and by 1954 TCOA was forced to admit two Afrikaner coal owners into the cartel. New power stations were being constructed and the coal supply contracts were increasingly being awarded to Afrikaner-owned coal-mines. Federale Mynbou's Coalbrook colliery supplied the new Taaibos and Highveld stations. Overall, however, Afrikaner capital was still on the fringes of such activity. The major problem of the 1950s was in meeting the power demand of the gold mines and this was ultimately resolved by 1960 through the building of three power stations on the coal fields themselves, thus circumventing the need to transport huge quantities of coal around the country.

The construction of new power stations strengthened the MEC but this development was constrained by a lack of capital and machinery. Even when power station construction was approved, the demand from the Korean war (1950–3) mopped up supplies of imported power generation equipment. To some extent, this was countered by the strategic needs of the United States for South African uranium. For example, in return for the import of much needed uranium, institutions such as the US Export-Import Bank provided loans, like the £7m loan in 1952 for US power generation equipment, thus facilitating the construction of the Wilge station. Enormous long-term loans were raised in the 1950s, mainly through the World Bank, for power plant (1950: $30m; 1954: $30m) and railway infrastructure (1950: $20m; 1954: $30m). In 1950, a further $10m was raised from eight US commercial banks, which also raised $20m to finance mining equipment for the OFS mines. By 1960, the Vierfontein (360MW), Taaibos (480MW) and Wilge (240MW) stations had been built and the Highveld (480MW) station was under construction. New capacity totalled 1560MW, a huge increase compared to 1950 capacity of 1290MW (Escom 1990). Of the £105m of long-term liabilities raised by the Union government in the 1950s (Union Statistics for Fifty Years, U3), more than half (£58.5m or $117m) was incurred before 1955, specifically for energy and railway infrastructure. Macroeconomic balances were then significantly affected by the investment demands of the MEC.

In the 1950s, the development of an indigenous fuel-chemical industry was the second conscious industrial strategy by the state. This coincided with the expansion of the existing chemical industry, which was heavily dependent on demand from the mining industry and had long been dominated by the AAC subsidiary AECI. Most of AECI's capital expenditure in the 1950s was aimed at increasing ammonia production for the explosives required by the new OFS gold mines. While diversification did take place – the Saiccor Rayon plant joint venture with the IDC in 1954, the manufacture of PVC in 1955 and expansion in fertiliser production – most chemical production served the mining industry.

The construction of the Sasol I oil/chemicals-from-coal plant was a substantial bolster to the MEC. An indication of its impact on the chemicals sector and on the state budget is its cost of about £40m between 1950 and 1956 when it began producing (IDC Annual Report 1956). In comparison, this was almost double the *total* authorised capital (£23m in 1956) of the dominant producer AECI and it dwarfed AECI's £10m ammonia plant expansions between 1958 and 1960 (Cartwright).

Set up in 1940 to encourage secondary industrialisation, the IDC was heavily involved in developing the synthetic fuel and chemical industries. Table 7.4 provides an indication of the focus of its attention in industrial sectors associated with the MEC. By 1956, the IDC had invested £40.7m in Sasol, representing 77 per cent of its total investments in industry.

Table 7.4. I.D.C. FINANCING OF
THE MINERALS ENERGY-COMPLES (%)

1960	1965	1970	1975	1980	1985
68.3	64.6	52.3	53.5	37.4	48.0

Note: Figures are for the cumulative proportion of outstanding capital advanced to industrial undertakings in the following sub-sectors: chemicals, rubber, plastics, non-metallic mineral products, basic iron and steel industries, non-ferrous metals.

Source: IDC Annual Reports (various years).

These and subsequent IDC interventions contributed significantly to the growth of the MEC core. The IDC historically chose to finance the establishment of infant industries which fell largely within the non-mining sectors of the MEC. These included phosphates (1952), Palaborwa copper (1963), coal-based chemicals, Sasol I (1951), synthetic rubber (1962), Soekor oil exploration (1965), Alusaf aluminium smelter (1967), industrial chemicals (1967), Sasol II (1976), Sasol III (1979) and Mossgas (1986). While the IDC promoted other industries, including armaments such as Atlas Aircraft Corporation (1964), most resources were deployed to promote the MEC (Table 7.4), with 68.3 per cent going to the complex in 1960, a gradual decline to 37.4 per cent in 1980 and a subsequent rise to 48.0 per cent in 1985. The IDC's political role in furthering the interests of Afrikaner capital is discussed below. The upward trend since 1980 appears set to continue. In 1991, the IDC indicated that its next targets include steel and stainless steel beneficiation, wood pulp, chemicals and petrochemical products.[6]

In summary, the boundaries of the MEC had been substantially broadened by 1960 and this was a process that was to continue subsequently. In sectoral terms, it encompassed mining, mineral processing (mainly steel at the time), electricity, chemicals and liquid fuels. GDP contributions from these sectors rose from 18 per cent in 1953 to 21.5 per cent by 1960 while non-MEC manufacturing continued to fluctuate between 14–15 per cent (Figure 4.5, p. 83).

As a system of accumulation, the MEC represented the means by which Afrikaner fractions of capital sought to involve themselves in mainstream economic activity. While the 1950s saw Afrikaner capital consolidate its position within the financial sector and gain footholds in the coal mining and fuels–chemical sectors as a junior partner, the 1960s would witness its much wider sectoral penetration of the economy, mainly within the core MEC sectors. In addition, there would be an increasing interaction between itself and English capital.

The interpenetration of English and Afrikaner capital in the 1960s

The erosion of the disjuncture between English and Afrikaner capital was spurred on by the withdrawal of foreign capital after the Sharpeville massacre. It resulted in the interpenetration first of English and Afrikaner capital and secondly of different fractions of Afrikaner capital. However, the erosion was insufficient to support significant industrial diversification out of the MEC, which dominated economic activity and continued to determine the pattern of industrial development. This process was accompanied by increasing state-led investment in the MEC around energy, chemicals, processed minerals and armaments. Thus, as the direct contribution of mining to the economy fell from 13.7 per cent of GDP in 1960 to 8.8 per cent in 1971, the contribution to GDP of non-mining MEC sectors rose from 7.9 per cent to 8.5 per cent (Figure 4.5, p. 83).

The share of Afrikaner ownership of the mining sector increased significantly in the 1960s. Initially, these were served by coal contracts from the growing state electricity giant, Escom. Of the five stations commissioned in the 1960s, four coal contracts were awarded to Sanlam's Federale Mynbou (the mining subsidiary of Sanlam's industrial arm, Fedvolks), whose coal interests were subsequently placed under the Trans Natal Coal subsidiary (TNC) through Genmin. By 1962 Federale Mynbou was the second largest coal company in the country after AAC.

[6] *Financial Mail* (1991) 17 May. In 1994, the IDC again reaffirmed its support for MEC projects.

Table 7.5. ESCOM COMMISSIONING SCHEDULE

Coal-fired stations	Location	Rating (MW)	Mining house	First set	Last set
Komati	Middelburg	1,000	TNC	1962	1966
Ingagane	Newcastle	500	TNC	1963	1969
Camden	Ermelo	1,600	TNC	1967	1969
Grootvlei	Balfour	1,200	AAC	1969	1977
Hendrina	Hendrina	2,000	TNC	1970	1977
Arnot	Middelburg	2,100	AAC	1971	1975
Kriel	Bethal	3,000	AAC	1976	1979
Matla	Bethal	3,600	TNC/GFSA	1979	1983
Duvha	Witbank	3,600	RM	1980	1984
Lethabo	Vereeniging	3,708	AAC	1985	1990
Tutuka	Standerton	3,654	AAC	1985	1990
Matimba	Ellisras	3,325	ISCOR	1987	1991
Kendal/Khutala	Kendal	686	RM	1988	1993
Majuba	Volksrust	0	RM	1996	2001

Source: Escom.

With the exception of a few large and lumpy investments, mainly in MEC sectors, diversification out of mining took place through acquisition rather than through new investments. Federale Mynbou diversified into asbestos in 1962 through the acquisition of Msauli and Gefco. The outflow of foreign capital after the Sharpeville massacre provided the opportunity for Afrikaner and English finance capital to buy into existing concerns. The AAC, flush with cash from the OFS goldfields, began a pattern of domestic and international acquisitions that has continued unabated. In 1958, AAC took control of Central Mining, subsequently placing it under the London-based subsidiary Charter Consolidated. In 1962, Charter took control of the Hudson Bay Mining and Smelting Company in Canada at the same time that AAC was blocking Federale Mynbou's bid for control of JCI by taking over JCI itself. There were two reasons for this move. (Innes, p. 158) First, JCI had substantial holdings in De Beers and the Diamond Producers' Association. Secondly, JCI controlled Rustenburg, the world's largest platinum mine and also had substantial copper mining interests. Clearly, uncontrolled penetration of Afrikaner interests in AAC's sphere of influence was not welcome.

Thus the acquisition in 1964 of Genmin by Federale Mynbou with the help of AAC signalled a conscious accommodation of Afrikaner by English capital or compromise in the face of conflict. It is no coincidence that the assistance given to Federale Mynbou followed the setting up of a Commission of Inquiry into the affairs of the AAC in 1964.

Table 7.6. DOMINANT MINING AND INDUSTRIAL GROUPS, 1960–70

	1960 Market capitalisation (£m.)	*1970 Ultimate controller*
AAC	87.3	AAC
JCI	15.1	AAC
Rand Mines	12.7	AAC
Central Mining	15.5	AAC
Genmin	15.3	Sanlam
Union Corporation[1]	32.8	Sanlam/Rembrandt
Anglovaal	5.7	Hersov/Menel
Goldfields	33.7	Goldfields

1. Genmin took control in 1975.

Source: Innes (p. 165).

as a result of lobbying by the largely Transvaal-based, Afrikaner petty-bourgeois fraction of the NP. Innes (p. 158) argues that: 'participation for Afrikaner interests in one of the main gold mining groups was a way in which these criticisms might be muted.' However, the growing accommodation with English capital increased the strains on the NP alliance and as O'Meara observes:

> Initially this took the form of regionalism. Attacks on the geldmag (financial power) of the Cape – on Sanlam and Rembrandt – gathered force in the 1950s. By the time of Sharpeville, these divisions were explicit... Throughout the early 1960s...the Cape party, its organ *Die Burger*, and the Sanlam interests were virtually an official opposition within the NP. With the assassination of Verwoerd in September 1966, this conflict burst into open struggles between so-called verligtes (the enlightened) and verkramptes (the reactionaries). In 1969, the leading verkramptes were expelled from the NP and...they formed the Herstigte (reconstituted) National Party. (p. 251)

While Afrikaner capital had made inroads into the mining industry by end of the 1960s, the AAC still dominated gold mining through its own mines and through control of JCI, Rand Mines and Central Mining. Interpenetration was evident through the minority holdings the AAC held in Genmin, Union Corporation and GFSA.

Given the political strains outlined above and despite the erosion of the disjuncture, it was still not possible for the state to adopt industrial strategies to diversify out of the MEC. Instead, the policies adopted in the 1950s through state corporations and joint ventures between the IDC and private capital in and around the MEC continued to provide the main impetus to industrial development.

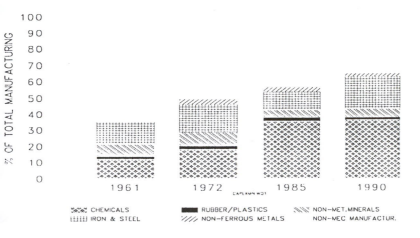

Fig. 7.2. M.E.C. FIXED INVESTMENT (YEAR-END VALUE)

Source: South African Statistics; IDC (1992).

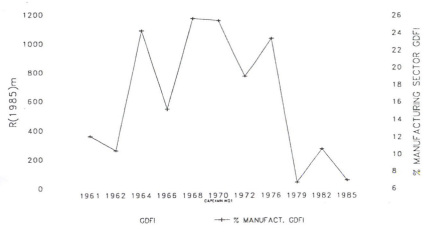

Fig. 7.3. G.D.F.I. IRON AND STEEL SECTOR FIXED INVESTMENT

Source: South African Statistics.

Although the manufacturing sector is generally acknowledged to have grown significantly in the 1960s, most of the expansion was associated with large, lumpy investments in the MEC, as it had been throughout the post-war period. A considerable proportion of manufacturing sector fixed investment in the 1960s was concentrated in MEC sectors like steel, chemicals and processed minerals, rising from 35.5 per cent to 49.8 per cent of manufacturing fixed investment between 1961 and 1972 (Figure 7.2).

For much of the decade of the 1960s, the iron and steel sector absorbed more than a quarter of all annual fixed investment in the manufacturing sector (Figure 7.3). Specific investments in the steel industry included that in 1964 to the AAC-owned Highveld Steel and Vanadium plant costing R127m, as compared to the total 1964 manufacturing sector fixed investment expenditure of R241m. Highveld prompted a second round of investment as AAC vertically integrated its steel and engineering activities (Innes, p. 195). Scaw Metals, a speciality steel producer, was also acquired in 1964 and by 1969 had assets of R40m.

The ferrochrome industry was created in 1964 by RMB Alloys, a subsidiary of Rand Mines, using local chromite ore. This was followed by the Southern Cross Stainless Steel plant, built in Middelburg with IDC assistance between 1964 and 1965. However, the state-owned primary steel maker, Iscor, still remained the major producer and investor in the sector.

In the mineral processing sectors, large investments were made in the Alusaf aluminium smelter. Construction of Alusaf began in 1967 and came into production in 1971 with 53000 tonnes per annum capacity. The plant's R59.5m cost in 1970 compares with the total 1970 manufacturing sector fixed investment expenditure of R371.8m. Increasing interpenetration and collaboration is evidenced by the fact that Alusaf was a joint venture between the state, domestic English and transnational capital, involving the IDC, AAC-controlled Rand Mines and Alusuisse. The project included an additional aluminium rod plant, Alustang, a joint venture between Alusaf and state-owned Iscor subsidiary, USCO.[7]

The chemical industry was also an avenue through which Afrikaner capital grew and interpenetrated with English capital. Apart from Sasol and Klipfontein Organic Products, chemical production in 1960 was dominated by the AAC subsidiary AECI and by transnational oil companies. Economies of scale prompted early integration at Sasolburg with a polythene plant joint venture between AECI and Sasol. In 1964, the SA Nylon Spinners (SANS) plant was built. In 1966, AECI spent R80m on a petrochemical complex at Sasolburg; this was in comparison to the total 1966 manufacturing sector fixed investment expenditure of R386.5m.

---

[7]   IDC *Annual Report* 1970.

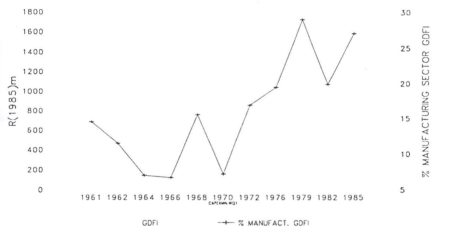

Fig. 7.4. G.D.F.I. CHEMICALS SECTOR FIXED INVESTMENT

Source: South African Statistics.

Afrikaner capital furthered its investments in chemicals with the assistance of the IDC. In 1964, a synthetic rubber plant was set up by the Fedvolks subsidiary Karbochem and the IDC. In 1967, the Sanlam subsidiary, Sentrachem, absorbed Karbochem, Klipfontein Organic Products (KOP) and the UK Distillers Corporation subsidiary, National Chemical Products (NCP). This newly-formed Afrikaner-owned chemical giant formed an association with Hoechst of Germany in 1969 and expanded into polyethylene. The Natref inland crude oil refinery was built between 1968 and 1971 and was a joint venture between initiators IDC and the National Iranian Oil Company and Compagnie Française de Petroles. Domestic investors invited included Rembrandt, Volkskas and SA Mutual. Though less than in the 1970s, the magnitude of chemical sector investments in the 1960s were significant (Figure 7.4).

The imposition of an international arms embargo in the early 1960s provided other manufacturing opportunities for Afrikaner capital. Again, the IDC's assistance in the formation of Armscor subsidiaries such as Atlas Aircraft Corporation in 1964 was invaluable.

The emphasis on the MEC does not detract from attempts made during this period, or any other period for that matter, to diversify out of the MEC. However, such efforts were not effective. Between 1960 and 1970, the GDP contribution of non-MEC manufacturing sectors rose from 15 per cent to 17.5 per cent and then fell below 16 per cent in 1972 (Figure 4.5, p. 83).[8]

This non-MEC growth can be attributed to the motor industry (0.6 per cent of GDP directly) and the textile industry (0.4 per cent of GDP) to a lesser extent. In the case of the former, many commentators have cited the local content programme initiated in the early 1960s as providing a boost to the manufacturing sector.[9] The evidence presented in Figure 7.5 indicates that the impact has perhaps been exaggerated in relation to the MEC. Apart from the direct growth in GDP contribution of about 1.8 per cent, the motor industry would have stimulated growth in the fabricated metal product sector and in the non-electrical machinery sector. While the latter two grew to 2.2 per cent and 1.6 per cent of GDP, respectively, they are equally likely to have been stimulated by the impact of large-scale MEC projects during this period.[10]

In the case of textiles, growth during the 1950s was partly encouraged by the now discredited apartheid decentralisation policies (Clark 1987b, p. 335). By the early 1960s, the lessons of this experience were abundantly

---

[8] For further discussion, see Chapter 4.

[9] The IDC provided direct support by forming Wispeco, a joint venture with the Australian firm Repco, to manufacture motor components.

[10] See Rustomjee (1993) for a discussion of linkages between the economy and the fabricated metal and machinery industries falling within the ISIC 3800 category.

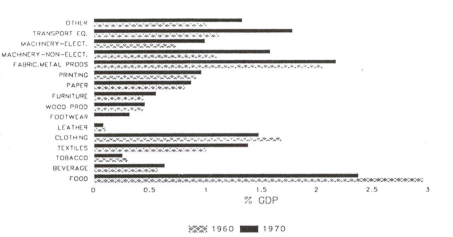

Fig. 7.5. NON-M.E.C. MANUFACTURING:GROWTH IN
G.D.P. CONTRIBUTION, 1960–70

Source: South African Statistics.

clear to the IDC, the actual creator of the industry in the 1950s.[11] However, the linkage effects created by the new nylon plant of SANS (South African Nylon Spinners), a company formed in 1964, provided a boost to the downstream textile industry (Figure 7.5).

Adopting a more historical perspective, non-MEC manufacturing's GDP contribution grew from about 4 per cent in 1924 to above 15 per cent in the early 1950s and it has fluctuated around that point ever since (Figure 4.5, p. 83). In contrast, a conventional and false perspective is that manufacturing's GDP contribution grew from 7.5 per cent in 1924 to 26 per cent in 1990 (Figure 4.1, p. 72). In the 1960s, the financial sector grew rapidly, its GDP contribution rising from 10.8 per cent in 1960 to 14.9 per cent in 1971 (Figure 4.5, p. 83). This was partly due to the role played by the sector, particularly by newly formed merchant banks, in channelling profits from mining into acquisitions of and investments in MEC and non-MEC manufacturing sectors.

In conclusion, then, and without dismissing their importance, non-MEC manufacturing industries as a whole did not acquire an independent momentum from the weight of activities within the MEC in the 1960s. Nor were the institutional conditions favourable to the adoption of policies to achieve such an objective. With the rise in gold and energy prices in the early 1970s, the possibility of this receded even further.

MEC expansion in the 1970s

The erosion of the disjuncture between English and Afrikaner capital by the 1970s allowed the state to adopt extensive co-ordinated industrial policies for the first time. These revolved primarily around the MEC, following the gold and energy price rise of the early 1970s but co-ordination was uneven, varying across sub-sectors. In contrast to previous periods, a significantly greater degree of co-operation was evident between private capital as a whole and the state.

In the 1970s, MEC industries benefited from both booming commodity prices and stable and conducive relations governing the profitability of internal markets. Non-MEC industries, while playing a supportive role to MEC mega-projects either as suppliers of inputs and capital goods or as consumers of intermediate goods produced by the MEC core, were partly boosted by military demand during the Angolan civil wars (1974–6) and partly cushioned by conglomerate ownership and tariff protection.

Perhaps the best example of state co-ordinated policies and the eroding disjuncture between English and Afrikaner capital is provided by coal utilisation, both in the expansion of Escom power generation and in the

---

[11] See van Eck cited by Gerber (p. 113).

development of the coal exports through Richards Bay. Coal output grew rapidly from the early 1970s, driven by electricity demand, demand from the Sasol II and III plants and coal exports (Figure 7.6). Through the patronage of Escom contracts, Genmin's TNC had become the largest single producer of coal in Sough Africa by the early 1970s. Subsequent Escom contracts were integrated within broader policies for the development of the then fragmented coal industry as a whole. This led to the coal industry's consolidation and modernisation around three major groups: AAC's Amcoal, Genmin's TNC and Rand Mines' Randcoal.

The coal export industry could not have developed without closely co-ordinated policies which facilitated the pooling of large-scale resources. At the time, the TCOA, of which TNC was an important member, entered into a long term coal supply contract with Japanese steel producers and subsequent negotiations with the state and the development of coal export policies resulted in enormous state and private sector capital investments. Capital expenditure in the coal industry averaged more than 13 per cent of mining investment for most of the period between 1975 and 1988 (Figure 7.7). The state developed infrastructure to facilitate rail transport of coal from the developing Eastern Transvaal coalfields to Richards Bay, ensuring that the harbour would be developed to accommodate large coal carriers. The TCOA undertook to develop the mines and to build, maintain and operate the coal-loading terminal. Thus the MEC was both the most important site of accumulation and the platform from which the economy was propelled in the 1970s and on which it faltered in the 1980s.

Perhaps the most decisive industrial policy since the formation of Iscor was the decision by the state to construct Sasol II and III. These plants, built with considerable assistance from the IDC, came on stream between 1979 and 1983 and further enhanced the role of the MEC within the economy. Sasol's output of approximately 50 per cent of domestic liquid fuel consumption was forced upon the existing transnational oil refiners who were compensated through a secret agreement that has continued to regulate the fuels industry until 1993.

The disjuncture between English and Afrikaner capital in the chemicals sector did not fade to as great an extent as it did in others. The construction of the Sasol plants did assist integration across some sub-sectors in downstream chemical processing. It provided new and stable sources of raw materials which would could be further processed within a policy framework that would protect downstream investment, the latter requiring enormous commitments of capital which could only be secured through the pooling of resources. For example, Sentrachem formed a joint venture with AECI in 1979 to produce PVC from coal at the Coalplex plant in Sasolburg. On the other hand, the Sasol project partly

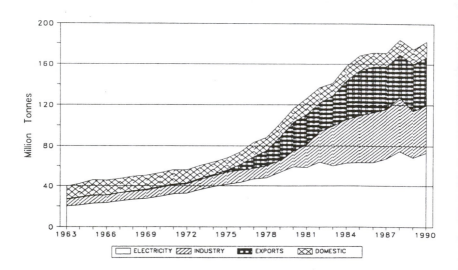

Fig. 7.6..COAL SALES (*million tonnes*)

Source: DMEA (various years).

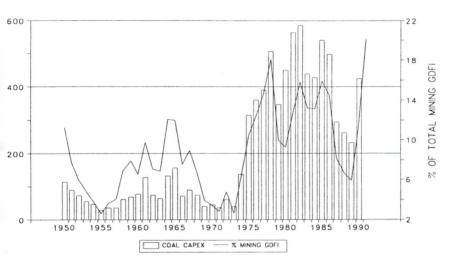

Fig. 7.7. G.D.F.I. COAL MINING FIXED INVESTMENT

Source: *South African Statistics.*

undermined co-ordination and further development of the chemicals industry in the 1980s, as shown below.

By the 1970s Afrikaner capital in conjunction with English capital, was also confidently reorganising other important sections of the mining and manufacturing industry, although not without favourable assistance from state institutions. Clark (1987b) incorrectly interprets this reorganisation as purely state-led by the IDC. Acquisitions of fragmented chrome mines in the early 1970s were consolidated and recapitalised, leading to the development of the ferrochrome industry on a large scale with a major role played by private capital itself.

After embarking on a joint venture with Union Carbide, which led to the construction of the Tubatse ferrochrome smelter, Genmin took control of its main rival Samancor in 1984 in controversial circumstances. Samancor, formed by a merger between SA Manganese and AMCOR in 1975, was controlled by Iscor (39.6 per cent) with AAC as the largest private shareholder and Genmin as a smaller partner (7 per cent). In 1977, both AAC and Genmin bid for Iscor's 40 per cent share but each was blocked by the state. In 1983, Genmin instituted a R120m court case against Iscor on a coal supply contract at the tied Hlobane colliery where Iscor was demanding reductions in supply. To resolve this, Iscor exchanged 50.25 per cent of AMCOR (which controlled its share of Samancor) in June 1983 for Hlobane and 70 per cent control of Dunswart Steel, despite the fact that AAC would have paid more for the stake. In June 1984, Samancor bought the remainder of Iscor's share.

Several other manufacturing industries within the MEC core grew in the 1970s, including aluminium, titanium and platinum smelting. Alusaf's capacity was doubled in 1974 and a further expansion was carried out in 1983 by importing an entire mothballed Japanese smelting plant. The titanium smelting operation at Richards Bay was initiated in 1972 as a joint venture between the IDC, Genmin, SA Mutual and QIT of Canada (a subsidiary of mining conglomerate RTZ).

While large-scale English and Afrikaner capital were increasingly entering into joint activities, they competed in the scramble for acquisitions in order to accrue scale advantages. In 1975, Genmin acquired control over the Union Corporation in circumstances which symbolised emerging relationships between conglomerates. In 1974 GFSA announced a takeover bid for Union Corporation, then one of the largest 'independently owned' mining houses.[12] Previous interpenetration had resulted in AAC and Genmin having 10 per cent and 7 per cent strategic stakes respectively in the company, with AAC holding its share through

---

[12] 'Independent' in that it was not within the controlling sphere of any of the South African conglomerates.

London-based Charter Consolidated. To complicate matters, AAC also held a strategic stake in Genmin.

Threatened by GFSA's bid, AAC initially offered its holding in Union Corporation to Genmin but after the latter had raised its holding to 29.9 per cent, AAC switched its support to GFSA. Since Genmin's parent Sanlam was not prepared to bear the full risk, Genmin was only able to acquire control with the financial assistance of Rembrandt. This resulted in increased interpenetration between large-scale Afrikaner concerns, with Rembrandt subsequently taking a 25 per cent stake in Genmin, which then reorganised itself and Union Corporation into Gencor in 1980. Through Union Corporation, Afrikaner capital acquired footholds in two important sectors, pulp and paper through Sappi (South African Pulp and Paper Industries) and platinum through Impala, the latter later growing into the world's second largest producer after AAC's Rustenburg Platinum.

Interpenetration took place within Afrikaner capital too but was not without associated conflicts. Having jointly financed General Mining's takeover of Union Corporation in 1975 and the subsequent formation of Gencor in 1980, publicly antagonistic relations developed between Rembrandt and Sanlam.[13]

In summary, the 1980s witnessed the emergence of five interpenetrated 'axes' of capital straddling the mining, manufacturing and financial sectors (see Chapter 5).[14] Their origins differed ethnically and sectorally. AAC had moved from gold and diamond mining into domestic manufacturing, domestic finance and regional and international mining. Sanlam had used its pooled Afrikaner financial resources to break into mining and manufacturing. Rembrandt had grown domestically and internationally, retaining a focus on cigarettes, tobacco and liquor production but also diversifying its investment portfolio. Anglovaal, the smallest group, had retained a historical base in manufacturing. Thomas Barlow had developed its manufacturing interests, diversified into mining through acquisition of Rand Mines in 1971 and had retained the financial backing of SA Mutual, mainly to prevent itself from being taken over by other conglomerates. Only Liberty/Standard remained purely financial, as it had been originally.

Thus, the disjuncture between English and Afrikaner capital had eroded sufficiently by the early 1980s to allow co-ordinated industrial

[13] While less relevant to the arguments here, this antagonism stemmed from Sanlam's heavy-handed ousting of Gencor chair, Wim de Villiers, apparently because he had opposed a Sanlam directive to purchase a company owned by the son of the Sanlam chair, Wassenaar. By then, Rembrandt had increased its stake to 30 per cent of Gencor.

[14] Discussion of the number of such 'axes' is complicated by their changing patterns over time and the extent of interpenetration. Historically, there have been six mining conglomerates, although JCI has now been absorbed by AAC. On the other hand, Liberty/Standard has emerged as a new conglomerate, but with limited mining and manufacturing interests.

policies to be effected and for the interpenetration between the two fractions of capital to proceed apace. Chapter 5 discusses the outcome of these developments.

Post-1980 paradoxes of the MEC

Six axes of private capital entered the 1980s with increasing strength and cohesion, particularly through extensive oligopolisation of the most productive sectors. The disjunctures between economic and political power had been eroded across a wide range of economic sectors. While the benefits of scale economies through acquisition and the reorganisation and concentration of production were far from exhausted, conditions had become more open to state-co-ordinated industrial policies to exploit economies of scale and scope (coordinating across sectors), the crisis of apartheid began to foreclose possibilities for state-co-ordinated industrial strategies which sought to diversify out of the MEC as monetary policy came to the fore following the debt moratorium of 1985. Equally, paradoxical was the fact that conglomerate control of the financial sector led to increasing speculative domestic investment activity and illegal capital flight at the expense of productive investment. While large investments have been made in the late 1980s and early 1990s, these have been solely in core MEC sectors, with corresponding consequences for broader future economic growth.

After the gold price peak in 1980, the GDP contribution of the MEC fluctuated around the 25 per cent level rising with the devaluation of the rand to average 27 per cent until the fall in the gold price after 1990, when its contribution was 25 per cent (Figure 4.6, p. 83). There is little empirical evidence of diversification out of the MEC core. Investment in non-MEC sectors declined relatively in the 1980s (Figure 7.2, p. 163). Non-MEC manufacturing's contribution actually fell from 18 per cent in 1980 to 15 per cent in 1985 but rose slightly to 16 per cent by 1990. This was probably due to increased engineering sector activity during the construction of the Mossgas project.

However, state industrial co-ordination during the 1970s had been uneven across sectors and was short-lived. As MEC projects such as mineral processing and Sasol were completed in the early 1980s, export commodity prices declined. Since there was no structural or institutional basis laid down to diversify into non-MEC sectors, the latter declined according to the fortunes of the MEC, except for some sub-sectors driven by military and mega-project expenditure, whose buoyancy was prolonged until the late 1980s.

A confluence of factors in the 1980s contributed to impede diversification out of the MEC. The orientation of the corporate sector and the nature and structure of the financial sector, together with policies of deregulation in the latter, were not conducive to diversification. With most major mining and manufacturing assets having been acquired by conglomerates in the 1960s and 1970s, a flurry of financial sector acquisitions followed deregulation in the 1980s, consolidating conglomerate power at the level of the financial sector. This is reflected in financial service contributions to GDP rising from 11 per cent in 1980 to almost 15 per cent in 1990 (Figure 4.5, p. 83).

Prominent among the efforts in centralising and concentrating financial sector interests in the 1980s has been the recent emergence of the ABSA banking group. As the largest group in South Africa, it is a testament to the success of such objectives, representing the merging of Volkskas, United, Allied, Bankorp and Trust Bank, historically Afrikaner-oriented institutions.

Paradoxes of the financial sector. One of the consequences of the way in which Afrikaner capital has been promoted and ultimately integrated with large-scale capital in general is the creation of a particular relationship between finance and industry. While there are close ownership linkages between mining/industry houses and finance houses, these have not been conducive to long-term investment in industry. Rather, the South African financial system has been much more geared towards the creation of financial services, dealing more in the buying and selling of productive assets than in their creation. Roux *et al.* (1991) address the role of the financial system. They recognise that it has been subject to criticism, being accused of: 'allowing excessive speculation, of not financing productive investment, of ignoring the needs of important sections of the population, of channelling too much saving through the contractual institutions, of overextending its lending activity, and of being dominated by a few powerful operators. (p. 2)

Such issues tend to be addressed in a framework of the supply of and demand for funds. This leads almost inevitably to the conclusion that inadequate levels of manufacturing investment are primarily due to lack of demand for funds, not the conditions for manufacturing or the extent of availability of funds. The financial system would respond to signalled investment opportunities if these were profitable, even if the funds have to filter through a series of intermediaries which effectively convert short-term speculative activity into sources of long-term manufacturing investment. Indeed, it can even be argued that the complexity and variety of financial intermediaries can serve to enhance the types and levels of investment funds available.

The logic of this view is more attractive than its reality. A complex and sophisticated financial system may operate in this way, especially if the real economy is booming, although it is assigned an extremely passive and reactive rather than active role in generating manufacturing invest-ment. In actual fact, finance can be trapped within speculative activity that is self-sustaining. Therefore, a more satisfactory approach is to reject supply and demand as a starting point and to examine the institutional context within which investment takes place. For the distinction between supply and demand is obscured once it is recognised that there is a close relation between saving and investment within those corporate structures that control both, whether it be through internal financing or the relation-ship between financial and non-financial branches of the conglomerates. The appropriate question then becomes somewhat different. To what extent does the financial system serve both to fund and direct the level and restructuring of manufacturing investment?

In this context, Roux *et al.* (p. 11) draw a parallel with the UK financial system: 'Financial arrangements in South Africa are largely modelled on the British banking system. Within this framework banks are primarily confined to short-term lending and money market activity. The stock exchange occupies a distinct, but equally central position, since it is assigned the dominant role within the capital market.'

It is thus not surprising that the *Financial Mail* rejected the IDC's role as an industrial financier in the early 1980s:[15] 'Whether the IDC was necessary or successful in the past is now a fatuous question. There are as many pros as there are cons. The point is whether it will continue to be useful in the future now that the country enjoys developed capital markets and has a core of developed technical skills.'

There are similarities between the two banking systems both in institu-tional organisation and in the structure of finance. Yet, there are also, significant differences between the South African and UK systems which makes each of them unique. For example, South Africa demonstrates a high level of concentration and intimate connections to other corporate structures, especially with mining, which might have been expected to lead to more direct avenues to manufacturing investment. Even if the United Kingdom could be taken as an appropriate model, this raises questions of the suitability of the South African system for promoting industrial investment, given its higher level of development of banking relative to its general level of economic development.

In reality, however, the UK *cannot* be taken as a model to emulate. It has suffered from low levels of ineffective manufacturing investment, exactly like the South African economy. There has been a long tradition of debate that this is due to the nature and power of the financial system in its influence over economic policy and in its greater commitment to speculative global short-term financing as opposed to long-term financing of investment in domestic industry. Fine and Harris (1985) argue that this

---

[15] *Financial Mail* (1982) 29 January, p. 398.

is both a cause and effect of the structure of the British economy, in that the financial system does not itself serve directly as an agency for the restructuring of British industry, unlike German and Japanese banking for example. Nor does it respond more passively to the needs of industry, given its preoccupation with short-term, speculative financing. A similar if not identical situation has prevailed within South Africa. Further, macroeconomic policy, partly inspired by the ideology of monetarism, has been geared around support to the financial sector under the guise of an otherwise neutral commitment to stabilisation of inflation, the exchange rate or the balance of payments. Thus has arisen the paradox that the financial structure, although greatly concentrated in the 1980s, did not encourage productive investment but encouraged speculative activities instead.

Further, both English and Afrikaner capital have begun to adopt an outward orientation since the early 1970s, investing off-shore. Illegal capital flight, always part of the structure of South Africa's politically charged, mixed economy, increased dramatically, largely through the mechanism of transfer pricing (see discussion in final chapter). It has also been accompanied by a publicly vociferous campaign by corporate capital for the lifting of capital and exchange controls. Capital flight has been estimated to have run at around 25 per cent of the value of non-gold exports, most of which were raw and processed minerals from MEC sectors aimed at export sectors and open to transfer pricing and false invoicing.

Increasing capital flight through transfer pricing, a mechanism much favoured by transnational corporations, is directly linked to the internationalisation of domestic capital. This has not only been confined to English capital, as represented by AAC. For example, Rembrandt had internationalised from an early period. By 1961, it had operations in more than a dozen different countries. In 1981, it sold a share of Rothmans to the US cigarette maker Phillip Morris and used the proceeds to finance further off-shore diversification.

While internal opposition to apartheid had always been important, it was strong enough by the mid-1980s to prompt a withdrawal of foreign capital, with the latter also affected by the global financial crisis involving Third World debt. Thus instead of co-ordinating the privately owned financial sector together with cohesive industrial policy, the state first deregulated the sector, which was flush with gold revenues in the early 1980s. It then focused more on monetary rather than on industrial policy after the fall in the gold price and the debt moratorium in 1985.

Paradoxes of the manufacturing sector. Despite the shift in the orientation of some state agencies towards liberalisation in the 1980s, a more cohesive industrial policy was maintained almost until 1990 for the production of armaments. Several sub-sectors of manufacturing associated with arms production remained buoyant, despite recessionary conditions prevalent in the economy between 1981–3 and 1984–6 and after 1988. While fixed asset values of the engineering sector declined in the 1980s, the value of assets held by Armscor actually grew over the same period. This reflects a paradox in policies of industrialisation in South Africa, uneven as they have been across sectors. Given the unsustainable political policies of apartheid, both domestically and regionally for which arms production was both supportive and dependent, such a strategy was always unlikely to diversify industrial activity significantly away from mining, processed minerals and chemicals in the long term. Thus concerted industrial policy has been possible for armaments, but it has not been extensive.

Another paradox of state co-ordination around the MEC is evident in the chemicals industry. In the 1970s state co-ordination fostered a synthetic fuel industry. Although it regulated and mediated between the interests of English, Afrikaner and transnational capital, the competition between the former two undermined the extension of industrial co-ordination around fuels to cover chemicals. Base organic chemical production is of course usually a joint activity of fuel refineries, whether crude oil- or, as uniquely in South Africa, coal-based. The chemical industry had been the site of competition between the two largest entities, AECI and Sentrachem, with the latter never having been a serious challenger. On the other hand, Sasol became a threat by its sheer size and its association with the IDC and Afrikanerdom as its output increased after 1982. It lobbied for and achieved deregulation of the explosives industry and, with burgeoning production, made increasing inroads into explosives and fertiliser markets, long the preserve of AAC's AECI.

On the one hand, state co-ordination of the national chemicals industry became possible in the mid-1980s, particularly through Sasol's production of a considerable proportion of national bulk chemicals such as ethylene, alcohols and other intermediate feedstocks. On the other hand, deregulation considerably undermined the potential for a co-ordinated industrial strategy around chemicals. It also undermined the achievement of economies of scale at the national level and very little new investment was subsequently made in the chemicals industry until the mid-1980s.

In the 1980s state policy-makers were more concerned with ensuring liquid fuel supplies to South African industry as a whole and less inclined to adopt a strategic approach towards co-ordinating fuel output with chemicals production and bulk chemical output with the development of downstream industries. The lucrative nature of these heavily regulated synthetic fuel projects also made them the subject of private capital's attention in the early 1980s. Several private sector consortiums, involving various combinations of English, Afrikaner and transnational corporations, put forward proposals for synthetic fuels project that were to follow

Sasol III into the 1980s. Not surprisingly, the state approved the construction of the Mossgas synthetic fuel plant, a design which used Sasol's synthetic fuel process under licence. Gencor was also offered the option to take a share in the project on completion. Private sector interpenetration in the fuels and chemicals sector also continued. In 1989, Gencor purchased the refining and fuels interests of the divesting transnational Mobil; it has subsequently developed this into Engen, a diversified fuels exploration, production and refining division with significant off-shore interests.

In 1993, the commitment to co-ordination has receded through the partial privatisation of Sasol and policy proposals for the deregulation of the fuel industry. A large proportion of Sasol stock is now held by various financial arms of the private sector axes. Cost overruns on the Mossgas project have also been a focal point of criticism of state intervention. While valid as far as it goes, it represents an ideologically-based attack by private capital on the co-ordinating role of state institutions. For private capitals have benefited from the contracts attached to the project.

Institutional paradoxes

State institutions previously coordinating industrial policy were not unaffected by these historical developments. The BTI, administrator of tariff policies, was emasculated in 1992 by the BTI Amendment Act and the IDC assumed the role of industrial policy formulator and implementor (see discussion in next chapter).

This is not surprisingly since it was the IDC's role historically to foster and further the interests of large-scale capital; it seems only natural that large-scale capital, having acquired a cohesion as never before, should find a corresponding institution within the state apparatus to pursue its appetite for big foreign exchange generating projects, requiring state support and guarantees but not co-ordination with other sectors. Large-scale private capital has been collectively antagonistic to co-ordinated state industrial policies, particularly in the present period of transition and in the global and domestic climate of deregulation and privatisation.

Before transitional government in the 1990s, the apartheid state appears to have withdrawn from any active co-ordination of industrial policy. In the absence of concerted state policies to diversify out of the MEC, the weight of past investment and the present institutional orientation have acted to keep the trajectory of industrialisation firmly in and around the MEC core. The stagnation of the economy and political paralysis in adopting coherent, long-run industrial policies are leading to mega-project investments around the MEC core. These can be regarded as strategic and subsidised staging posts for future private sector operations lying, as far as is technically possible, outside the reach of a future post-apartheid state and its political constituencies. Highly capital-intensive projects dependent on export marketing, with the prospects of foreign exchange earnings, are liable to be least susceptible to government control and effective trade union pressure other than for wage bargaining. In this respect, such investments are the domestic counterpart to capital flight and disinvestment which place resources outside the reach of a future government altogether through the continuing financial conglomerates. Along with mergers and acquisitions, these are central features of the MEC as a system of accumulation in the period of transition.

This historiography of the post-war period has been dictated by: the centrality of the evolving MEC; the transition from a situation of political and economic disjuncture between Afrikaner and English capital to one of interpenetration and co-ordination through the state; and the uneven but distinct chronology of these activities across the range of economic activities. In the next chapter, the role played by industrial policy is considered. It is complemented in the following chapter by a review of the debate over South African industrialisation and industrial policy, a debate that is found to be limited by the failure to acknowledge the historiography that has been identified here.

8

POST-WAR INDUSTRIAL POLICY

As a system of accumulation, the underlying thrust of the MEC over the post-war period was the empowerment of Afrikaner capital, ultimately fostering the latter's successful interpenetration and co-ordination with English capital. As shown in successive sections of this chapter, this has had a profound impact on industrial policy from the 1950s, reducing it to three relatively unco-ordinated and even incoherent components: the creation of state corporations, mainly around the MEC; the application of trade policy through tariff protection; and policies to promote industrial decentralisation and small businesses. This has led to policies which both supported the MEC's core sectors and precluded the adoption of other industrial policies of diversification away from heavy reliance on South Africa's resource base. This was despite numerous recommendations to the contrary by official Commissions of Inquiry into industrial performance. Finally, it will be demonstrated that the industrial policies that actually were pursued, particularly by two key institutions of the IDC and the BTI, followed a separate path from that promoting industrialisation.

State corporations in the 1950s

The creation of state corporations as instruments of industrial policy began in the early 1930s with the creation of Iscor. This had an enormous propulsive impact on the economy, both directly and indirectly. Most subsequent state corporation investment was made in this and other MEC sub-sectors, with considerable downstream activity through joint ventures with private capital. Despite this, the broader role of state corporations in industrialisation has usually been overlooked or viewed separately from privately owned industries upstream and downstream of the parastatal.

Clark (1987a) provides the most comprehensive discussion of the role of state corporations in South Africa, focusing especially on Escom and Iscor (see Chapter 6). There is little evidence that these corporations were set up to act or could operate as stepping stones predominantly for the promotion of national capital at the expense of foreign or mining capital.

The latter were essential to their operation, especially as customers: 'Indeed, it was difficult even for the state-sponsored industries to diversify economic development away from the mining industry.' (p. 345)

Thus the inter-war period witnessed varying degrees of co-operation and conflict between Iscor and private capital. Coming out of the Second World War, the state corporations saw private capitalists as potential competitors, undermining their own commercial viability. This seems to have been more important than establishing a more or less favourable relation to firms in the private sector. For the BTI (*Annual Report* 1946, p. 64), the curtailment of Iscor's activity was motivated by the wish to minimise its competition with the private sector, indeed to serve it through providing its basic input:[1] 'In view of the fact that the primary object in establishing the Corporation was to provide the country with cheap steel, the Board feels that under no circumstances should the Corporation undertake the processing and manufacture of secondary products which can be economically provided by independent undertakings.'

Nonetheless, the symbiosis between the corporations and private capital was subject to some scrutiny after 1948, since there was suspicion of subsidy to private capital through joint ventures. This was not without foundation; for example, Victoria Falls Power Company was only purchased by Escom in 1948, having been owned previously by mining capital that had benefited from wartime profiteering. The purchase was made with finance underwritten by AAC which had also entered into a joint venture with Iscor to form Vecor, a heavy engineering company utilising steel output from Iscor.

It is against such a background that the development of both state and private industry must be assessed. There is no doubting the widening scope of state corporations such as Iscor and Sasol, both in their exclusive activities and in their collaboration with the private sector. Phillips (1974, p. 242) refers to Iscor's 'far flung activities and the depth to which it had penetrated the economy even before 1939'. Norval, the chair of the BTI during the 1950s, stated: 'It is difficult to over-estimate the importance of the role played by Iscor, with all its ramifications, in the economy of South Africa. There is hardly a sector in the country's economy which its activities do not permeate and influence to a greater or lesser extent.' (p. 17)

Webster (1985) illustrates how by the 1970s, 'the ownership of the seven largest foundries was concentrated in the South African state through Iscor and IDC, international capital and local mining and industrial finance.' (p. 130) Joint ventures and the all too familiar feature of interlocking ownership involved companies such as British Steel, GEC International, Barlow Rand, ACC and Genmin. Similarly, Sasol has

---

[1] See also p. 66. For an account of how the state-owned steel corporation in Britain was used to promote private steel companies prior to its privatisation, see Fine and Poletti (1992).

proved the basis for diversification into heavy chemicals, again through involvement with the private sector.[2]

In this light, large-scale state investments and corporations must be assessed in relation to the broader context within which industrial development has been taking place. To what extent have they served to foster dynamic economies and new industries and linkages, both sectorally and in support of private capital? Nor are these questions that can or should be asked only in retrospect. For example, Norval anticipated a bright prospect for South Africa in iron, steel, engineering and metal industries, including exports, as long as appropriate policies for training and research and development were adopted. A similar stance is adopted in relation to chemicals, again on the basis of the availability of indigenous natural resources and the initial development of state and private corporations. In the event, his hopes proved futile, although such goals are even now re-emerging, with significant privatisation of state corporations. Thus, while there has necessarily been an integration between state and private capital, it was one which has largely been confined to the MEC core.

The IDC has played a major role in implementing those aspects of industrial policy concerned with the creation of state-owned industries around the MEC. It also conducted the now-abandoned industrial decentralisation programmes and has continued to administer policy in support of small business.

Its promotion of large-scale investments in Sasol and Foskor in the 1950s are seen by Clark to have accepted the limits of the form to be adopted by South African industrialisation: the use of minerals to produce industrial goods and provide support for skilled white, as opposed to unskilled, black employment. She cites the example of the promotion of the manufacture and export of rayon pulp but without its extension to rayon manufacture (Clark 1987a, pp. 337–8). Influential policy makers also seemed wedded to an industrial trajectory explicitly based on increasing both capital and energy intensity and hence mechanisation. Sectors were targeted according to perceived comparative advantage and lay largely within the MEC. Addressing a delegation from the California Institute of Technology in 1962, H.J. van Eck (the then Chairman of Escom and IDC) stated:[3]

In South Africa, far from relying on so-called cheap labour we believe in the application of power. The generation of electricity per head is just about 1500 kWh per annum. It is equal to the per capita generation of a very highly industrialized country like Great Britain only six years

---

[2] For an early illustration, see Houghton and Dagut (1972, p. 195).

[3] The seminar was hosted by the South African Foundation and included the president of the CSIR, Meiring Naude.

ago. In other words in the development of power and the use of power, we compare favourably with the countries of western Europe. The fields in which we have comparative advantage are iron and steel, foundry products, ferro-silicon, ferro-chrome, ferro-manganese, timber as a cheap raw material because of the high rate of growth of trees in certain areas. (Van Eck in Gerber, pp. 105, 112)

Writing in 1962, Norval noted:

> It would be extremely unwise for South Africa to enter into long-term contracts for the sale of its base minerals, even in a semi-processed state. In the chemical field South Africa possesses a vast potential for the manufacture of a large range of chemicals, which are presently being imported by a considerable number of industrialists as raw or semi-manufactured materials for use in their respective manufacturing processes. It is a field too which, next to iron and steel, will, in course of time, lend itself to the development of large-scale exports, not only to adjoining territories, but to other parts of the world, as has already been demonstrated by some of the concerns operating in the chemical field. (pp. 25, 39)

The heady optimism of the time is clearly reflected in a startling statement by van Eck on the need to *curb* growth; this same statement also records the early recognition of problems of skill shortages and high import propensity:

> Our growth rate should not be very much faster than an average over the years of 5 per cent per annum because a high growth rate sets up difficult strains in the economy. A high growth rate increases our imports because of our high marginal propensity to import... I don't think we should grow much faster than 5 per cent because of the problems of social adjustments, housing conditions, town and regional planning and all the other factors that enter into development in a highly complicated multiracial society with vastly different stages of cultural and economic development... I regard it [5%] as a pretty good rate...we cannot move faster unless we train our people better, unless we have more managers skilled in various directions, scientists, technologists, engineers and people with high managerial ability. (Van Eck in Gerber, p. 106)

By 1960 the creation of state corporations and their support for related industries had played a pivotal role both for the MEC and industrialisation but its potential was subsequently never fully exploited in extending the scope of manufacturing.[4] Thirty years later, the IDC's priorities in 1991 have remained tied to the centrality of the MEC. Mineral beneficiation

---

[4] With regard to industrial policy and performance, many recognise the existence of state-owned industries but view them as being inappropriately targeted (Moll 1991)) or inherently inefficient compared to privately-owned industries (Fallon *et al.* 1993; Levy 1992).

targets included financing the Columbus stainless steel plant, the Alusaf aluminium smelter project and Foskor's potash/alumina project. Chemicals and paper projects include Sappi's Saiccor expansion and Sasol's acrylic fibre plant.[5]

Tariffs as industrial policy

Tariff protection was neither all pervading nor was it ever central to determining the pattern of industrialisation. It is the disjuncture between English and Afrikaner capital, the formation of state corporations and the latter's interplay with private capital that have been central in influencing post-war industrialisation. The erosion of the disjuncture between the two fractions of capital as the former grew in strength and interpenetrated with the latter has partly undermined the rationale for tariffs, as is evident in the demise of the BTI and the IDC's present overtures in negotiations on the General Agreement on Tariffs and Trade (GATT).

The BTI, the state agency wielding the tariff instrument of industrial policy, mainly interfaced most directly and continuously with the private manufacturing sectors. Norval (pp. 121–2) is emphatic on the role played by tariff protection to ensure the viability of local production; he observes that such support was strengthened following the Second World War once duties could be offered by the Board in advance of the setting up of productive facilities. Institutionally: 'It is doubtful whether in any country in the world there is a closer contact between the body dealing with tariff matters and industry than exists between the Board of Trade and Industries and the manufacturing industries in South Africa.'

Opposition to tariffs in the 1930s had been rooted in the disjuncture between English and Afrikaner capital. Iscor, created in the face of intense opposition by mining interests who would rather have built their own plant under protection or to have imported without protection, was undermined by dumping of surplus production from abroad in the mid-1930s. Dumping was common for a wide range of goods in the 1930s and lowered input costs for mining capital. The influence of the latter after the political defeat of the Nationalist and Labour Pact government in 1933 is evident in the report of the Holloway Commission of 1934–5. Holloway argued that protected industries were not internationally competitive because their white labour costs were much higher than in Europe (Zarenda 1977). Clark (1987a), however, has demonstrated that Iscor, which would have been the most likely industry to retain the 'civilised labour' policy, was busy substituting cheaper black labour at this time to reduce costs.[6]

---

[5] IDC senior general manager, Malcolm MacDonald, quoted in *Business Day* (1991) 1 November.

[6] Iron ore mining and steelmaking processes involved an extensive division of labour and

Even if tariffs were meant to provide a propulsive effect to industrialisation, they were ineffective due to poor management and a failure to appreciate the importance of linkages between protected sectors. After the Second World War, the BTI (1945) recognised the extent of protection, yet viewed this as a temporary necessity to protect infant industries during post-war reconstruction. Thirteen years later, in 1958 the Viljoen Commission issued its report. Unlike Holloway, Viljoen did not evaluate the effects of past tariffs on the manufacturing sector. His brief was to report on (*a*) whether existing tariffs were adequate to ensure growth and employment creation; (*b*) whether growth could be sustained without imposing a burden on mining and agriculture; (*c*) the constraints to accelerated growth; and (*d*) the adequacy of policy machinery to combat dumping by importers.

Since possibilities were limited in the mining and agricultural sectors, Viljoen believed that the burden of employment creation would have to fall on the manufacturing sector. Manufacturing's high import propensity was viewed as a constraint on high rates of growth and therefore, Viljoen's recommendations were to restrict imports, raise exports and increase capital inflows. Viljoen's recognition of the need to raise exports is not overlooked by Brand (1976). He has argued that the debate at the time on industrial policy was not between *either* ISI *or* export-orientated industrialisation (EOI) but can more usefully be seen as being over the balance of emphasis between each. Viljoen obviously falls into the group favouring emphasis on the former. The policy instruments to achieve this emphasis included retaining import tariffs but Viljoen went further, recommending targeting of sectors to be protected and singling out industries for special protection. These included the motor industry, which would forge economic linkages downstream of the steel and chemical industries. (Viljoen Commission PI, SI, sch 28, III)

Although this approach appears to be a most sensible reconciliation between inward and export orientation, it leaves the entire onus of policy making on the ill-defined practice of selectivity. This raises the issue of the selection of industries to receive state support, whether through tariff protection or by being created from scratch as state-owned enterprises. In fact, this process was not based on an adequate assessment of each of the targeted sector's potential to fulfil the objectives of economic policy. These objectives might have been a combination of balance of payments constraints, employment generation, industrialisation to diversify out of dependence on gold, protection of infant industries, or more short-term

---

such policies did not apply to all categories. Moreover, Iscor's policy was fluid, contingent on political lobbying and sensitive to the lessons of strikes by black power station workers in 1943.

measures in response to the unfair competition associated with various forms of 'dumping'.

Early on, Laight (1955, p. 222) had argued against protection as a general policy and warned that its selectivity for infant industry so to broaden the industrial base, either in response to 'unfair' competition or as a temporary measure in response to cyclical unemployment, had to 'be very carefully defined and constantly reviewed'.

The intention was that selectivity should be determined by economic goals and potential but how well could these be both identified and put into practice? The evidence on the first is far from satisfactory. Samuels (1959, p. 181), criticised Viljoen along these lines for both understating the linkages between primary and secondary sectors and failing to disaggregate the manufacturing sector adequately to determine sectoral sources of growth. He argued that a considerable portion of demand for manufacturing output came from mining and agriculture and furthermore, increased international demand for mineral and agricultural output could not be excluded as a source of economic growth. He pointed out that since much of 1950s industrialisation involved capital-intensive investment in sectors such as chemicals and steel, the scope for employment creation was limited if this trajectory continued.

Tariff policy was poorly managed, bringing into question the basis of discretionary decisions, even in the case of targeted sectors such as the motor industry. This was noted by Norval:

> The then Minister of Commerce and Industries made provision in the Enabling Act of the Board of Trade and Industries in 1947 for the establishment of costing systems, in a manner approved by the Board, in any particular industry or branch of industry enjoying customs tariff protection or receiving any form of State aid. Unfortunately *not much has been done in this respect*, but it is a matter which, in the interest of industry and in order to provide the Board with more reliable costing material to determine the measure of tariff protection needed, should receive earnest consideration. (p. 8, emphasis added)

This is a particularly damning indictment of the lack of scientific criteria for conducting industrial policy. Given Norval's acknowledgement of the centrality of tariff protection to industrialisation, a range of unnamed and presumably unquantifiable criteria other than cost were used to evaluate applications for tariff protection.

However, to divorce this choice of policy instrument from the political and economic issues of the day is to miss important causal factors. Departmental discretion in licence and scarce resource allocation was exercised in favour of Afrikaner-owned concerns as early as 1949 and continued after the NP secured electoral victory again in 1953. In a complaint to Ernest Oppenheimer MP in 1949, the African and European

Company (a subsidiary of AAC, chaired by Oppenheimer) stated that advisers of the Department of Commerce and Industry were:[7] 'Mostly young men of the Stellenbosch University type very sympathetic towards the new low-grade [coal] producers.' Import and export permits, scarce railway freight space and power during periods of shortage were favourably allocated to these Afrikaner concerns.

Despite the warnings of the former chair of the BTI, poor management continued into the 1980s. Twenty-six years later, the BTI (1988) revealed how poorly tariff policy had been administered, that tariff applications were dealt with in a reactive manner with no continuity:

> It was realised by the BTI that the approach adopted by the Government in the [1985] White Paper for continuous [sectoral] studies to be undertaken was a *major policy deviation from the policies applied in the past.* Previously the BTI reported from time to time on industrial sectors after having completed investigations into those sectors. There was, however, not a continuous involvement. In respect of tariff protection the BTI responded to applications by the private sector and initiated revisions of previously recommended duties. Even in such cases there was *no attempt at continuous monitoring actions. It was a reactive rather than a pro-active procedure.* (p. 4, emphasis added)

Although tariff discretion may have favoured large-scale Afrikaner capital at the aggregate level, particularly after 1948, its application was uneven. During the 1950s, sectors that benefited most were mining, agriculture and the motor industries. These sectors were treated as special cases, each with separate arrangements around the method of licence issue.

Any impact that trade policy might have had on industrialisation was mediated by its frequent use as a mechanism to protect the balance of payments, through increasing quantitative restrictions (Viljoen 1958). This increased during the capital outflow crisis of the 1960s. Petrol, oil, coffee and yarn imports were not restricted under the import control regulations of 1958. However, 75 per cent of imports were subject to licensing (with a few quotas from time to time) on the basis of meeting national market needs rather than for processing for export. In the 1960s, the policy instrument used to stimulate the targeted motor assembly industry was simply an extension of the scope of the permit system. For manufacturers with an acceptable local content programme, full requirement permits were issued. For others, CKD (completely knocked-down kits for assembly) permits were only issued for nine months' stock at a time.

While Viljoen intended tariff protection and import licensing to be a

---

[7] Cited in Christie (1984, p. 153).

temporary state of affairs, Lachman (1974) has outlined how these specific instruments became a permanent feature of industrial policy. South Africa's GATT membership in 1947 imposed limits on tariff levels; to by-pass this, import licensing was extensively used. Between 1949 and 1973, it grew to cover 80–90 per cent of imports, with raw materials and capital goods being given priority licence allocation over consumer goods.

Citing Little, Scitovsky and Scott (1970), Lachman argued that the usual disadvantages of bureaucracy, rent-seeking and misallocation made licensing an inefficient mechanism for the allocation of scarce foreign exchange. His alternative, which reflected the concern of the time, was to use the price mechanism as a policy instrument and to allow the exchange rate to float.

Thus, tariff policy was neither coherent nor decisive as a policy to shape industrialisation. Instead, it was reactive to interests of various fractions of capital. An empirical indication of the extent to which and the ease with which the BTI has granted trade protection is revealed by the numbers of applications for support and the proportion of these that were successful (Table 8.1).

Table 8.1. B.T.I. TARIFF APPLICATION RECORD

	Supported	*Rejected*
1990	155	198
1989	65	253
1988	140	226
1987	151	83
1986	137	96
1985	269	20
1984	198	151
1983	177	115
1982	119	7
1981	128	2
1980	142	125
1979	115	127
1978	160	142
1977	172	135
1976	140	169
1975	150	174
1974	157	121
1973	212	150
1972	187	112
1971	121	112
1970	81	115
1969	139	140
1968	111	97
1967	116	72
1966	147	85
Av. % of 1958–67	47.8	52.2

Source: BTI (various years) *Annual Report.*

In terms of its criteria of operation, the BTI offered eight considerations to be taken into account when granting assistance.[8] Even though these were counterbalanced by a list of grounds, running from (*a*) to (*m*), on which an application could be refused, this only served to increase the discretion exercised by the BTI. However, as early as 1945, the BTI was hopeful that protection would decrease as manufacturing competitiveness was attained:[9]

> The Board wishes to reiterate that the future of the Union's manufacturing industry does not lie primarily in the granting of protection in the form of assistance through customs duties or otherwise. Protection has, the Board fears, in some cases, enhanced immediate profits, without sufficient stimulation being given to the industry to improve its methods of production and marketing with an eye to its future stability. The future lies much more in the rationalisation of industry...and the consequent reduction of the high cost structure. (p. 225)

Such hopes have not been realised. In its 1989 *Annual Report* the BTI divides export composition, excluding gold, into the following proportions: raw materials (42 per cent); processed raw materials (45 per cent); intermediate goods (8 per cent); and finished products (5 per cent). On the other hand, imports remain dominated by capital and intermediate goods, especially chemicals for the latter. Excluding arms, oils and miscellaneous goods, the share of machinery and equipment in imports has risen from 20.7 per cent in 1946 to 49.3 per cent in 1985, having peaked at 54.4 per cent in 1980.[10]

In implementing the tariff component of industrial policy, there appears to have been little cohesion with industrial policies around state corporations and their joint ventures with the private sector. In addition, policy was usually implemented reactively and was poorly managed. Little or no continuous monitoring existed to provide a concrete basis for policy and to measure the effectiveness of such policy over time. In what was essentially a discretionary process, there is evidence in scrutinising Reports that Afrikaner capital was preferentially favoured.

---

[8] See Appendix II to the Viljoen Commission (1958). See also the discussion of the levels at which protection could be granted (pp. 7–8). The BTI's policy and practice remained essentially unaltered until the mid-1980s. Contrast the statement in their *Annual Report* for 1985 (pp. 5–6) with those for 1989 (p. 12) and 1990 (pp. 5–6). A shift in emphasis from protection to meet normal competition from abroad to one of export-orientation is clear. Such statements of intent have to be assessed against the policies adopted in practice and their ultimate impact.

[9] Significantly, the last sentence of this quotation represents wishful thinking in that the BTI has not intervened to realise these goals. It might even be interpreted as impeding them through featherbedding tariff protection.

[10] Figures calculated from Lewis (1990, p. 59). See also Kahn (1987).

Thus industrial policy has proved resistant to interventions over and above those that operate at the level of revenue, whether subsidising profits through protection against imports or compensating for the higher costs that these imply for manufacturing inputs. Nor have these interventions been sustained by a careful economic calculus, it long being recognised that no account has been taken of effective levels of protection. For example, protection for the textile industry has led to higher costs to the clothing industry which, accordingly, itself requires corresponding support to sustain its profitability. Balancing the relative costs and benefits to the two sectors has taken priority over transforming and advancing the connections between them.[11]

In short, the use of tariffs to target industrial sub-sectors selectively was not accompanied with a range of additional supportive policies to overcome the numerous problems of industry identified by official investigations. Thus, contrary to the commonly held view of the importance of protection as industrial policy, the overall pro-active thrust at the institutional level came not from the BTI's tariff protection but from the support given to the MEC through the offices of the IDC.

Decentralisation as industrial policy?

The academic discussion around decentralisation in South Africa has been remarkably unanimous both in its conclusions and its divergence from official pronouncements over an extended period. It is perceived to have been an expensive failure. As it is not dealt with in any great detail here, the reader is referred to the relevant literature.[12] A brief example only will be given here.

One early foray in the early 1950s involved creating a decentralised textile industry and this proved disastrous. The IDC was then and is still concerned with decentralisation and small business support, although its role has been devolved to or been supplemented by other organisations such as the Small Business Development Corporation (SBDC), formed in 1983, and the Board for the Decentralisation of Industry, formed in 1960. In textiles, the IDC was unable to control its costs, insufficiently funded and unable to guarantee a stable, low-waged, docile workforce. The industry also encountered intense competition from private capital, which set up in developed urban areas under tariff protection.

---

[11] For example, see the 1983 Government Report on textiles and clothing.

[12] There is an extensive literature on the decentralisation of industry. For a selection with its own further references, see the June 1990 issue of the *South African Journal of Economics*, Addleson (1990), Dewar *et al.* (1986), Dickman (1991), Geyer (1989a; 1989b), Holden (1990), Maasdorp (1990), Rogerson (1982; 1987; 1988), Tomlinson (1990), Tomlinson and Addleson (eds) (1987) and Wellings and Black (1986).

Subsequent industries promoted by the IDC tended to be the more capital-intensive process industries, such as Sasol and Foskor, whose costs were more easily controlled. Mining operations were based on well-known coercive labour management techniques and supportive legislation, requiring little commitment to training as had been required for textiles, while the processing operations required higher skilled white labour.

Political and ideological rather than economic and industrial imperatives have driven decentralisation policy. In regard to its role in South Africa's industrial trajectory, three points emerge. First, the scope for such policy, even outside the context of apartheid, has been heavily contingent upon the success of national performance and policy; the faster the economic growth, the greater the stimulus to the number and location of jobs away from traditional centres of industry. As growth in the sorts of employment that could be decentralised has been minimal within South Africa, in part as a consequence of its lack of industrial policy more generally, so the potential for decentralisation has been negligible even if it had been appropriately pushed with greater commitment.

Secondly, policy has in actual practice never been sufficiently nor coherently funded. It has always been based upon or dominated by other objectives than a genuine commitment to 'homeland' development.

Thirdly, as a consequence, it is hardly surprising that the rationale for and efficacy of decentralisation policy should have become entirely subverted by lack of economic effectiveness and left open to bribery and corruption. In the absence of any internal coherence and external direction, detailed decisions in implementation have become more or less arbitrary. As such, they are not so much random or misguided as a remarkable synthesis of South Africa's political economy, reflecting an overall lack of industrial policy as well as the increasingly byzantine compromises between the economics, politics and ideologies of the apartheid system. In short, decentralisation policy has both reflected and consolidated the weaknesses of industrial development more generally.

Small-scale industry

Compared to the MEC, the IDC has in practice committed few resources in support of decentralisation or for small-scale industry. Norval (p. 98) observes that: 'In 1959 the Corporation had investments in 75 companies for a total amount of just under R130m of which just under R104m was invested in three major concerns. The balance...was invested in 72 companies in the normal course of its business.' In other words, at a rate of R26m for 72 companies, the average support to smaller companies was less than R300,000, as compared to the average of over R30m to Iscor,

Sasol and Foskor. State corporations in and around the MEC had been hugely supported by the IDC as discussed in the previous chapter, its role otherwise has been, and continues to be little short of token. Limited support to small-scale business is also evidenced by examination of the beneficiaries of present tax incentives under Section 37E of the Income Tax Act and export subsidies. Ben Vosloo, Managing Director of the SBDC, *Business Day* (1992) argued:

> In the Budget for the 1991/92 fiscal year, R1.411bn was allocated to export trade promotion. This amount is distributed to about 2500 beneficiaries, most of which are large companies, under the General Export Incentive Scheme [GEIS]. In the same Budget, only R75m was earmarked for small and medium size enterprise [SME] development through the small Business Development Corporation [SBDC]... In this year's Budget...R2bn has been allocated to the GEIS, but only R3.8m has been set aside for small business development.

Thus the agency entrusted with supporting small-scale business, the IDC, has never accorded the sector any significant priority. That has principally gone to the MEC.

In summary, the two prongs of industrial policy of state corporations and tariff protection were operated by the early 1960s in favour of large-scale, capital and energy-intensive industries within the MEC. Afrikaner capital was also favoured, resulting in greater penetration of several industries which were formerly the preserve of English capital. The latter's distinctiveness was further eroded in the 1960s as it bought up shares in industrial companies as foreign capital withdrew and as interpenetration with English capital increased. Industrial policy conduct did not alter this trajectory significantly during the 1960s.

Promoting the MEC – from Reynders onwards

In 1972, the Reynders Commission presented its report, fourteen years after that of the Viljoen Commission. Highlighting the need to shift to an outward orientation (a reflection of the economic debate of the time), Reynders (1975) later identified a wide range of structural impediments to further industrialisation:

> If South Africa is to maintain its export momentum and to stop balance of payments constraints from becoming an obstacle in the national development process, continuous attention will meed to be directed to import replacement on the one hand, particularly in the intermediary and capital goods sectors, and on the other hand, to the promotion of experts. The latter may perhaps best be secured by the process of export targeting through which the national export earnings are assessed and

evaluated against the export potential of each economic sub-sector. And this in sum was the basic proposition of the export Commission. (p. 131)

Recommendations included improved productivity monitoring by the government's National Productivity Institute (NPI), government support in raising skill levels, export marketing assistance, improving the transport and port systems and removing labour market rigidities including apartheid restrictions. The concept of export processing zones was supported by Reynders together with recommendations for freight concessions for export inputs. Reynders also argued that industrial decentralisation policies should not undermine the economies of agglomeration and that policies should not hurt export industries in metropolitan areas. Ten years earlier in 1961, van Eck had identified the same problem (van Eck in Gerber):

> As far as the Bantu border areas are concerned, the pace of development is still tragically slow, particularly with our high rate of population growth. The industrialist has to decide to go to a border area...where there are no cinemas, cafes, schools, or other amenities for his supervisory staff, no water, no roads, no communications, no power, no housing, no sewerage, inadequate health services and police protection. Why should anybody want to go there where he is far from his market? Of course he comes to Johannesburg instead. (p. 113)

Ratcliffe (1975), however, warned that Reynders had underestimated the extent of internal structural change that would be required to shift to an export orientation:

> The essentially one-sided approach of the Commission to the expansion of exports causes it to underestimate the extent of the internal transformation of the South African economy which is required for exports to lead growth. Again and again the Commission tentatively considers various aspects of the matter, notably in the chapters dealing with production costs, fiscal measures, finance, and transport. Nevertheless it does not fully accept the proposition that domestic economic changes are the essential precondition for increased exports and for sustained growth. (p. 80)

In response, Reynders (1975) argued that it would be the implementation of export incentives that would lead to the structural changes, not the reverse:

> My fundamental hypothesis is that the newly introduced export incentives have in fact introduced a structural change in the whole of South Africa's export environment. However, since this is a very recent change; since the package of incentives is not yet complete; and since

the understanding and acceptance of the new package has not yet worked its way through to all exporters and potential exporters, it is rather premature to look for a statistical quantification of the extent of the change which I am hypothesizing. (p. 123)

To date there has never been an adequate analysis of the impact of these policies. More than a decade later, the same debate has been played out between policy makers in the BTI (1988), who proposed industrial restructuring, and IDC (1990), who supported export incentives to induce structural change, as discussed below. It is thus unlikely that the effect of the tax incentives of section 37E and the GEIS export incentives will have been coordinated coherently with other policy initiatives.

In any case, the government rejected Reynders' call for a cabinet committee on exports and for a white paper which outlined official positions and strategies on export-oriented industrialisation. Instead, it appointed an interdepartmental committee on exports consisting of heads of relevant departments. The private sector at the time was represented on the state's Private Sector Export Advisory Committee.

Despite Reynders' wide-ranging recommendations on raising manufacturing exports, no diversification away from the MEC took place in the 1970s. Instead, the very reverse occurred after the gold/energy price boom increased industrialisation around the MEC (Fig. 4.6, p. 83). These industrial policy decisions were partly IDC-led, including Sasol II and III, Escom expansion and Armscor. They were increasingly propelled by the growing interpenetration between English and Afrikaner capital in specific sub-sectors, as detailed in earlier chapters.

The increasing dependence of the economy on the MEC became apparent by 1975. Main (1975) and Zarenda (1975) attributed this to the fact that Reynders had not focused adequate attention on the internal structure of the economy. While agreeing on the need to bring down tariffs gradually, Zarenda (1975, p. 117) pointed out that protection was more complex and that it would be more useful to use effective rather than nominal measures of protection, mainly because past policies had favoured intermediate input and capital goods imports. This had the impact of masking very high levels of effective protection and emphasising the lack of cohesiveness of tariff policies.

Main pointed out the linkages between mining, mineral processing and other manufacturing and was concerned with the failure to accord equal state incentives to each, particularly in activity around mining. He described how mineral processing was hampered by a small local market, low capital returns, high freight charges, inadequate port loading facilities, difficulty in competing with developed market producers and penetrating their markets, and a shortage of skilled labour.

Despite Main's criticisms, many segments of the MEC benefited from

Reynders' recommendations. A 20 per cent power subsidy was allowed to the ferro-alloy industry in mid-1974, retrospective to October 1973, and this contributed to the growth in ferrochrome exports. Government implemented a number of recommendations, including finance charge aid to exporters of some minerals, but it rejected private sector proposals to lower export finance charges below domestic interest rates in a scheme which involved the SARB raising off-shore loans. Instead, the SARB allocated R95m per annum for foreign exchange forward cover losses during 1973–4 and the IDC allocated R40m per annum to subsidise export production capacity creation. Some of Reynders' recommendations on transport were also implemented. Rebates were granted on the transport of unprocessed or semi-processed raw materials destined for export either directly to ports or via processing plants. Government also increased tax allowances on market development expenditure, capital investment, initial allowances and beneficiation allowances.

When viewed in the context of the social, political and economic forces of the day, it is not surprising that only a selective implementation of Reynders' recommendations occurred, one that benefited and enhanced the MEC over and above non-MEC manufacturing and which might have occurred independently of the Commission's deliberations.

Industrial policy in the 1980s – the Kleu Report

By the 1980s, the disjuncture between English and Afrikaner capital had largely been eroded, manifesting itself in the increasingly influential economic roles played by Sanlam and Rembrandt. By the late 1980s, increasing conglomeration and interpenetration were being accompanied by the privatisation of state corporations, such as Iscor and Sasol.

The policies of the 1970s that supported the MEC had led to a cul-de-sac once the benefits from the gold and energy boom of the 1970s were exhausted. The economic crises of falling global demand for MEC exports and the structural impediments to diversification out of the MEC core overlapped with the political crises of apartheid. Ironically, just when internal political conditions amongst fractions of capital were most conducive for the adoption of coherent economic policies for diversifying out of the MEC, economic conditions were unfavourable, with the state subordinating policy to countering the post-1985 debt crisis. For example, Kahn (1991b) has shown that resulting exchange rate movements had differential impacts upon the profitability of one sector as opposed to another, depending upon their relative dependence upon imports for their inputs and exports for their outputs. Little account was taken of this as the industries stagnated. Priority lay with the balance of payments.

It was perhaps because MEC growth adequately sustained the

economy for much of the 1970s that the next official inquiry into the state of South African industry reported only ten years after Reynders, despite the dramatic changes in economic conditions and the continuing failures of industry and industrial policy. The time that it took for the report to be produced indicates both the limited inherited expertise and research on which the group was able to draw and the limited urgency with which industrial policy was being treated. The Study Group, led by Kleu, was set up in 1977, with its deliberations emerging in 1982,[13] and a White Paper on industrial policy not until 1985!

Kleu's lack of realism and the Report's ideology is apparent from its opening page: 'It must be said at the outset therefore that an industrial strategy for South Africa must be determined within the framework of a system in which free enterprise, consumers' freedom of choice and private ownership play a fundamental role.' (p. 1)

In effect, the Report did point to a broad framework for the formulation of industrial policy, although this was ambiguously, if not inconsistently, combined with a commitment to 'the private entrepreneur to decide *what* he will produce, *how much* he will produce and *how* and *where* he will produce' (pp. 317–18), even if subject to indicative planning. As such, the Report suffers from two drawbacks. First, it is so general as to be meaningless except as a statement of good intent; we are given little indication of what, how much, how and where *he* is liable to be producing either within any one sector or across them. Secondly, by the same token, the recommendations have been studiously ignored in practice, having themselves been based on an analysis that has devoted little attention to the political and other forces that had in the past shaped the path of both industry and industrial policy.

Joffe (1987, p. 1) detected a shift away from state intervention in industry in the rhetoric of the Kleu report, interpreting this as a reflection of a global trend towards liberalisation. This process in fact began in the early 1980s when the state liberalised the financial sector, an act which by itself failed to give impetus to the industrial trajectory. Instead, it heavily benefited the cash-rich mining conglomerates, heralding speculative booms, capital flight and accelerating imports. More damaging policies to confront a subsequent fall in the gold price would have been difficult to design even in retrospect! Yet Moll (1992) suggests that macroeconomic policy was successful, given the 'exogenous' constraints under which the economy operated.[14]

Even before the 1982 Report Kleu (1973) had argued for policy to enhance competition by reducing government interference in the economy and shifting towards a more even balance of support between

---

[13] Even so, the report is itself poorly produced, with many publishing errors.

[14] See Chapter 10 for further discussion.

import substitution and export promotion. Greater productivity increase was to be encouraged through the startling measure of initiating studies by the NPI in collaboration with industry.

Whatever its other deficiencies, the Kleu Report examined industrial policy from a wide perspective, just as its predecessors had. It called for a balanced promotion of exports and import replacement, a more vigorous effort towards decentralisation, enhanced labour skills and a concerted technological policy.

Kleu's 'multidimensional' view of industrial policy recognised the proliferation of responsible government agencies and called for a co-ordination both between these various agencies and with the private sector, implicitly recognising how this had been absent in the past (1982):

> At present a number of bodies naturally share the task of dealing with numerous policy aspects that influence industrial development. These bodies include the Department of Industries, Commerce and Tourism, the Board of Trade and Industries, the Decentralisation Board, the Competition Board, the Economic and Physical Planning Branches of the Prime Minister, the Department of Manpower and Finance, the South African Reserve Bank, the Industrial Development Corporation, and others. (p. 318)

However, with the exhaustion of revenues from the gold-price boom of the early 1980s and the crisis of apartheid, industrial policy co-ordination, never cohesive in the first instance, evaporated further. First, Kleu's narrow vision of 'industry' excluded mining and energy, sectors which had long been co-ordinated through the Chamber of Mines and, more recently, in conjunction with the Department of Mineral and Energy Affairs (DMEA). They had even made the attempt to extend co-ordination to mineral processing. Reynders' 1972 proposal to reduce imports of intermediate and capital goods while raising sectorally targeted exports necessitated continuous monitoring of the latter; thus the Minerals Bureau was set up in 1972 to monitor mineral resource management and mineral processing (Main, p. 109).

Secondly, the responsibility for co-ordinating energy policy concerning liquid fuels rested with the DMEA, although Sasol and its creator, the IDC, also played decisive roles. Thirdly and most importantly, responsibility for industrial policy for most 'other' industries (non-MEC) fell to the Department of Trade and Industry (DTI) and, in particular, to the BTI whose tariff policies were both diffused across MEC and non-MEC sectors and were also unco-ordinated with the MEC-oriented policies.

Industrial policy into the 1990s – the demise of the BTI

Industrial policy in the 1980s cannot simply be described as a shift from an inward to an outward focus. In fact, industrial policy thrusts around the MEC continued, creating and supporting large-scale MEC industries continued. While some Escom projects were postponed because stagnation reduced electricity demand, the co-ordinated strategy around liquid fuel energy was sustained. Shortly after the release of the 1985 White Paper on industrial policy, the cabinet evaluated several private and public corporation proposals for developing the nation's offshore gas reserves and the Mossgas proposal was selected. This IDC-led mega-project involved the transfer of Sasol's technology and provided a major short-term boost to the economy between 1988 and 1992.

On the other hand, the economic crisis of apartheid, particularly after the 1985 debt crisis, began to have an impact on the unco-ordinated trade policies of tariff protection. Lacking an overall economic rationale and coherence as well as being disconnected from other aspects of policy, tariff policy through the BTI had been reactive to the individual levels of profitability of domestic industry, even if apparently more stringently applied over the most recent years. Levy takes the fate of applications to the board as an index of 'the responsiveness of the BTI to entreaties from the private sector' (p. 17), 65 per cent proved successful in 1987 compared to 40 per cent in 1988 and 20 per cent in 1989.

In the late 1980s, the BTI attempted to reduce tariff protection substantially by linking this sector-by-sector to interventionist and inappropriately named structural adjustment programmes (SAPs). This was in part to ease the path of adjustment; more significantly, it aimed to secure productivity increase without relying exclusively upon the competitive coercion of the market.

In the BTI (1988) view, the decline in the economy's performance as measured in terms of GDP growth was due to several factors. First, despite Reynders' (1972) emphasis on export promotion, South Africa did not adjust its exports away from primary commodities ('stage 1' goods) in response to falling real prices and increasing world imports of advanced technology products ('stage 4' goods). Secondly, low productivity, high capital intensity, low personal savings and high tariffs were contributing factors as were currency overvaluation which occurred between 1979 and 1983 (p. 37). Using the negative trade balance of 'stage 4' complex manufactured goods as an indicator of poor industrial performance and orientation, the BTI crystallised the debate over policy orientation at the time into three alternative options (p. 42): liberalisation through removing tariff protection; stimulating a free trade regime in the belief that this, by itself, would shake industries into competitiveness – the envisaged instruments were tax rebates on industrial inputs or the adoption of export processing zones; and adopting a sectorally targeted strategy to support industries while tariffs were gradually lowered (p. 47). The last option (SAPs) were favoured by the BTI. In essence, these:

...would fundamentally be founded on principles similar to those underlying tariff protection and would, therefore, essentially also exhibit similar characteristics (except for...various forms of assistance pertaining to the different functional areas of business and different competitive factors). In short, it embraces an infant industry approach to export development assistance. (p. 48)

However, with the continued stagnation in South African manufacturing throughout most of the 1980s and into the 1990s, two important influences have altered ways of thinking about future industrial policy. First, the prospect of a post-apartheid government has opened up a Pandora's box as far as analysis, policy and strategy are concerned. Theory and experience from many different sources have greatly enriched the terms within which South Africa's past, present and future manufacturing performance is being assessed. Secondly, as a specific and central example of this, the success of the NICs has exposed the limited terrain upon which South African industrial policy has been both conducted and discussed.

The pressure for action in the face of economic stagnation was most acutely felt by non-MEC sectors and by their co-ordinating institution, the BTI. Here, the sectoral SAPs proved less acceptable, especially to the DTI, even if the department was more amenable to tariff reform (i.e. reduction). As Levy (pp. 17-18) quotes from the department's Annual Report for 1989: 'The Department experienced problems with the acceptance of the BTI's first recommended "structural adjustment programmes"...government policy implies the reduction of state involvement with the activities of the business sector – not an evergrowing involvement.' This statement was followed in 1990 by the DTI withdrawing ninety personnel seconded to the BTI, thus crippling the latter's SAP work. Simultaneously, new SAPs were forbidden by the Trade and Industry minister.[15]

The IDC appears to have stepped into this policy vacuum, publicly challenging the BTI's interventionist approach. The IDC (1990) attributed the problems of poor industrial performance to the tariff policies administered by the BTI: 'For almost 70 years, the industrial development policy of successive governments was based on import replacement.' (p. 1) In its recommendations, which were more in keeping with the liberalising elements of the Kleu Report,[16] the IDC conveniently ignored

---

[15] *Business Day* (1991) 14 June.

[16] For a review of the IDC report along the lines presented here, see also Black (1991). He sees 'a key instrument of industrial policy is the availability of long term capital and that this has to be made available on a concessionary basis to targeted sectors' (p. 17). This raises a

its own interventionist role in creating and nurturing a range of MEC industries. As argued here, these industries played a greater role in shaping South African industry than tariffs. There is also an astonishingly frank but possibly unconscious admission of the limited scope of what constitutes industrial policy for the IDC; it is effectively identified with trade or, more exactly, BTI-administered protection policy. As if as a matter of terminological convenience: 'In this report the terms "trade policy" and "industrial policy" are used synonymously and interchangeably.' (p. 1)

The logic lying behind the IDC's push for greater export orientation is that protection policy is mere featherbedding of inefficient industries which need to feel the coercion of competition to shake them out of a low level of performance; industries are not expected to be infants for seventy years. Irrespective of the presence of such competitive pressures, such logic fails to recognise that there is also the incentive to reduce costs in order to enhance profitability; more pragmatically, removal of protection may have the effect of eliminating the fittest enterprises without necessarily inducing the entry of alternative producers in the same or other sectors, except by imports from abroad. But the IDC must bend to international pressures, and it has recommended a progressive reduction of import duties and surcharges to bring about a more uniform and lower level of protection in line with the fashion for export orientation. Equally significant, the stiffening attitude to protection almost certainly reflects a shift in the balance of internal economic interests and political balance.[17] Favour has swung away from small-scale Afrikaner manufacturing (never highly supported in any case) towards large-scale, corporate MEC activity. It is also apparent that the mega-projects currently being put in place under the imperative of generating foreign exchange incorporate a logic arising out of their capital-intensity. This places them more readily outside the reach of organised labour and the state other than in the form of an incorporated and elite-based dependence. This is all the more remarkable given the desperate need for labour-intensive job creation through state expenditure.

---

number of issues. By what criteria are those sectors to be selected? How are they to be identified given those criteria? And, if this can be done, why should intervention not be more extensive and not necessarily centred on cheap finance which serves more as a mechanism of implementation of policy to guarantee the realisation of goals within the firms and sectors selected for the economy more generally? In short, Black appears to substitute selective finance for trade policy as the Midas touch in the formulation of industrial policy. This is all the more remarkable given his correct emphasis on the need to create comparative advantage, as seen in the South Korean experience. See Black (1992) where he draws similar, if more general, conclusions to our own concerning the scope of industrial policy and the lessons to be learnt from the Asian NICs.

[17] Of course, it can be convenient to project policies as being imposed externally and so beyond domestic control, whether favouring or harming the balance of sectional interests.

The exact incidence of support across sectors and its determinants requires further study. The shifts in balance are themselves masked by limited coherence in policy and the more general withdrawal of support to all as a response to economic stagnation. While the BTI (1988) proposed sectorally based adjustment programmes, the IDC (1990) favoured a three-pronged approach. First, reduce tariffs, the basis of BTI's discretionary power. Secondly, support export-oriented capital investment through tax incentives. Thirdly, target industrial sectors which offer static comparative advantage; in particular, mineral beneficiation industries. Not entirely dissimilar to the debate between Reynders and Ratcliffe in the mid-1970s over the sequencing of restructuring measures, this policy disjuncture was publicly highlighted by BTI Chair, Lawrence McRystal, in a newspaper article 'Industry must be restructured before tariffs are lowered' (*Business Day* (1991) 17 July). After this last ditch stand, McRystal resigned in August 1991 and the BTI was emasculated by the BTI Amendment Act of 1992.

Thus, after apparently occupying centre stage in industrial policy for much of the twentieth century, the BTI was renamed the Trade and Industry Advisory Board in 1992 and its functions were curtailed to advising the Trade and Industry minister on tariffs and dumping duties.[18] Even so, by 1993 it was the IDC that appeared to be providing the basis for South Africa's tariff position at the GATT negotiations.

With the demise of the BTI, the IDC administers the only significant pro-active industrial policy in the 1990s: the promotion of an industrial trajectory around the MEC, supporting large-scale mega-projects including Sasol's expansions, aluminium smelting, stainless steel and potash. The only difference is that the process is now driven by private sector interests, especially following the privatisation programme.

Discretion still remains at the heart of decision-making as in the selection of projects qualifying for Section 37E tax incentives, the subject of opposition by senior officials of the Finance Department (*Business Day* (1991) 2 August). In 1991, section 37E incentives initially covered projects beneficiating locally-sourced minerals. Its susceptibility to the powerful coalition of private sector interests around the MEC is evident in its 1992 extension to projects beneficiating imported material; in particular, this included the Alusaf project, which did not previously qualify because it utilised imported alumina.[19]

Of more interest are the exceptions that the IDC (1990) brought to the fore. Apart from acknowledging that some sectors would adjust to tariff

---

[18] *Business Day* (1992) 3 March. Previously the BTI made recommendations directly to the Finance Department, by-passing the Trade and Industry minister.

[19] The rationale for Alusaf also reflects its heavy use of electricity, which is in considerable excess supply.

reduction with greater difficulty than others according to the level of previously sunk capital, for example, as well as highlighting the case for inward industrialisation, the report also emphasised the need for what might be correctly termed industrial policy for capital goods:

> The active promotion of capital goods manufacture is therefore a desirable direction for development in the long term...in a modified trade policy, new development, including capital goods manufacturing, must be actively promoted but with less reliance on protection alone and greater use of pragmatic and innovative development schemes. (p. 25)

Like many previous recommendations for diversification out of the MEC core, such 'active promotion' has never been carried through. Given the orientation of the IDC, the strength of private sector interests around the MEC core and judging from past experience, it is unlikely that any sectors falling outside the core would be 'actively promoted'.

The most recent official policy document, the Normative Economic Model (NEM) (Keys 1993), confirms this. It represents a synthesis of a model developed by CEAS (1993).[20] CEAS firstly adopts an incorrect and essentially false framework to conceptualise productive economic sectors. The model bases its analysis on a traditional conception of the economy, dividing it into primary (mining and agriculture), secondary (manufacturing, construction and electricity) and tertiary sectors (transport and communication, financial services and social services). The sectors are essentially treated as independent entities, with the policy objective being to shift away from the primary sector, according to the aggregated international developed market economy norm. There is no recognition of interlinkages and interdependence within the MEC core sectors. First among its limitations, the model incorrectly interprets industrial development as having followed a path of ISI:[21]

> The development of the manufacturing sector in South Africa during the 1960s and 1970s is typical of a country that has adopted an import replacement strategy. This strategy implies a progression from non-durable to durable consumer goods and then to highly sophisticated intermediate products and capital goods. Measured against the objectives of such a strategy, the results achieved cannot be considered a clear success. (p. 301)

Secondly, the model considers only a narrow range of factors which have contributed to the pattern of industrialisation. The problems of the

---

[20] The ineffective role of the BTI (Board of Tariffs and Trade), the successor of the BTI, is evident in its apparent lack of participation in developing the synthesis document.

[21] This is discussed at length in the next chapter.

economy are interpreted in terms of capital- intensity versus labour-intensity at a level so highly aggregated as to render the analysis meaningless:

> The capital or labour-intensity of the economy is dependent, *inter alia*, on the country's production structure, on the one hand, and the production and management techniques as determined by the stance of the technology, on the other. The production structure is, in the first instance, a function of the composition of the demand for South African goods and services, which in its turn, is subject to changes in the pattern of income distribution. (p. 42)

These are inappropriate analytical tools to interpret causality in the process of industrialisation. The economy's high capital-intensity is attributed to inappropriate state-led investment in strategic projects (p. 44) as well as low nominal interest rates in the 1970s (p. 14). Although the model only considers industrial development after the 1973 gold and energy prices rise, Fig. 4.5 (p. 83) shows the capital-intensive pattern around the MEC to have been evident from the inter-war period. Otherwise, the CEAS argues in a tautologous fashion that economic stagnation was due to low levels of investment in the 1980s (p. 25) which fell because growth fell (p. 27). This led state sectors to cut capital expenditure in a regime of stricter fiscal discipline after 1980 (p. 28). Clearly, this is descriptive rather than analytical.

Thirdly, the conduct of past policy is only superficially examined. Its failure to be cohesive, the problems of poor monitoring and its determination by social and political factors is ignored (p. 289): 'In the past, the manufacturing sector in South Africa was stimulated by means of large-scale investment in capital-intensive, import-replacing and export-oriented industries. Another characteristic was the high level of protection that was granted to specific industries producing mainly for the domestic market.'

The proposed CEAS corrective policies are defined at a highly aggregated macroeconomic level. It identifies two problems which policy has to overcome: first, the failure to specialise in specific exported manufactured products; secondly, declining factor productivity, which the model only measures at an aggregate level.

Without any substantiation of its differing impact at the sectoral level, the model assumes that an outward-oriented policy will automatically lead to improved productivity and increased exports simply because of the resulting increase in competition. The net impact of such an approach is the reduction of tariff protection and the abandonment of the sector concerned to market forces.

Keys further develops the criteria for selectivity, subordinating them to more abstract macroeconomic ideological objectives.

The extent to which selective assistance to particular industries will be needed depends largely on the tempo at which policies such as the phasing out of exchange control, the lowering of tariff protection, cooperation in wage bargaining, price competition and fiscal and monetary discipline in general are realised. Progress in these areas would reduce and possibly even eliminate the need for selective assistance to industries with proven competitive advantage, such as in agriculture, mining and minerals beneficiation. The instruments to be used over a broadly defined spectrum of more advanced industries, probably mostly category 3 and 4 products of the GEIS, and should meet the criteria of investment, employment and efficiency in their impact on development. (p. 15)

While Keys expects a free trade regime to benefit the primary and processed commodity sectors, its impact on the rest of the economy is unquantified, even in CEAS (1993). Those that do survive the shocks of liberalisation may or may not be supported, depending on some discretionary judgement at that time.

To conclude, little has changed in the problems hampering manufacturing industry growth that were identified back in the 1960s. These included skills, training and research development deficiencies and the need to target beneficiation and exports.

[South Africa] must step up and step up rapidly its secondary and university training and adjust and direct it more towards the exploitation of the economic potential of the country. In particular the country should train scientists and engineers to a considerably greater extent and with much more deliberateness than has been the case up to the present. The country's engineering facilities should be strengthened and the State should make available substantial funds for attracting deserving students to such training. It is imperative, too, that the country's research programme should be stepped up and that it should be more purposefully directed towards the development and exploitation of such resources in the country in respect of which it has the greatest potential and comparative advantage for taking advantage of foreign markets.... The country needs to become far more outgoing in search of foreign markets and more aggressive in its salesmanship in the development of such markets than has been the case hitherto. Orders much be fetched, they do not come to the timid. (Norval, pp. 25, 27, 28)

Three decades later, the same warnings and recommendations by Norval are being dusted down and recommended in Keys (1993) and CEAS (1993). Yet the obvious question of why these warnings were not heeded thirty years ago has rarely been addressed. The reality is that such general prognostications serve to veil a continuing lack of coherence and commitment in industrial policy and, more sinisterly, the desire to retain the ability to respond with discretion to shifting, uneven and fragmented economic and political imperatives.

Our discussion of industrial policy has drawn predominantly upon the empirical evidence available to us and the arguments to be found in government reports. In particular, the latter part of the chapter has been concerned with the formulation of industrial policy by the apartheid government that was itself increasingly aware that the horizons over which it was liable to exercise control were far from distant. This questions the relevance of such a detailed discussion of policy proposals and frameworks that were both doomed to be short-lived and overshadowed by the immediacy and crisis associated with the coming transition. Thus, the government's normative economic model (CEAS 1993) has provided little more than a momentary contribution to debate over economic policy, with those concerned merely going through the motions.[22]

There are two important and related reasons why this review of the moribund remains an important exercise. First, the industrial policies of the 1980s, even in the second half of the decade, shed considerable light on the whole evolution of industrialisation and industrial policy over the post-war period as a whole. Indeed, the decade can be viewed as heralding the culmination not only of the apartheid regime but also of a particular and peculiar period of economic development. At the expense of repetition, it is worth emphasising how industrialisation and industrial policy witnessed the interpenetration and co-ordination of large-scale Afrikaner and English capital; this had been dependent on the prior development of Afrikaner financial institutions and on an industrial policy centred around integration with rapidly growing state corporations. The MEC has remained the key component of the economy and has been associated with industrialisation primarily around its core activities rather than through tariff and other policies. Finally, industrialisation has not proceeded, even in fits and starts, through ISI with backward integration from simple consumer goods to more sophisticated capital goods.

With these perspectives, it is possible to unscramble the apparent incoherence and incompetence of industrial policy and to make sense of the most recent proposals in terms of their seeking to sustain a continuity with the past, even if in the context of a break with the apartheid system itself. For the apartheid regime has sought to guarantee the interests of the

---

[22] The limited significance of the NEM is also explained by the inconsistencies between its short and long versions and the generally analytically superior and more progressive stances adopted even by the World Bank and IMF.

large-scale capitals organised around the MEC even as it has released the reins of immediate political power.

Secondly, the policy proposals emerging in the 1980s are not simply of academic or historical interest because they were the product of a moribund government. The political and economic interests and how these are structured and functioning remain in place to a large extent and are the inheritance of the transitional government. Those debating the merits of and prospects for policy proposals need to be grounded in the economic realities that we have identified. As detailed in the following chapter, policy discussion and debate over industrialisation has unfortunately been and continues to be distinguished by a persistent failure to acknowledge the true nature and source of South Africa's industrialisation.

9

DEBATING INDUSTRIALISATION
AND INDUSTRIAL POLICY

In reviewing past debates over South Africa's industrialisation, the first section of this chapter demonstrates that on the one hand, these have changed in parallel with more general shifts in the theory of industrialisation and development. On the other hand, it reveals how the themes of the debate and their interpretations of industrialisation have remained remarkably unchanged, often being resurrected from time to time, albeit from different theoretical perspectives. The rhythm of debate is discussed in the following section. It is found that past debates over industrialisation have been based both on a false perception of the pattern of industrialisation and on a partial and even false recognition of how industrial policy has been adopted and implemented in practice.

Two specific examples are used to illustrate this. First, the commonly accepted past and prospective trajectory of import-substituting industrialisation, backward from consumption goods, to intermediate and then capital goods, is shown to be contrary to the actual form of post-war industrialisation in South Africa, as this has run in the opposite direction, even if to a stunted extent. Secondly, a false dichotomy has been drawn between mining and manufacturing activities, masking the evolution of the MEC that straddles both. The concluding remarks examine the implications of our analysis in the light of recent developments in the theory of industrialisation.

Perceptions of industrial performance

There have long been fierce debates over the successes and failures of South Africa's industrialisation. These have evolved and exhibited a rhythm corresponding to the perceived performance of the economy itself, although protagonists within South Africa have often picked up and run with the analytical batons passed on by those following the fashions of externally determined theory. The shifting marriage forged between internal empirical developments and external theory has given the debate a dynamic that has apparently endowed it with a progressive evolution. This is dramatically illustrated by the Pandora's box of analyses that have been opened up by the prospects of a post-apartheid economy. Drawing upon a range of experiences of strategies from other countries and their corresponding intellectual baggage, an astonishing variety of industrial strategies has been proposed. This stands in sharp contrast to the previous, now supposedly sterile, debate over whether apartheid had been functional or not to South Africa's economic development and, subsequently, why the apartheid economy had proved incapable of sustaining itself.

Despite these swings in the content and the terms of the debates, the intention here is more to stress what they have had in common. Unfortunately, the apparent sensitivity to the most immediate empirical developments has been misleading in so far as the deep-rooted realities of the economy have paradoxically been overlooked. This is in part because of a lack of attention to detail in terms of what has actually constituted industrialisation in the South African context. It is also due to the failure to acknowledge the underlying economic forces that have driven industrial policy.

These deficiencies have been reinforced by dependence upon external theory. Beginning with Rostowian notions of industrial transition, South Africa's performance was judged on the basis of a programmatic sequence, attached to the notion that manufacturing would ultimately be self-sustaining. Although such determinism has long since been discarded, some of its nostrums have persisted within the continuing debate. In particular, the idea has persisted that industrialisation will take the form of backward integration from consumer goods, with a declining role for the primary sectors of the economy made up predominantly of agriculture and mining. The issue of industrialisation has continued to be very much one of how far this process has or has not gone and why.

The perspective from which we assess this literature is diametrically opposite. First and foremost, the South African system of accumulation has been dominated by the core activities of mining and energy but increasingly has incorporated other directly integrated manufacturing such as processed minerals and chemicals. Secondly, the extent of the MEC across the economy has been more or less limitless since, in corporate structure, it has been highly concentrated around mining houses, each of which has owned its own finance house, and these have been engaged in acquisition and mergers. In addition, private corporate capital has been heavily integrated with parastatals.

Thirdly, the broad categorisation of the economy into sectors such as primary and manufacturing has been extremely misleading since from an analytical point of view, much of the latter does not correspond to industrialisation in the sense of backward integration from consumer goods. Rather, industrialisation has primarily been based upon *forward* integration from the core activities of the MEC. Consequently, industrialisation should be debated in terms of the reasons why this has not processed further. As a corollary, the notion that South Africa has failed to make the step from ISI to international competitiveness is equally misguided for the greatest part of industrialisation that has been achieved has been related to core MEC activities that have served both domestic and foreign markets, whether directly or indirectly.

Rostowian determinism. Many analysts were blinded by the spectacular growth in the 1950s and 1960s, of the aggregated manufacturing sector relative to mining and agriculture (Fig. 4.1, p. 72). Falling growth after the 1970s was initially seen in cyclical, rather than structural, terms. Writing before the crisis in the South African economy became fully exposed, Houghton (1973, pp. 130–6) was optimistic over the prospects for industrialisation. In Rostowian fashion, he regarded 'take-off into self-sustained growth' as having been achieved between 1933 and 1945, with the economy engaged in 'a drive to maturity' ever since. 'According to Rostow, economic maturity is reached some sixty years after the take-off begins. If this holds true in South Africa's case the national economy should be reaching maturity about the year 1990!' (p. 18)

By the early 1980s, flagging growth was attributed to low productivity, poor economic management and ISI trade policies, preventing a shift to an export orientation in the 1960s. Yet Viljoen (1983, p. 33) still maintained that 'South Africa is clearly approaching the stage of industrial maturity': 'On the whole South African manufacturers were more interested in exploiting the protected and rapidly expanding local market than in competing in the highly competitive overseas markets. They were also penalised by the internal location of the main centre of industrial activity' (p. 47). He observed the 'remarkable fact' that growth was based on the combined use of more factors of production rather than on increased output for the same inputs, attributing this failure to 'the quality of management' (p. 42). Such problems were expected to be overcome over time by the formation of the Productivity Advisory Council and the NPI in 1967: 'experience has been that improvements in productivity is a long-term problem of many dimensions that can be solved only over a considerable period of time' (p. 48).

Rostowian positions did not go much beyond this in explaining why industrialisation, itself perceived in highly aggregated terms, had not been more efficient nor penetrated deeper. Although Viljoen recognised the disproportionate weight of steel and chemicals in the economy with the future potential to develop downstream linkages, there was no explanation of why this had not occurred. In the case of the motor industry, its low productivity was not attributed to poor management but to its fragmentation which impeded the achievement of scale economies.

Viljoen simultaneously pointed to the high and growing concentration in ownership of the manufacturing sector yet he drew few conclusions about its impact on the pattern and process of industrialisation except that it 'naturally raised serious issues in regard to the maintenance of competition and, ultimately, of the free enterprise economy' (p. 51). Here conglomeration was viewed as a potential impediment to industrial growth rather than as result of a particular form of industrialisation.

Liberalism challenged. In the face of flagging industrial performance during the 1980s, Rostowian optimism began to give way to a view that attributed industrial failure to the impediments imposed by apartheid. For D. Kaplan (1977), the Second World War promoted manufacturing, especially textiles, metal processing and engineering, and gave rise to a bi-modal structure in the size of manufacturing firms: the large-scale open to a degree of foreign control and dependence and the small-scale particularly dependent upon protection. In his view, however, economic policy was primarily concerned to promote the interests of mining and agriculture as a compromise between English and Afrikaner interests.

This is a judgement that is difficult to sustain without a detailed study across different sectors of the economy. Even then there is the problem of whether the distinction between the identified fractions of capital can be so sharply demarcated. Just as there is a necessary relation between state corporations and the mining sector, so the latter increasingly incorporates manufacturing. For example, Cartwright (p. 221) highlights one consequence of the development of the new goldfields in the OFS after the war: 'The chairman and directors of African Explosives and Chemical Industries...were quick to grasp what was happening. The steps they took in those days were eventually to increase the issued capital of the company to no less than £29,000,000 and to make it the biggest manufacturing enterprise in the country.'

It merely needs to be added that AECI had long been substantially under the control of Anglo American; Ernest Oppenheimer chaired it almost to the day of his death in 1957. Thereafter, it necessarily occupied an integral part in the development of the heavy chemicals sector in conjunction with Sasol. Cartwright's narrow conception of manufacturing ignored the far larger capital investment of £41m in state-owned Sasol by the end of the 1950s.

For liberals poor industrial performance reflected the intensified constraints imposed by apartheid upon market forces and, for Marxist-revisionists,[1] the crisis of the apartheid system that was previously functional for capitalist profitability. A compromise position is possibly to be found in the stance of Nattrass (1988). She sees state intervention from 1924 onwards as having shifted the economy 'to develop in its own

---

[1] For example, see Wolpe and Johnstone.

right and on a broader basis than that of the mining industry alone' to become 'something more than a peripheral area in the British Common-wealth' (p. 232). However, state intervention also entrenched white privilege so that the positive impact on industrialisation had to be set against the economic inefficiencies and injustices associated with apart-heid. In short, Afrikanerdom is seen as essential to break out of under-developed dependence on foreign capital but its associated state intervention, especially in the labour market, had become increasingly dysfunctional to economic performance.[2]

Inherently rejecting Rostowian determinism, Moll (1991) has argued by a range of criteria that the South African economy did not perform well in the post-war period even before the 1970s, so that the economy might be better considered to have been in a prolonged slump. His attention focuses on growth rates, relative both to other countries and to South Africa's own past experience, productivity growth and the contribution of exports.[3] Whatever the merits of his empirical account, it still leaves open the issue of why the economy should have failed. For example, the following offers more of a description than an explanation:

> Manufacturers were protected from some import-competition by a variety of direct controls and tariffs, and had access to cheap capital good imports. Not being encouraged to compete internationally via exports, they settled down to enjoy internal markets and in some cases returns to scale could not be achieved. Many 'infant' industries seem never to have grown up and required tariffs and protection decades after being started. The 'easy' stage of import-substitution in light final and intermediate goods industries ended in the early 1960s, but pos-sible shifts towards exporting light manufactures and the efficient production and export of capital goods (for example mining equip-ment) did not take place. Meanwhile, there is abundant evidence that many state industrialisation initiatives were inefficient (for example Sasol) or misguided (the industrial decentralisation policy). (p. 283)

Essentially, the argument is that the tempering of market forces and the inadequacy of state intervention were at fault. But why should protec-tion not lead to take-off? Indeed, limited domestic markets and access to imports might imply intense competition rather than featherbedding. Given extensive state economic intervention, why should it not have been more conducive to growth?

Moll (1990) ultimately offers a number of explanations without claim-

---

[2] See also Nattrass and Ardington (eds) (1990).

[3] See also Nattrass (1989a; 1989b; 1992) for an account of the failing South African economy based on falling profitability from the 1960s. Some doubts are cast on these calculations in view of profit in the form of capital flight.

ing to be comprehensive. These divide into two types. First, there is appeal to restrictions in the labour market, created by the commitment to apartheid, whether it be in the geographical, sectoral and occupational immobility of black labour or its limited access to informal self-employment and to state-provided education and training. Secondly, there is the argument of inappropriate economic policy within the confines of the apartheid labour system. In particular, devaluation of the rand would have proved more favourable to export of manufactures. He points to the separation between trade and industrial policy as well as the separation between each and the conduct of balance of payments and exchange rate policy:

> Balance of payments and exchange rate policy was seen as the preserve of the South African Reserve Bank, its aim being to deal with monetary flows...Industrial policy was dealt with by the Board of Trade and Industries, largely using tariff and decentralisation policy. The linkages between trade and industrialisation seem never to have been explicitly considered on either side.[4] (p. 142)

Moll suggests that the reason for this compartmentalisation of policy is to be found in the short-term relationship between the exchange rate and the distribution of income and the favour to be bestowed on underlying economic interests. In short, devaluation would have enhanced the position of black workers since they were disproportionately employed within the traded sector, as opposed to the whites located predominantly within non-traded, particularly state, employment.

Such a view is problematic. First, it ignores the role played by the IDC, instead attributing responsibility for industrialisation almost solely to tariffs administered by the BTI. Secondly, it presumes that the separation between arenas of policymaking and the content of policy is primarily determined by the distributional interests of different fractions of workers. It also sets aside the other factors determining the distribution of income and levels of wages and employment. Should export promotion have proved so favourable to black workers, the evidence is that compensating adjustments could well have been adopted by the apartheid state to support white workers. More generally, the problem with Moll's counterfactual arguments is that they are almost inevitably dependent upon very heavy *ceteris paribus* assumptions. The economy would have performed better with more skilled and less fettered black workers and with an exchange

---

[4] Moll (1990) quotes an interview with Simon Brand, head of the (DBSA) Development Bank of South Africa and leading development specialist for the apartheid government: 'Dr M.H. de Kock, governor of the Reserve Bank, would have been horrified if the Board of Trade and Industries had come to him in the 1950s and asked him to devalue to encourage industrialisation.'

rate policy more favourable to exports. But the economic and political conditions to allow such policies to be put in place would not have allowed such *ceteris paribus* assumptions to hold. The skill composition of the workforce and the structure and content of policymaking were themselves products of the underlying balance of economic and political forces.

Similarly, McCarthy (1988) finds it easier to identify than to explain South Africa's economic malaise:

> It would appear that South African industrial development has reached an impasse. Import-substituting development has taken the manufacturing sector a long way up the ladder of development but has not lowered the average import propensity of the economy. In order for this to happen large-scale replacement of intermediary and capital goods will be required, a development which is accepted to be difficult and costly in the comparatively small market. (p. 21)

Here, we find a number of commonly cited factors for South Africa's difficulty in promoting further growth in manufacturing: a structural obstacle to further industrialisation which has exhausted the scope for import-substitution; continuing import dependence especially as a consequence of weak capability in capital and intermediary goods; and the constraints imposed by the level of domestic demand.[5] As such, it leaves unanswered a number of questions, not least why the industrialisation that has taken place should not have gathered its own momentum, whether through spin-offs into other linked sectors or through the attainment of international competitiveness and export growth, especially given dependence upon limited domestic markets. As South Africa's export performance has been dramatically poor in manufacturing, with export growth limited to processed minerals and chemical sectors, the notion of insufficient demand cannot legitimately be isolated from consideration of export markets (Wood and Moll, 1994). Why could these not have been sought out and captured?

Schumpeterian interpretations of industrialisation. Poor economic performance is also reflected in perceptions of technological underdevelopment based loosely on Schumpeterian paradigms. D. Kaplan (1987; 1990) points to the weakness of the capital goods sector, focusing upon the subsectors of machine tools and telecommunications. For the former, he argues that traditional explanations of failure based on limited markets and insufficient R & D are inadequate by themselves. He points in addition to the failure to develop indigenous design capability, insufficient protection and commitment to export markets and their ineffectiveness in view

---

[5] See also Archer (1987), Black and Stanwix (1987) and D. Kaplan (1987).

of exchange rate movements and the lag in the South African business cycle compared to other countries. Meth (1990) takes a very different view. He emphasises the extreme diversity of the capital goods sector and argues that, given the structure of the South African economy, it is quite appropriate for it to import a large variety of capital goods and foreign technology, especially since these are used profitably in production for protected domestic markets:[6] 'South Africa has a competent engineering (capital goods) industry which is as large as one could reasonably expect. Given the size and diversity of the manufacturing sector, it is unrealistic to believe that a local capital goods industry could produce anything more than a narrow selection of the core machines required.' (p. 308)

But why should those subsectors in which competence does emerge not also lead to international competitiveness and exports? What determines which subsectors should benefit from competence? For example, the two sectors of capital goods and telecommunications highlighted by Kaplan, are very different from one another, quite apart from their own internal heterogeneity. Capital goods have in part had a close and longstanding connection with the core activities of the mining, minerals processing, chemicals and energy industries; the determinants of developments in telecommunications have been very different with much stronger links to foreign capital and technology and greater scope for diversification into new technology around electronics. Such considerations raise the issue of how general an explanation for industrial success or failure can be, given the wide diversity of the subsectors concerned.

In the context of industrial development and industrial policy, it is more useful to avoid a narrow focus on capital goods and to consider the broad engineering industry as a set of heterogeneous and closely linked sub-sectors whose role it is to deliver capital goods, repairs and other services essential to the efficient functioning, reproduction and further development of core productive sectors. In the specific South African context, the engineering industry and, consequently, the capacity to produce capital goods, has failed to develop as a productive sector in its own right. This is not solely because of the reasons advanced by Kaplan or Meth. It is also associated with concentrated conglomerate ownership of the engineering and other sectors. These have tended to confine engineering's linkages to dependence upon mining, mineral processing, chemicals and energy

---

[6] Meth also questions the notion of 'appropriate technology', suggesting that this is only meaningful in the context of a more fundamental transformation of the economy: 'A major restructuring of the pattern of demand (which is distorted by gross income inequality and South Africa's natural resource endowments) is required before the potential for a larger more 'appropriate' capital goods sector can be realized.' (p. 308)

industries, which have historically absorbed a significant proportion of GDFI.[7]

Monopoly capital interpretations of industrialisation. As with Schumpeterian perspectives, the trajectory of South African industrialisation has only been partially explained by those operating within the monopoly capital paradigm. Here, an attempt to force the observed trajectory to 'fit' the imported model of advanced capitalism has reinforced the false dichotomy between 'mining' and 'manufacturing'.

In rejecting both the liberal arguments of apartheid constraining industrial development and the Marxist-revisionist view of apartheid being functional to the growth of all industrial sectors, Innes has been less favourable in interpreting the achievements in industrialisation. He regarded it as being 'relatively backward' for, even in the early 1950s, apartheid encouraged:

...[A] particular form of industrialisation based largely on labour-intensive methods of production. The immediate result was the expansion of the labour-intensive light industries rather than the more mechanised capital goods sector. For instance, during the early 1950s it was industries like food, beverages, paper and textiles that expanded (together with the more labour-intensive mineral processing group of industries), while in the late 1950s, when there was little growth, the trend to labour-intensity became more marked. (p. 170)

According to the model, diversification out of mining became possible through development of financial institutions, capital markets and a burgeoning credit system particularly after the 1950s: 'What the growth of the local money market represented in particular was the clearest form yet of the merging together of bank capital and productive capital – that is, of the emergence of the phase of finance capital' (Innes, p. 182). For Innes (p. 191), industrial expansion of a capital-intensive nature could only take place in the 1960s.

As with ISI assumptions, the sequencing of events in reality does not fit the monopoly capital model. Investment in certain highly capital-intensive manufacturing industries has been a feature of industrial development since the late 1920s. By 1960, 35 per cent of fixed assets in manufacturing were concentrated in the three MEC sectors of steel, non-metallic mineral products and chemicals, (Fig. 7.2, p. 163)

In summary, while describing the centralisation and concentration of the economy through the group structure of conglomerates with their historical roots in mining, the monopoly capital approach offers a false explanation for the pattern of industrialisation and only partial reasons for

[7] For a review of the engineering sector, see Rustomjee (1993).

poor industrial performance. Why, for example, did centralisation and concentration not lead to greater economies of scale and outward orientation; why did the economy stagnate in the 1980s after 'finance capital' had achieved even greater concentration and dominance? As in other contributions considered here, particular theoretical paradigms have been appropriated and 'confirmed' by confronting them with judicious selection and interpretation of empirical evidence, usually organised around success or failure in ISI.

Regulation School and racist Fordism.   Such is the case with Gelb's (1987) attempt to explain poor industrialisation through an appeal to a variant of Regulation School theory.[8] His marriage of the external theory with internal empirical evidence adopts the seductively attractive terminology of 'racist Fordism'. Theoretically, the Regulation School provides for the economy to sustain accumulation systemically until it enters a 'structural crisis'. The apartheid system gives the South African economy its peculiarly distorted form of Fordism, the predominant structure of accumulation for the post-war boom. Essentially, then, South African Fordism as the unity of mass production and mass consumption is doomed to run its course but only upon the restricted basis of mass consumption for privileged whites. Consequently, apart from relying upon a stereotyped version of Fordism as a system of accumulation, there is ultimately reliance upon underconsumption even if this is reinforced by reference to the poverty wages of blacks.

The theoretical and empirical underpinnings of the Regulation School have already been extensively criticised for such leanings.[9] From our perspective, the notion of the South African economy as a restricted or distorted form of Fordism necessarily suffers from a reductionism of the apartheid system to the limited *consumption* of the majority, even if this is in turn related to the failure to sustain Fordist production, with, as in other contributions covered here, a neglect of the 'Fordist' industrialisation that was in fact typical of production around the MEC core sectors.

---

[8] See also Gelb (ed.) (1991) in which the racist Fordism approach serves as an uneasy, possibly reluctantly adopted, framework for the separate contributions. More significantly the approach has sunk without trace in the rush to post-apartheid economic policymaking, not least in Gelb's own work!

[9] See Brenner and Glick (1991) and Mavroudeas (1990). The obvious question to address to the putative crisis of the racist Fordism regime of accumulation is why it should prove incapable of serving continuing expansion in privileged, white, domestic markets, especially given high import propensities and protection for domestic production of consumption goods and/or serve export markets. It is worth observing that regulation theory has increasingly become eclectic and middle-range in which, for the latter, stylised empirical observations are interpreted as structures which are more than capable of explaining the empirical evidence from which they have been derived.

The themes and rhythm of debate

Debates have covered two trajectories. The first concerns the interpretation of the *conduct* of industrial policy. The second traverses the observed *pattern* of industrialisation and its associated performance.

The literature that is widely available on the formulation and conduct of industrial policy is limited, especially if, as here, only literature in the English language is covered. This itself reflects a deeper problem, though one that is less relevant today. The economic disjuncture between English and Afrikaner capital has had a counterpart in academic debates over the content of industrial policy. South African industrial policy formulation and control has, until very recently, been the preserve of a handful of Afrikaner bureaucrats, academics and industrialists. Brand highlights this in passing (our emphasis):

> It is widely accepted that high growth rates of manufacturing output will continue to be essential. This assumption has occupied a central place in such forums for the formulation of government policy with regard to economic development as the Viljoen Commission (1958) and the Reynders Commission (1972), as well as in the spelling out of development targets in the successive Economic Development Programmes issued since 1963. It also features prominently in the writings of *economists outside the official sector*...e.g. in T. Bell (1975). (p. 166)

The context of debate has thus been one where 'unofficial' academics based at English-speaking institutions have usually criticised the conduct of industrial policy from the sidelines relying upon the findings of numerous Commissions of Inquiry and parliamentary bills, from the preparation of which they have been excluded. Key milestones in this chronology include the Holloway Commission (1934), BTI Report No. 282 (1945), Viljoen Commission (1958), Reynders Commission (1972), Kleu Commission (1982), White Paper (1985), BTI Report No. 2614 (1988), IDC (1990) and the NEM of 1993 (Keys) and CEAS (1993). As argued above, the analytical tools used have often followed the fashions of externally determined theory.

In this light three specific but overlapping issues have dominated debates on industrial performance in the past. The first has already been discussed and concerns the liberal perspective that industrial performance has been constrained by apartheid. The more recent debates on post-apartheid industrial policy have essentially discarded this issue. A second set of issues has weighed up the balance between inward and outward orientation of industry and the selectivity of sub-sectors in industrial strategy. A third issue has been the extent of state- versus market-orientation of the economy.

Inward versus outward industrial orientation.   Debates on inward and outward orientation have pivoted around the widely accepted proposition that South Africa followed an ISI path. Observers and policymakers hold that after exhausting the 'easy' industrial activities by the early 1960s, the 'growth path' of ISI became progressively difficult in the 1970s and contributed to the crisis and stagnation of the 1980s.[10]

Houghton (1973, p. 18) points out that the need to shift away from ISI and to develop an export orientation was recognised and advocated in a number of successive government reports, beginning with the Third Interim Report of the Industrial and Agricultural Requirements Commission (1941). He identified several of the more common reasons for the failure to diversify out of mining, including the low productivity of production, which was partly linked to both the small domestic market and poor economies of scale and the inward mentality of South African industrialists.

It is generally accepted that South Africa had completed the first stage of industrialisation (domestic production of consumption goods) during the 1950s. As Scheepers (1982, p. 20) claims in retrospect: 'The studies of both T.A. du Plessis and the author during the sixties proved that this country entered the second phase of the import-substitution process during the fifties.'[11] For him, this should have led to the increasing domestic production of intermediate and capital goods. It was certainly anticipated to be the prospect at the time and also during the following years. Such was the case for Marais (1960). As others have done subsequently, he recognised that import substitution does not necessarily reduce the propensity to import, thereby easing pressure on the balance of payments, since import dependence shifts from consumption goods to their input requirements. Similarly, Lumby (1983) notes:

> Although South Africa became nearly self-sufficient in the production of many consumer goods and certain equipment for mining, agriculture, construction and transport, industries which produced consumer goods continued to import a large percentage of their raw material requirements... The contribution of manufacturing to the Gross Domestic Product may have outstripped the combined contribution of agriculture and mining for the first time in 1965, but that industrial growth which was possible was not self-supporting or independent. (p. 227)

[10]   For example, see Moll (1991, p. 283).

[11]   Zarenda (1975) quotes from the Scheepers' study, noting that only 16 per cent of growth was accounted for by import-substitution between 1956–7 and 1963–4, as compared to 52 per cent between 1926–7 and 1956–7. Zarenda suggests that industry and exports should be promoted rather than protected, thus opening the way in principle to a variety of policies and not just price support.

Lachman also accepted that the early stage of easy import substitution had been completed and so sought greater export orientation. In fact, he must have been one of the first commentators to suggest South Korea as a potential model of export orientation from which lessons could be learnt, however correctly that model was understood. For Reynders and van Zyl (1973), there is a recognition that there had been more than enough import policy, especially in the form of protection, but an absence of export policy on the grounds that 'gold sells itself '. Reynders himself had just completed chairing the commission examining export policy.

Some, however, did not agree that inward policies were exhausted but pointed to the issue of the *selection* of sectors to benefit under import-substitution protection. For Marais (p. 67), blanket ISI had run out of steam by 1960 and required targeting: 'It therefore does not seem necessary to protect and stimulate a whole range of industries, but to concentrate on a few industries only, such as, for example, the production of rayon, synthetic rubber, and motor vehicles, parts and accessories.' In response to the Reynders Commission Report on the export trade, Bell argued in favour of more import substitution into intermediate and capital goods in order to accrue dynamic economies rather than seeking larger potential markets through blanket support to exports, as the report recommended. But Bell went further, recognising that the international climate had grown more hostile to exports from developing countries after the 1973 gold and energy price rise.

A synthesis of or, more exactly, a compromise between these competing views is to be found in Brand's (p. 172) contribution, which is even-handed between ISI and EO. He argues that proponents of both inward and outward strategies base their respective arguments: '...on the basis of very much the same evidence about the country's past patterns of development, and very similar perceptions of the present structure of its economy.'

We will argue below that this basis is falsely conceived. However, Bell also raised the issue of selectivity, that there should not be a general disposition either towards protection for import substitution or for export promotion but rather the decision should be based on their potential to fulfil the objectives of economic policy, whether these be employment creation, easing balance of payment constraints, protection of infant industries of short-term considerations, such as anti-dumping. Moreover, Bell (p. 173) recognised the unscientific basis on which debates had been conducted and selectivity had been exercised in the past, pointing to the lack of 'intensive micro-economic study of individual sectors and products' concerned. As argued here in earlier chapters, decisions around selectivity were bound up with the patronage that the state offered to Afrikaner capital during much of the post-war period.

Also from our previous chapter, it is apparent that the policies that were actually implemented in the decade of the 1970s greatly strengthened the role of the MEC core within South Africa's economic structure. In this sense many who have engaged in the debate over industrialisation have based their observations on a false perception of the pattern of industrialisation on backward linkages from consumption goods. Similarly, the political factors that influenced decisions around industrialisation have only been partially appreciated and this goes some way towards explaining why effective policies were not taken despite the recognition of the same manufacturing sector weaknesses time and time again in the post-war period.

Fifteen years ago the report of the Viljoen Commission into the South African commercial policy was criticized for repetitiveness; the inclusion of superfluous details, incoherence, incompleteness and partiality in the presentation of economic arguments; and excessive concern with immediate decisions on the implementation of policy whose general direction had already been determined, instead of a scientific and reasoned analysis of alternative policies. These defects are also to be found in the report of the Reynders Commission.[12] (Ratcliffe, p. 75)

Clearly, the terrain of debate has focused narrowly on the perceived exhaustion of ISI. However, it is our contention that the ISI concept is far too blunt a methodology to be used to interpret the specific form that industrialisation has taken in South Africa even if it were appropriate for other countries and those of Latin America in particular. First, ISI's presumed path and chronology does not match the pattern of industrialisation in South Africa. Secondly, the descriptive categories of light (consumer) and heavy (producer) goods used to sub-divide industries conceal other important sectoral linkages around the mining, mineral processing, chemicals and energy sectors which have imparted a greater impulse to industrialisation in South Africa than has blanket ISI protection. Thirdly, contrary to ISI logic, South African industry has long demonstrated a considerable capability in capital goods manufacture.

Examining industrialisation in South Africa beyond ISI

The empirical evidence reveals flaws in the presumed path and chronology of ISI in South Africa. Fig. 9.1 shows that 'import substitution' had largely taken place before 1945 even at the most aggregated level. After this, imports ran at about 40 per cent of gross manufacturing output.
Important sub-sectoral trends are revealed in Figs 9.3 and 9.4 which

[12] The reference is to Samuels (1959), who was less overt in his criticism than is suggested but did raise the issue of how selectivity is to be determined.

show the real division between light, mainly consumer goods and heavy, mainly intermediate goods, industrial consumables and producer durables manufacturing activities. From 1932, heavy activity output grew at a faster rate and caught up with consumer good production by the end of the Second World War.

Thus the idea that imports of light or 'easy' consumer goods were first substituted for and that this 'stage' was exhausted by the 1960s is inaccurate.[13] Fig. 9.2 reveals that the ratio of imports to value added for 'easy' consumer good sectors fell from 265 per cent in 1924 to 75 per cent in 1945 while the heavy or 'difficult' capital-intensive sectors (mostly associated with the MEC) fell from 330 per cent to 50 per cent over the same period. While a greater proportion of consumer goods were wholly manufactured domestically, considerable inroads into local manufacture of difficult, capital-intensive goods were also being made. Data are not available for the period between 1958 and 1970, but Fig. 9.4 shows that only a slight decrease in import/value added ratio for both 'easy' and 'hard' sectors was achieved.

This is not to deny that imports declined with the flourishing of local production behind tariff barriers. However, the pattern of industrialisation in South Africa cannot be reduced to an ISI model which in fact grew out of theories based on patterns of Latin American industrialisation.[14] Interpreting industrialisation in South Africa as ISI is misleading for two reasons.

First, the dynamic potential of linkages *between* economic activities is not recognised by aggregating specific sectors. ISI analysis has been based on a conceptual divide between industries which manufacture consumer and producer goods. Other linkages within the economy, for example between mining and manufacturing or between manufacturing subsectors, have usually been ignored. Yet linkages around a MEC were emerging even as early as the turn of the century, when the largest dynamite factory in the world was constructed at Modderfontein. This was subsequently to impart a propulsive effect on the chemicals sector. The impact of the primary steel industry which began production in 1933 is clearly evident in Figure 9.3 and led to industrialisation across a wide range of sectors.

Secondly, ISI analysis has tended to reduce the political factors that have influenced the pattern of industrialisation to the strength and ability of indigenous capital to impose protection. But inter-war diversification in industrialisation was constrained in South Africa by the disjuncture

---

[13] This sequencing was suggested for developing countries by Little, Scitovsky and Scott.

[14] These concepts are associated with the work of the Economic Commission for Latin America in the 1950s and 1960s. For a review of Latin American contributions to the political economy of development, see Kay (1991).

between the political and economic power of Afrikaner as opposed to mining capital. Hence, the heavy, capital-intensive industries were developed early on relative to the conventional pattern for ISI, reflecting an uneasy compromise between serving the MEC and promoting national capital. The creation of Iscor is a case in point. The development of the steel industry went some way in stimulating other sectors but industrial policies could not be cohesive enough to carry industrialisation extensively downstream out of the MEC core.

State versus market in industrial performance. The debate over state versus market has and continues to be sterile, ideologically driven, of limited scope and based on a false conception of the realities of state–capital relations in South African industrial development. In more recent debates, attacks on any active role for the state have become a component of a range of contemporary policy studies (see below).

Two issues have dominated the debate on the role of the state in industrial performance. The first has already been discussed: the liberal assault on state intervention in labour markets which is held to have impeded industrial performance (Moll 1990). The second has been around the creation of state-owned industries. This policy instrument has long been opposed on ideological grounds, with protection, let alone more extensive state intervention, also opposed by free-market positions. This leads to reliance upon static comparative advantages in mineral exports.

Others such as Black and Stanwix have seen state corporations in a broader economic context. They recognise that state-created industries were among a number of factors which historically promoted industrialisation. Others included tariff protection, state repression of labour, the demand from mining activities, diversification using mining surpluses and South Africa's relatively open economy stimulated from time to time by events in the rest of the world. The pattern of industrialisation that resulted from these factors is seen as having led to the structural constraints to growth which emerged in the 1980s. These included: inadequate demand from a limited domestic market; exhaustion of easy consumer good import-substitution at the cost of raising capital goods import dependency; an anti-export bias through overvalued exchange rates; uncompetitive industries featherbedded by protection; the promotion of capital-intensive investment; and the concentration of ownership, coupled with capital strike and flight.

However, such perspectives tend to overlook the more obvious political and economic linkages forged by state-owned industries. The actual process of industrialisation in South Africa involved a symbiotic relationship between the state corporations and private capital around the MEC. Central to the process of post-war industrialisation has been the erosion of the disjuncture between English capital's economic power and

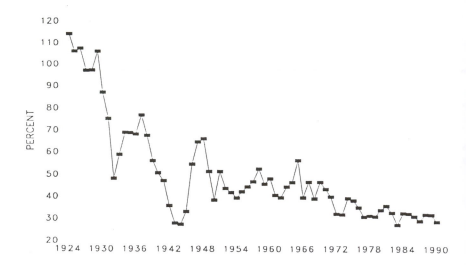

Fig. 9.1. TOTAL IMPORTS/GROSS MANUFACTURING OUTPUT

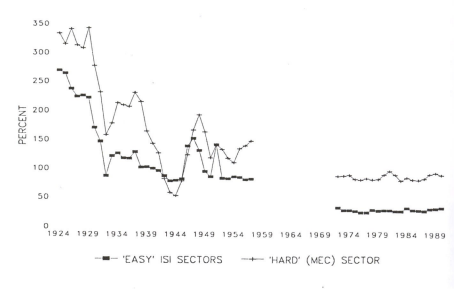

—■— 'EASY' ISI SECTORS   —+— 'HARD' (MEC) SECTOR

Fig. 9.2. SECTORAL IMPORTS/SECTORAL VALUE ADDED

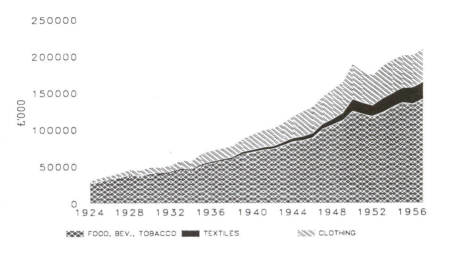

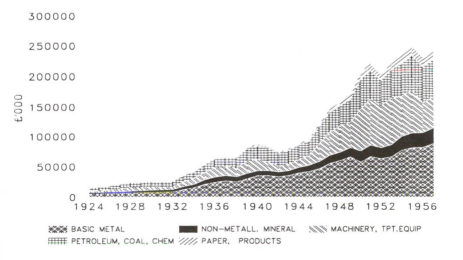

Fig. 9.3, 4. MANUFACTURING GROSS OUTPUT
(*Constant: 1924*)

Afrikaner capital's political power. The creation of state-owned corporations should be viewed in the context of this process which involved the creation of large-scale Afrikaner capital around the MEC core, its interpenetration with English capital and, ultimately, their combined collaboration and co-ordination through the state. It is quite inappropriate to view South Africa's industrialisation as a balancing act between state and market provision, adjudicated on ideological grounds over the relative merits of intervention or not. The error is compounded if this approach is wedded to a notion of conformity or not to a normal pattern of industrialisation, reflecting the transition from ISI to export orientation, and backward integration from consumer to capital goods as the economy becomes more technically sophisticated and internationally competitive.

Industrial financing and industrial performance. Industrial performance has also been associated with developments in the financial sector and debates on the impact of industrial finance on industrial performance have been dominated by the conventional market-based, neoclassical perspective. This holds that industrial development proceeds smoothly along a well-worn path, lubricated by the financial system:

> Institutions canalizing savings – including mutual funds – and the functions of the new issues market...together with the position of the stock exchange as the facilitating mechanism through which the burden of waiting and risk bearing was shifted to those most able to bear it, and which facilitated the transfer of capital from those who possessed it to those who could employ it more profitably. (Dickman 1973, p. 373)

The absence of capital markets is held to have resulted in relatively labour-intensive industrialisation. Norval (p. 97) argued that industrialisation was constrained until the Second World War because industries had: 'to rely on what they could scrape together themselves or obtain from friends, legal firms, boards of executors and trust companies, one of whose main functions was to administer estates of deceased persons and invest the savings of their clientele.' For Norval, the inter-war period was marked by the development of labour-intensive industries like clothing, tanning (coarse leather not requiring capital equipment), canning, confectionery, cigarettes using primitive machines, foundries and engineering repair shops. From our perspective, this is incorrect, for a significant proportion of inter-war industrial activity was due to capital-intensive investment in the steel industry through the creation of state-owned Iscor and an ensuing range of downstream joint venture metal industries with private capital (see Chapter 6).

Martial control of production during the Second World War interrupted the 'normal' process of industrialisation according to conventional thinking and state intervention spurred industrialisation for war production. For Norval (p. 53) the Second World War and not 1925–39 was the turning point: 'the country went from a labour-intensive to a capital-intensive basis of its manufacturing industries.' This occurrence was attributed equally to a speculative bubble in industrial financing:

> No efforts were spared, nor funds for the equipment of industries. In many cases it could be no more than improvising. The remarkable phenomenon was that there was no lack of capital. Capital was forthcoming like rabbits from a hat. With the most favourable prospects of profits and dividends the general public had no hesitation in placing their savings at the disposal of industry by taking up shares based on nothing more than the optimistic assurances of industrialists of whose credentials very little was known and still less regarding the basis of the security offered. It was a real bubble and many came out the poorer, but the wiser, from these speculations. (Norval, p. 53)

Dickman (1973) also refers to constrained industrialisation in the 1950s due to the fact that:

> Disillusionment with the stock exchange was rife following the 1948 debacle on the share market, when the hesitation that was to continue characterizing the investment scene for many years to come had as its counterpart the fact that the capital market mechanism remained relatively dormant and underdeveloped, and profit re-investment continued to be a major source of industrial finance. (p. 373)

In contrast to the financial constraints to industrialisation that typified the 1950s, the boom in aggregate manufacturing sector activity in the 1960s is attributed to the freeing of impediments in financial markets. For Viljoen (1983):

> A large number of new financial institutions have appeared on the scene, such as merchant banks, general banks and investment houses, and, in the late 'fifties, an increased interest began to be displayed by pension funds and insurance companies in investment in industrial equities. This was a major element in permitting the market to fulfil its role of efficiently transforming the savings of the community into capital formation. The result has been the broadening of share ownership and marketability, and the increased ability of companies to look to the market for their capital needs. (p. 50)

Despite these conducive institutional conditions, even Dickman (1973) acknowledged that finance did not flow as smoothly into expanding manufacturing activity in the 1960s. Long-term insurers, pension and

provident funds almost doubled the proportion of assets invested in equity
between 1961 and 1965. Yet:

> Just how much of the new capital that flowed from the public and the
> institutions in the two major new issue booms of 1963/65 (when a net
> R371 million was raised from the public) and 1968/9 (when a net R719
> million was raised) was destined actually to finance new fixed invest-
> ment or fund existing borrowings is another matter... And even if, as
> it will be argued, the majority of issues was designed either to attract
> savings for further but diversified investment in existing securities (as
> in the case of investment trusts) or to enable local entrepreneurs or
> foreign investors to reap the benefit for a successful profit record in
> their personal or foreign corporate capacity and yet retain effective
> control (as in the case of offers for sale, techniques similar to this but
> classed as new issues, and pyramid companies), one should not com-
> plain. (p. 375)

Dickman thus draws attention to the simultaneous emergence of the
speculative nature of financial markets in South Africa and their overlapping with growing ownership concentration, facilitated by the very financial institutions whose purpose, according to theory, was to mobilise and
allocate savings according to market-determined investment needs.

His failure to connect the two occurrences is partly noted by Viljoen,
for while developed financial markets supposedly enhanced industrial
performance during the 1960s, it apparently also contributed to growing
market defects, particularly through rising ownership concentration. In
noting the spate of mergers and acquisitions in the 1970s, Viljoen (1983)
suggests that the latter partly contributed to subsequent poor manufacturing performance:

> The Commission of Inquiry into the Regulation of Monopolistic Con-
> ditions Act found that according to the 1971–72 census...virtually
> every industry investigated by it could be considered as either monop-
> olistic, duopolistic or oligopolistic in structure... The measure of con-
> centration in South African industry naturally raises serious issues in
> regard to the maintenance of competition and, ultimately, of the free
> enterprise economy. (p. 51)

More recently neo-liberal positions have extended this to argue that
economic stagnation was caused first by the concentration of state, rather
than private, ownership in the productive sector which prevented the
financial sector from efficiently deploying resources. Secondly, it is
argued that the financial sector itself was constrained by a variety of
regulations, such as foreign exchange control and prescribed assets.

A number of theoretical positions which are not rooted in neo-classical exchange theory have drawn different conclusions from rising ownership concentration and evolving financial markets. According to the theory of monopoly capital (Innes 1983), industrial financing did receive a boost in the late 1950s as mining houses re-directed profits from mining into manufacturing through new financial institutions; however, this was seen as a consequence of the attainment of the stage of finance capital. Nevertheless, it is not clear why either the achievement of monopoly capital or the emergence of capital markets did not lead to a dynamic and self-sustaining manufacturing sector after the 1960s.

On the other hand, Black and Stanwix view the rising concentration as an 'organic' response of capital: 'The mergers and takeovers which were the hallmark of the process of centralisation of capital during the 1970s were spurred by recession as financially strong groups sought to expand their market share by buying companies weakened by adverse economic circumstances.' (p. 52)

A curious feature of debates on industrial finance is the way state and private sector finance and investment have been compartmentalised. Although many acknowledge the existence of the IDC in providing finance for industry, its activities are hardly referred to by Dickman (1973), for example, even though its investments, while sectorally focused within the MEC core, constituted more than 50 per cent of manufacturing sector fixed investment. Instead, the financing of state-sector industries have often been portrayed as the creation of monopolies rather than as sectors with extensive upstream and downstream linkages with the private sector, imparting a propulsive effect on a broader industrial trajectory.[15] For Viljoen (1983):

> The state has played an important role in further enhancing the already undue measure of concentration. This has been effected through the Public Corporations and certain State departments, which dominate or monopolize the basic iron and steel and chemical industries, the supply of electricity, and the provision of rail, air and postal services. (p. 51)

Others, such as Levy (1981) cited in Black and Stanwix view state-owned industries as capital intensive, as opposed to private sector investment which, presumably because they were more responsive to factor markets, have been more 'labour-intensive'. More recently, debates on the impact of industrial financing on industrial performance have focused on the reasons for the capital-intensive nature of South African manufacturing industry, with the neo-liberal position being that capital intensity is the result of state 'interference' in capital markets (see below).

[15] Significantly, even the World Bank (Fallon *et al.*) has recognised, against all its previous recent credo, the role of crowding-in of the private sector by public sector investment in the South African context.

From our perspective, the issues around financing and industrial performance have been discussed using too narrow a conception of the financial and manufacturing sectors. First, industrial performance cannot be explained solely by the extent of financial market development since considerable industrialisation took place before these markets emerged in their present form; furthermore, financial market liberalisation in the 1980s did not enhance industrial performance.

Secondly, it is our contention that past and present debates have been based on a false dichotomy between mining and manufacturing. The bulk of industrial finance in the 1950s, 1960s, 1970s and late 1980s has been concentrated in the core sectors of the MEC and continues to be so into the 1990s (Fig. 7.2, p. 163). Thirdly, the debates on industrial finance have largely ignored the role of state corporations and their symbolic relationship with private capital in industrialisation; simultaneously, they have not recognised the resonance between the pattern of industrialisation and its financing and the evolving and peculiar form of conglomerate ownership which incorporates the financial sector.

In terms of the MEC, the growing power of large-scale capital has taken place in the context of the erosion of the disjuncture between English and Afrikaner capital from the inter-war period. The particular conglomerate form that has evolved in the post-war period, enveloping the financial sector in the process, is to be seen as a whole rather than as operating in separate and distorted markets.

Contemporary debates on industrialisation.   Recently, more sophisticated understandings of the workings of the economy have emerged, focusing especially on the poor performance of the manufacturing sector Fallon *et al.*, Kaplinsky (1992), Lall (1993b) and Levy. While manufacturing is perceived to have been successful in the narrow sense of having increased its share of the economy at the expense of mining and agriculture, its overall performance over the past two decades is considered inadequate by a number of criteria, including many of those identified in past debates such as low productivity and ISI limitations.[16]

The consequences of adopting this false conceptual divide between mining and manufacturing has already been demonstrated and it applies equally to agriculture, although in practice, linkages between agriculture and manufacturing are not as strong as those of core MEC activities. Apart from this, these analyses also adopt ahistorical approaches, ignoring the roles of the financial sector and the evolving corporate form in shaping and reproducing the pattern of industrialisation.

---

[16] Indeed, memories and scholarship seem to be short with the unacknowledged rediscovery of economic deficiencies and remedying policies that had already been identified in the past.

An example of the former is Fallon *et al.*, who argue that had the state not intervened in creating and financing steel, chemical and mineral processing industries, scarce capital resources might have better been utilised for other purposes: to create more jobs in export-oriented industries etc., many of which would have realised greater returns to capital employed. Such an appraisal is reminiscent of Moll's *ceteris paribus* arguments discussed above. Levy implicitly accepts this, attributing heavy investment in steel, chemical and related industries to policies of state intervention which resulted in a manufacturing sector suffering 'distortion' from some ideal, if vaguely defined, labour-intensive norm.

In addition, Levy notes that while investment in the Sasol process might not be economically and financially justified *ex ante* once undertaken it may *ex post* support a market-driven rolling programme of high capital investments in downstream activities such as plastics, particularly since ownership has largely passed into private hands. In fact, chemical sector investments have not proceeded downstream but have remained locked into the capital- and energy-intensive MEC.

From our perspective, Levy self-admittedly fails to explain why investments have taken the direction that they have, understands industrial policy on too limited a canvas, [17] and forcibly disconnects manufacturing from the MEC as if, for example, the fortunes of the textile and clothing sectors have more in common with chemicals and steel than the latter do with mining and energy. His assessment of the past and of future prospects relies more or less completely on a theory of comparative advantage derived from (labour-intensive) factor endowments.

Kaplinsky (1992) and Lall (1993a), however, while noting the distortion, do not argue, as the others seem to do that state intervention is inherently misplaced. Instead it is argued that selectivity of state-led investment in South Africa's case was misplaced. Although such judgements are made on economic bases, there is an absence of consideration of the political contexts in which the investments were made.

Whilst many consider the creation of state corporations in South Africa to have been ill-judged and the consequence either of (unexplained) policy mistakes or of commitment to self-reliance in the face of potential sanctions, it is important to recognise that, the direction and content of such policies are not thereby predetermined. They reflect continuing capabilities and the response to economic and political interests as well

---

[17] By way of digression, note that he also observes that 'a producer that currently supplies one-third of local refrigerators estimated that production could be doubled with the addition of no more than 400 workers' (p. 8) – suggesting a considerable degree of excess capacity for this consumer durable at least.

as their becoming institutionalised in particular ways.[18] Our approach suggests that these observations have to be situated in relation to the MEC. The apparent consensus of contemporary debates on the triumph of outward over inward oriented policies in the late 1980s is premature and also a repetition of a debate which has been conducted on a very narrow terrain for much of this century between the interventionist and more liberal factions of orthodox theory. Levy (1992, p. 17) reports from the IDC that seven investigations into trade by government committees between 1958 and 1988 drew the conclusion that greater emphasis had to be given to exports at the expense of inward orientation by shifting the balance of incentives. Previously we have shown that the concepts of ISI has been inadequate in explaining the pattern of industrialisation. Similarly, the supposed shift to an export orientation is inadequate as a methodology to understand the recent process of industrialisation in South Africa.

First, export-orientation has not shifted industrialisation away from the MEC. Most new manufacturing sector investment is taking place in mega-projects within the established MEC core, which as a whole has historically been export-oriented. The MEC then has been the subject of considerable supportive intervention from the National Party government through tax (37E) subsidies and guarantees from potential future governing parties. Export incentives (GEIS) provide additional profits and guarantees to the close-knit conglomerates that are involved in such cast-iron investments. As *Trade Monitor* (1993) observes:

> GEIS provides a premium to companies that would have exported in any case. It is a bonus hand-out to large companies such as Iscor, Sappi, Mondi, Armscor, Sentrachem and AECI. Correspondingly, very little effective encouragement is given to potential first-time exporters in order to entice them into producing for the export market. (p. 6)

GEIS alone has had little impact in shifting export dependence away from the MEC, and its impact in future will be undermined when the heavy investments under 37E incentives begin production. Table 9.1 indicates a dramatic fall in primary exports, mainly gold. This has partly raised the relative percentage of non-primary exports. In addition some of the real rise in exports of Stage 4 Manufactured Products is unsustainable. A considerable proportion of 1990 and 1991 exports consisted of one-off or distress exports from dying shipbuilding and railway equipment industries

---

[18] See, for example, the discussion of South African nuclear power in Christianson (1990). He argues that whatever its rationale within South Africa, it is necessarily associated with an undemocratic and informationally closed process of decisionmaking, one which we would argue is open to manipulation by entrenched interests, most obviously the military but also the associated manufacturers. For a similar view of the British nuclear industry, see Fine and Harris (1985).

and from the armament industry. In the latter case, the product concerned is an artillery system that achieved an internationally competitive edge because it could be developed and tested in the Angolan war by the Defence Force. In the absence of continuing regional conflict in which similar systems can be developed and improved, it is unlikely that arms exports can be sustained.

Table 9.1. EXPORT TRENDS, 1988-91,
COMPOSITION OF TOTAL INDUSTRIAL EXPORTS

	1988	1989	1990	1991
Primary products	76.7	74.7	71.8	67.9
Beneficiated products	8.7	9.6	9.2	11.0
Material-intensive products	10.4	10.7	12.5	13.1
Manufactured products	4.1	5.0	6.5	8.0

Source: Trade Monitor (1993).

Secondly, those looking to export-orientation as the stimulus to renewed industrialisation have not noticed that industrial policy, other than for MEC sectors, has been increasingly divorced from the main policy making institutions like the IDC. In the past, non-MEC industry was in part promoted by the now defunct Board of Trade and Industry (BTI), which administered uncoordinated tariff policies.[19] These sectors seem to have been abandoned to their respective fates in various negotiating 'forums' involving labour, capital and the state, while the latter unilaterally reduces tariffs. There has, in effect, been no industrial policy for non-MEC manufacturing.

These assertions are supported by the inadequacy of policy management, even at the level of basic industry monitoring. In its investigation into the level and structure of export development assistance for industry, the BTI (1988) stated that:

> The nature of the present system of export assistance is such that sufficient information to monitor the effectiveness and efficiency of the system adequately is not forthcoming. (p. 44)

Since the policy making role of the BTI has now been downgraded, it is difficult to imagine any improvement in this sorry state of affairs.

To conclude, perceptions of industrial performance have ranged across ideological divides, have often been based on a narrow range of factors

---

[19] After a battle for institutional supremacy between the IDC and the BTI, the latter was effectively abolished in 1992. Whilst the conventional wisdom is that increased trade liberalisation has been a response to external pressure and fashions, we would emphasise the weakening representation of internal non-MEC manufacturing interests.

and have usually utilised highly aggregated analytical categories. Most important, however, they have failed to provide an adequate explanation of the pattern of post-war industrialisation. Only by unravelling its mode of operation and its intimate relations to the state and finance is it possible to address the issue of the nature of the weakness of manufacturing, which other analyses take as their unproblematic starting point or as a simple consequence of apartheid and mistaken policies.

The period since the early 1980s has been characterised by a paradox as far as the theory and practice of industrialisation and industrial policy are concerned. In policy terms, the thrust has been towards what is perceived to be market liberalisation, with privatisation, deregulation and decreasing protectionism in the ascendancy. On the other hand, serious academic work has shown empirically how important extensive state intervention has always been to successful industrialisation and development; see Chapter 2 for the literature around South Korea. At the same time, empirical studies have been complemented by significant theoretical contributions that both refute laissez-faire dogma and justify state economic intervention of various sorts under a wide range of circumstances. Broadly, the presence of economies of scale and scope, externalities and imperfect competition can explain why the patterns of trade and development – predicted by static, orthodox theory based on comparative advantage – break down.[20]

Further, when translated into a dynamic context, in which technologies and capabilities have themselves to be adopted and adapted, the focus moves to the policies or conditions necessary to create comparative advantage rather than to exploit it. While there can be no presumption, as in neo-Austrian theory,[21] that such dynamic economies are best left to the talents and animal spirits of private entrepreneurs, nor can it be assumed that *any* state intervention is preferable or that the form, extent and content of effective intervention is easily identifiable. For, as discussed in Chapter 3, the role of the state cannot be assumed to be ideal since it is responsive to the economic and political interests that act upon it – even if the recognition of this does not lead to the conclusion that the state should be encouraged to be minimalist. It does mean, however, that policy proposals need to be assessed in terms of the institutional and political capacity of the state to deliver them, because they will otherwise fail or be subverted

---

[20] See Baldwin (1992), Dornbusch (1992), Rodrik (1992), Ocampo (1986), Pack and Westphal (1986), Krugman (1983), and Greenaway (1991). For a recent review of the literature, see Krugman (1994) together with the complementary empirical studies, Krugman and Smith (eds) (1994).

[21] For a critique of which, see Fine and Harris (1987).

to different purposes (again this is recognised but only in unacceptably extreme forms by the scholars of 'rent-seeking' who support laissez-faire).

The literature on South African industrialisation has empirically recognised the failure to stimulate a broad-based industrial diversification. However, much of it has been based on a false perception of the pattern of industrialisation and a partial and even false recognition of how industrial policy has been adopted and implemented. In reviewing this literature, a variety of explanations have been found for the failure of the economy to diversify away from dependence on primary commodity exports. These apparent insights have recurred, raising the question of why was nothing done about the identified deficiencies in the past, and why have apparently identical analyses been rediscovered.

By way of answer, the literature is shown to have followed the rhythm of debates over the theory of industry and development. In general, when applied to South Africa, analysis has suffered from three inter-related deficiencies: overgeneralisation across the economy as a whole according to abstract principles, however valid, and at too aggregate a level; unsystematic use of 'lessons' from comparative experience; and insensitivity to the political and economic realities of the South African formation. In our view, these deficiencies arise from the failure to recognise the central presence of the MEC. While the infrastructural, technical and financial capabilities of the economy are extensive, their scope has only been exploited to a limited extent for reasons reflecting evolving economic and political conditions. Further, the outcomes for the future will be uneven and will cut across the paths associated with the continuing dominance of the MEC, on the one hand, and the policy perspectives currently being peddled in scenarios for a post-apartheid economy, on the other.

These points can be addressed in a slightly different way by considering both the content and scope of what constitutes industrial policy. First, observe that it has experienced a shifting economic meaning according to the ideology (or academic fashions) of the times. Paradoxically, as industrial economics and policy has come more to the fore recently, so it has become associated with, and increasingly confined to, competition and regulation policy in the domestic arena – with this serving to displace the debate over private versus public ownership through the proposition that ownership as such does not matter (relative to how competitive is an industry and how it is regulated).[22] On the international front industrial policy is now linked to trade policy and the virtues or not of protecting domestic markets and promoting exports. But at other times industrial policy has been attached to regional, technology, training, labour market, financial, and even macroeconomic policy etc.

As Chang (1994) recognises, the alternative to a narrow, single-issue

---

[22] See Fine (1990a) and (1990b) for a critical assessment of these propositions.

definition of industrial policy, dictated by the instruments or factors in vogue, is an all-embracing definition acknowledging that almost any economic policy will have some impact on industrial performance in one or more sectors. Accordingly, he suggests an alternative:

> The existing definitions of industrial policy, then, tend to be too over-loaded to be useful in practice. We propose to define industrial as a policy aimed at *particular industries* (and firms as their components) to achieve the outcomes that are *perceived by the state* to be *efficient* for *the economy as a whole*. (p. 60)

Of course, this more narrowly focused definition has its own purposes, but it continues to suffer from seeking a general categorisation of industrial policy whereas we judge this goal to be inappropriate. For if the way that industrial development takes place (and can be steered) is to be analytically targeted, then this must be the starting-point. From our general framework of linkages and agencies, and their dynamic interaction, it is essential to identify underlying economic and political relations upon which the form of industrialisation will depend.

It follows that industrial policy should not be generally defined, no matter whether on a broad or narrow canvas of issues and/or policy instruments. Rather, it should be drawn from the conditions specifically governing the economic formation under consideration. In particular, our own discussion of industrial policy (and industrialisation) in South Africa is focused upon the dynamic attached to the MEC.

Much of the discussion of industrial policy for the new South Africa has overlooked the new theories of trade and growth; the more conservative have been wedded to static, conventional analyses generally supportive of limited and decreasing state economic intervention, and the more radical – such as the ISP project – have been inspired by another rationale, that attached to a belief in the increasing predominance of flexible specialisation.[23]

Lall's work (1993a)[24] is something of an exception. Drawing upon a weight of experience, he constructs an approach based upon the dynamic creation of technological capabilities rather than this static efficiency:

> Even under its simplifying assumptions of perfect markets, the (orthodox) theory proves that free trade optimises static resource allocation rather than dynamic growth. As the proponents of 'new growth

---

[23] For a critique of flec-spec, see Curry (1993) and the references cited there. In our view, flec-spec has been shown decisively in the literature to be of limited theoretical and empirical validity and applicability. It is that much more inappropriate to the South African economy, dictated by the MEC, on the one hand, and characterised by the need to provide for basic needs and employment for the majority, on the other. See final chapter.

[24] See also his references to his own work and especially Lall (1991).

theories' note, under neoclassical assumptions trade liberalisation can only provide a once-for-all improvement in resource allocation – by itself, it cannot lead to the higher rates of growth that provide its empirical underpinnings. A sustained increase in the growth rate can only come from investments in human capital and technology that raise the productivity of other factors of production. Analysts of import liberalisation note, in a similar vein, that the theoretical link between a move to free trade and improved efficiency is tenuous, and the empirical support for the hypothesis is weak. (p. 9)

But, as often and rightly happens in such analyses, emphasis is placed upon how intervention must be selective, 'based on a detailed analysis of the competitive problems of each industry'. (p. 24)

This is an implicit acceptance of the proposition that industrial policy has to be country-specific and not just sector-specific – especially once account is taken of the political process of policy formation and implementation, which may make even sector-specific strategies less amenable in practice than they are in theory. The prospects for policy must be related to the broader economic and political context in which they are proposed.

Thus, whilst Lall's analysis is a welcome advance on much that has gone before, it does suffer from repeating the ill-examined generalities and oversights of the past. He perceives South African industrialisation as having been dependent on ISI for the past seventy years; this erroneous assessment is only possible because the decisive role played by the MEC is neglected even though it set the framework within which industrial policy, properly conceived, was both formulated and implemented selectively in detail.

Part IV

10

CONCLUSIONS AND FUTURE DIRECTIONS

Implications for research

During the course of this book, an attempt has been made to specify the MEC as something more than a group of core and satellite sectors, a configuration of economic and political interests and/or a set of institutions, strategies and policies in which the apartheid state has been central. Quite apart from these factors which have shifted in content over time, it has also been claimed that the MEC is a system of accumulation. It has imparted a particular character to the accumulation of capital; in addition, it has exercised a profound influence upon socio-economic and political life more generally. Essentially, much of our discussion has been devoted to filling out these perspectives in the particular arena of industrialisation and industrial policy, where the impact of the MEC is immediately discovered once it is sought.

However, our research has ranged over a wider canvas and we argue that the direct or indirect influence of the MEC needs to be uncovered in discussion of almost any aspect of the South African formation. What follows in this section is a selective indication of the scope of influence of the MEC. The topics highlighted reflect continuing research but, whatever progress has been made, space constraints do not allow a full account of what has already been achieved. Nonetheless, even an abbreviated discussion may shed some new light on issues in which other researchers enjoy considerably more expertise.

First are the implications for historical research. Our preoccupation has primarily been with the post-war period, although Chapter 6 addresses the 1930s as a means of providing a historical back-drop. However, the class structure attached to the MEC and its reflection in the state have long been the attention of scholarship over a much longer historical period. Analysis has more readily acknowledged the importance of economic and political divisions in the past along the lines that we have pursued for the more recent period. Thus there is Trapido's specification of the gold-maize

241

alliance,[1] the origins and consequences of the Boer War,[2] the subsequent granting of a Boer republic,[3] the white miners' rebellion,[4] the position of South Africa's gold reserves and its Reserve Bank in the international monetary system etc.[5] In each case the relationship between economic and political factors has been addressed. In learning lessons about the past from the more recent experience of the MEC, we would not emphasise a history of what was eventually to materialise, that these events and conflicts were the inevitable unfolding of the MEC as we know it today.

Rather, we would draw from the more recent experience of the MEC and how economic and political conflicts have been resolved or transformed and point to the need to recognise how conflicts, compromises and outcomes have been structured differently from one economic activity to another. This is no more apparent than in the different experiences of agriculture, industry, mining and services, let alone those within these broad categories. This is not to appeal for the complexity of detail at the expense of grander theory. Rather, a South African historiography can satisfactorily draw upon the notion of an underlying and shifting balance and structure of class interests only by acknowledging that their impact is uneven. By the same token, such heterogeneity cannot in and of itself negate an analysis based on class simply because it is not the sole determinant.

Such considerations apply equally to what has proved to be a declining area of interest in the most recent period: the political economy of apartheid's decline. It is perhaps unfortunate that one of the closing contributions in this area should have been Gelb's (1987) notion of racist Fordism. This quite clearly reflects the imposition of a questionable regulation theory originally developed for other purposes with limited purchase on the peculiar features of the South African economy. It is quite incapable of dealing with its complexities and differences at the level of detail.

For example, consider the apartheid labour system. No one can doubt that it has been heavily structured along racial lines, with considerable differences in wages, conditions and rights of access to and within the labour market. Nor can it be disputed that there have been dramatic changes within South African labour markets over the past two decades, with the emergence of trade unions, rises in the real wages of blacks and

---

[1]   See Morrell. Here and in the summary which follows we only cite selected references. For a recent review of issues, see Beinart (1994).

[2]   See Phimister, and from the perspective of the reconstruction of agriculture after the Boer War, see Krikler (1993).

[3]   Marks and Trapido.

[4]   Yudelman.

[5]   Ally (1990).

erosion of differentials between whites and blacks. In other words, the labour market has been restructured and is continuing to experience a restructuring of its wages and conditions, even if many of its structural features, not least dependence upon migrant labour, remain in place.[6] Unfortunately, even orthodox analyses of South African labour markets remain underdeveloped. This raises the issue of how we are to understand such restructuring, noting in the first instance that the various labour market structures are not confined to those of race, there being differences by gender, skill, occupation, location, unionisation, etc. To raise these causal factors is to acknowledge the role of the MEC irrespective of the direct influence that it might exert through economic and political pressure on the state. Each has been conditioned by the MEC. Further, just as economic development has been uneven in the light of South Africa's unique system of accumulation, so the same applies to the way in which the labour markets have been structured. This leads us to reject both orthodox neoclassical theories of the labour market and radical alternatives based upon segmented labour market theory.[7]

The latter does have more purchase on the most recent developments, but we propose an alternative in which labour market segments are perceived to be created out of their own specific economic and political circumstances and to be distinct from one another, rather than being structured simultaneously out of the common underlying determinants. In other words, although the labour markets for domestic servants and for steel workers, for example, share common causal factors in which we believe the MEC to be significant and at times decisive, they cannot be understood on the same analytical basis. Further, the incidence of job reservation in favour of whites and against blacks represents a delicate balance, however crudely implemented, between privileging certain workers in order to gain at the expense of the remainder and in securing skilled workers cheaply. Both in principle and in practice, this has meant that the racial division of labour by skill, tasks and wages and conditions has been drawn differently from one sector to another, irrespective of an unambiguous hierarchy in most instances.

One aspect of the labour market that now receives considerable attention is the level and distribution of skills. Formal and informal skills have been systematically denied to blacks. But again this should not lead to over-generalisations. It is important to examine how the apartheid system both produced the demand for particular skills and sought to provide them. The same applies to technological progress which is highly skewed within

---

[6] See Hofmeyr (1994) and Kraak (1993). We cannot accept the former's conclusion that institutionalised discrimination in South Africa's labour markets had practically disappeared by the early 1980s.

[7] See Fine (1987).

the South African economy.[8] In certain areas, especially in some of those attached to the MEC and to security, achievement borders on best practice. In others, most notably the general level of educational attainment of the majority of the population, capability is sorely deficient. Thus, the parameters of technological attainment are highly uneven and cannot be reduced to nor simply read off from the imperatives of apartheid.

How then are we to understand the determinants of technological progress either in general or in the peculiar circumstances of the South African economy? The most sophisticated approach to this issue is that based on the notion of distinct national systems of innovation (NSI). It is arguable that this framework is unduly descriptive in content, merely pointing to the various institutional components driving technical change, albeit breaking with received notions in orthodox economics. However, it can be complemented by a specification of the dynamic of capital accumulation associated with a particular NSI. Not surprisingly, we argue that the South African NSI is heavily influenced by the MEC, with the particular rhythm, level and composition of technical change circumscribed by the systemic imperatives of the apartheid economy.[9]

One way in which the MEC has had a direct and significant impact on technical capability is through its state corporations. Whether through Sasol, Iscor, Escom or other public investments, the state has devoted considerable resources to R&D, and has heavily influenced the way in which there have or have not been spin-offs for the rest of the economy. The importance of the state to the private sector has been highlighted by the programme of privatisation that was embarked upon in the late 1980s. The issue of privatisation has generally been debated in terms of whether ownership matters or not or whether market failure is worse than regulatory failure or not. Hence, the literature on privatisation is generally inadequate in posing the issue as a false dichotomy between the state and the market.

By contrast, our approach is founded on the notion that privatisation is a form, not a withdrawal, of state intervention which tends to favour large-scale capital, whether directly or indirectly. The successes and failures of the South African privatisation programme can best be assessed from this perspective. It reveals the continuing symbiosis between the apartheid state and the MEC, even as the former was in the process of being dismantled. The two main motives have been, first, to support the

---

[8] See Lall (1993a). Lall (1993b) has also contributed an outstanding survey of the current literature on the role of transnationals that in economic development is notable for the complete absence of any discussion of nationalisation with or without compensation. This is an accurate reflection of a complete switch in policy perspectives (i.e. how to get the best out of a partnership with foreign corporations rather than how to handle foreign, exploitative capital).

[9] See Fine (1993a).

power of large-scale private capital in the long run, whatever form and policies were to be assumed by a subsequent government. Secondly the short run motive of the continuing apartheid regime has been to mobilise finance to sustain its various strategies over the period of transition. From these perspectives, it is possible to explain why the privatisation programme should have taken the form and timing that it did, although these were by no means the only factors.[10]

Not surprisingly, given our emphasis on the uneven impact of the MEC across sectors, the latter need to be studied in detail and differentiated. For agriculture, for example, it has been usual and correct to stress the inequality in access to resources characterising the apartheid system but also to recognise how much of white agriculture is commercially unprofitable, only surviving through heavy subsidies. Our emphasis is different or complementary, investigating the presence of a manufacturing-agricultural complex (MAC).[11] We find that the technical linkages between the two broad sectors have been significant and account for a substantial proportion of non-MEC manufacturing. But we would argue that the MAC does not constitute a complex for accumulation in the sense defined by the MEC, for while it has involved technical linkages in the input-output sense, substantial state support and intervention, and the institutionalisation of economic interests across different fractions of capital, it has not imparted a particular dynamic to capital accumulation outside its own spheres of operation. Indeed, over the post-war period, the MAC has fallen more within the orbit of the MEC as a system of accumulation as the latter's control of much food manufacturing, distribution and retailing has been complemented by a more active role than previously within agriculture itself, with sugar and beer proving classic examples.

While these brief comments on the MAC are overgeneralised (e.g. overlooking differences between localities and products), they also provide lessons for examining the development of consumer goods industries more generally. These have been too readily lumped together and their competitive weaknesses treated as endemic and pervasive. We suggest that this is not always the case, depending upon the form and extent both of integration with the MEC and on an individual sector's own dynamic. Similar considerations can be drawn out for the analysis of the capital goods sector. Contrary to much commentary, South Africa's manufacturing is not uniformly weak across all its constituent sectors.[12] Rather, considerable capacity and success has been achieved, particularly in

[10] This has been argued in papers prepared for Economic Research on South Africa (EROSA) on behalf of the ANC's Department of Economic Policy.

[11] See the discussion in MERG.

[12] See discussion of capital goods in Rustomjee (1993).

activities in and around the core MEC sectors. This implies that general theories of the economy's characteristics, usually posited as inherited weaknesses deriving from the imperatives or obstacles imposed by apartheid, are empirically unfounded and analytically misguided.

Traditionally, capital goods have been seen theoretically either as the form taken by saving (as in models of growth), as a response to the relative prices of capital and labour (neoclassical theory), as a reflection of the balance of power in production (labour process literature) or as the means of incorporating technical progress (for example, in models of learning-by-doing). These are all important factors but need to be complemented in the South African context by consideration of the MEC's influence.

The same is true of the arms sector. It is well known that the apartheid regime developed considerable capacity in arms manufacture, including nuclear and export capability. Quite correctly, this is seen as a response to internal and external opposition to the regime and it has led some to suggest the presence of a South African military–industrial complex. But this cannot be the full picture, as the existence of the security and industrial imperatives do not in themselves explain the extent and composition of the defence industry. Rather, the development of the defence industry has been intimately related to the interests and evolution of the MEC. This adds to our understanding of what constitutes a military–industrial complex beyond a simple descriptive category. From this understanding, it can be argued that the notion of a complex as a system of accumulation, whether minerals–energy or military, must be based on the empirical identification of historically contingent linkages established between different sections of capital.[13]

Finally, consider macroeconomic policy. There has been a tendency to undertake macroeconomic analysis as if the apartheid economy were amenable to modelling like any other despite its peculiar character. This throws into doubt the frequently favourable assessments of South Africa's conduct of macroeconomic policy under the apartheid regime.[14] For this reflects an unduly narrow preoccupation with some of the standardised targets of policy, such as inflation and the balance of payments, neglects other targets, such as unemployment and equity and welfare, excuses poor performance as due to external shocks without acknowledging that these were often the consequence of the apartheid regime of which the policy making institutions were a part, and it also neglects the extent and institutional structure of the financial system in South Africa which both reflected the directions taken by the apartheid economy and consolidated its poor overall performance.

Such a view is confirmed by the liberalisation of financial markets that

[13] See Fine (1993b).
[14] See Moll (1993).

occurred in the early 1980s, mistaken and disastrous policies (including the forward exchange cover) that are too easily excused by a rush of enthusiasm for laissez-faire policies and overly optimistic expectations about the gold price. However, it is crucial to recognise how these policies enabled South Africa's corporate capital to disinvest at a time when the temporarily fortuitous circumstances might have been better exploited in promoting domestic investment. Nonetheless, the exercise of macro-economic policy on behalf of the mining conglomerates is believed to have been abandoned in the second half of the 1980s when the exchange rate was no longer devalued to sustain the rand price of gold.[15] However, such an assessment is partial, for it does not recognise that the desperate straits of the economy in that period were such that they would not have allowed gold-based profitability to be maintained. In view of other polices adopted at the time, it is not so obvious that corporate capital had fallen out of favour with macroeconomic policymakers.

In addition, the enforced abandonment of liberalisation in financial markets by the the debt freeze of 1985 has been complemented by a continuing lack of control over capital flight, especially illegal flows. Our own calculations indicate that the latter has amounted to as much as 7 per cent of GDP per annum on average between 1970 and 1988. While the figures remain contested,[16] two important implications follow. First, they indicate the global character of South Africa's major corporations and their longstanding failure to promote industrial diversification out of indigenous strengths in and around the MEC core. This both reflects and reproduces the MEC as a system of accumulation as we have characterised it. The lack of industrial investment and diversification has its counterpart in the over-bloated financial system and corporate capacity to transfer funds abroad whether through transfer pricing, false invoicing of trade or other methods. Secondly, capital flight of this magnitude is indicative of a singular failure of macroeconomic management if reasonably broadened in interpretative scope to include the mobilisation of domesti-cally generated surpluses for domestic investment.

Strangely, the significance of alternative perspectives on South Africa's macroeconomic performance is even borne out by the application of orthodox analysis drawn from what is for South Africa a surprisingly neglected branch of the literature. This derives from the 'resource-curse' thesis, a generalisation of insights from Dutch disease analysis in which a 'shock' boost from mineral exports leads to revaluation of the currency and de-industrialisation as manufacturing terms of trade deteriorate. The rise in gold and energy prices in the 1970s renders South Africa a suitable

---

[15] See Kahn (1991a).

[16] See Rustomjee (1991). For a more conservative estimate and a review of the literature, seeWood and Moll (1994).

case study, even if this is cloaked by the complications attached to the crisis of the apartheid regime. In the context of oil-boom economies, Auty (1993) did highlight five problems that need to be confronted by economies adjusting after the end of a resource-based boom. These are: to ensure sufficient saving to cushion adjustment in the downswing (the 1980s for South Africa); to ensure that tax rates and key prices do not lag behind inflation; to avoid over-ambitious large-scale investment projects; to promote non-mining tradeables; and to make adjustments to the downswing that are neither too little nor too late. It is arguable that on each of these criteria South African macroeconomic management failed miserably, even if it is perceived to have succeeded by the other traditional targets.

The previous discussion has presented an extremely cursory coverage of how many of a large number of issues might be addressed in the light of the systemic role that the MEC has played in the South African formation. Even so, our insights are not simply informed by a shift of empirical perspectives that have been overlooked by others. Rather, as is apparent from the way in which we have laid out research directions above, we are also concerned with the theory with which the various issues are broached. This concern arises out of both the general intellectual climate and the peculiarities of academic life in South Africa.

The intellectual climate in which South Africa's political economy is now being discussed is one dominated not so much by laissez-faire and its associated theory as by the analytical agenda set by this way of thinking. This has previously been established in covering the theory of the state (for example, in Chapter 3) and in the more general feature of addressing questions in terms of state vs market. To some extent, social science in South Africa has been insulated or cushioned from intellectual developments elsewhere, albeit in different ways from one discipline to another and incorporating the latest imported intellectual fashions from time to time. Economics has been underdeveloped even from orthodox perspectives and political economy has tended to be practised more by those originating in other disciplines. Sociology and social and economic history have been much more innovative and well-established and have experienced a degree of dominance over more orthodox approaches.

For these and other disciplines, conditions are liable to change. Orthodoxy is sweeping in both from the established Afrikaner centres of learning, as they strive for the transformed conditions of respectability as well as from outside the country, now that it can become one more case study. With many academics being incorporated into government, lack of experience in contesting orthodoxies and a long lag before new education policies yield results at the level of research, the prospects for scholarship based on the material realities of the South African economy and open theoretical enquiry appear to be bleak. Hopefully, despite these weaknesses, much can survive out of the innovative analyses that addressed the causes and consequences of apartheid, for many of those theoretical perspectives and explanatory factors remain relevant today, along with the inherited socio-economic conditions that they sought to uncover and examine, not least the relationship between race and class and its significance for the forms taken by state policy and the accumulation of capital.

Perspectives for the future

There has been an explosion of literature on economic policy for postapartheid South Africa. It has emanated from a range of organisations and individuals; it has been constructed from a variety of stances, interests and theoretical perspectives, with a corresponding mixture of analytical context and quality. It is beyond our scope to review this literature, although we have touched upon various parts of it throughout this volume. From our view, much of it has a common deficiency. Whether concerned with state vs market, export vs inward orientation, high or low levels of wages or state expenditure or getting the prices right or not, there has been a tendency to foist associated analytical predispositions upon the South African economy. In general, these have proved inappropriate because, as we have elaborated at length, the economy has been inaccurately specified in terms of its characteristics and dynamics. This is irrespective of the merits of the particular economic theories employed which have themselves often been open to doubt.

This is not, however, simply a matter of marrying an improved empirical understanding to an otherwise unchanging set of policy principles. Our characterisation of the economy goes beyond economic structure and dynamics in the narrow sense, for these are based upon the class interests to which they are attached. In other words, many policy prescriptions are ill-founded not just because of a skewed empirical understanding but also due to a corresponding, even if implicit, misunderstanding of class relations. This is so even where the attempt is made to promote particular class interests explicitly. The view that such and such a policy will be good for labour or for capital may be limited both by poor empirical foundations and by the way in which labour and its relations to capital are understood.

Before elaborating our own policy perspectives, these points will be illustrated by a brief discussion of the approach adopted by the ISP. This example is chosen partly because it is relatively well-known in South Africa and has commanded substantial research resources but it is predominantly used because it does serve by way of comparison to demonstrate the differences with our approach. We are all too acutely aware that, in practice, the individual components of ISP and individual researchers have wandered far and even severed connections from its initial analytical stance. To some extent, this has even been a consequence of its failure to match South Africa's socio-economic realities. Nonetheless, the focus here is with the theory employed, irrespective of the extent to which this has been followed in practice.[17]

Although the notion of flexible specialisation on which the ISP has been based is little more than a decade old, it has already experienced a leap forward in sophistication and scope. It has encompassed subjects as diverse as changes in technology and the organisation of production, contracting and subcontracting, the size distribution of industry, retailing, distribution, industrial districts, skills and training, retailing, automation, consumer tastes for difference, computer-aided management and design, and flexibility within labour markets as well as within production levels, composition and quality, etc. By the same token, the theoretical scope of flexible-specialisation has grown significantly and chaotically. It can be married with notions of post-Fordism and regulation theory to give rise to particular views of the relationship between economics and politics or it can form a partnership with post-modernism to give new meanings to production and, ultimately, consumption. At other times, shifting notions of flexibility and any variety of theoretical fragments can be and have been drawn together under the general umbrella of flexible-specialisation (affectionately dubbed flec- spec) or some other terminology.

Rogerson (1994) has provided a thorough review of the literature on flec-spec, including an account of its deficiencies and its potential implications for South Africa. But despite this, there is a lack of balance in his account. While noting that 'the majority of local manufacturing continues to be rooted upon Fordist principles,' he asserts that flec-spec 'represents an important new theoretical concept of significance to the agenda,' (p. 12). This is possible only because he essentially treats two arguments as being of equal status, irrespective of their actual or potential empirical weight. In other words, the world could be Fordist or it could be flec-spec or some combination of the two. Hence, each is of equal importance.

The problem with this approach is that much of the burden of the literature critical of flec-spec is to point out how limited the replacement of Fordist production has been, that flexible batch production has become more like mass production rather than displacing it, and that the virtues of flec-spec for commercial success and for the benefits of the workforce have been heavily exaggerated, depending as they do upon a limited number of success stories which are themselves heavily contested.[18] This

---

[17] Of course, analytically weaker and more compromising policy contributions might have been targeted for our illustrative purposes, but the strength of the ISP approach both analytically and in its objectives allows our own arguments to be that much stronger.

[18] See Curry (1993) for a review.

is not simply a matter of the empirical validity of appealing to one form of production or another, although the flec-spec school has tended to depend upon isolated case studies and to fail to engage with the presentation of the more extensive contrary evidence on its chosen terrain as well as where it fails to tread. Rather, an ideal type of Fordist production is constructed as mass, factory production through deskilled labour of uniform commodities for mass consumption. Partly because of its intellectual flexibility, any variation from this ideal-type is construed as conforming to flexible production. In other words, the conceptual balance is tipped in favour of viewing as flec-spec any divergence from an ideal-type of Fordist production. Consequently, to defend analytically the importance of mass production, factory techniques, tendencies to deskilling, etc. is not to be blind to the pervasive significance of new technology and organisational change. Instead, it is to reject the idea that there is only one immutable form of Fordist production and that all production must be Fordist for mass production to be in the ascendancy.

Thus flexible-specialisation holds to a view of the world in which the economic and social conditions associated with Fordism or mass production are in crisis and are possibly drawing to an ultimate close. Building on existing trends, there is in the future an alternative path of development associated with smaller-scale batch production, satisfying more specialised demand and offering more skilled and varied work. The classic statement is to be found in Piore and Sabel (1984). The approach has its policy and political counterpart in focusing upon small-scale enterprises, their co-ordination through industrial communities or districts and for capital and labour to compromise with one another to share the benefits of greater competitivity, flexibility and, consequently, profitability.

Although derived from different arguments and considerations, the flec-spec approach thus reaches similar conclusions to those put forward by cautious social democrats who seek limited state intervention and wage increases.[19] Capital and labour need to reach an accord in order to benefit mutually from the attached productivity or commercial gains.[20] ISP has adopted this stance with a particular emphasis on the importance of education and training in acknowledgement of South African conditions.

However, exactly the same reservations apply to ISP perspectives for South Africa as have been identified throughout the course of flec-spec's evolution. How far does it apply to the South African economy? Even to the extent that it does apply, what guarantees are there of progressive forms of flexibility, with the danger of low wages and low investment and productivity as the form taken by cooperation and compromise? In

[19] For a critique in the South African context, see Fine (1995), for example.
[20] For a critique of this in the context of the Greater London Council's industrial strategy, see Nolan and O'Donnell (1987).

essentially leaving aside the issue of large-scale capital, will flec-spec policies not merely support, however successfully and however much in conformity with its ideal types, the emergence of a 'rent-seeking' strata of small-scale capitalists?

The purpose of this discussion of flec-spec is less to assess its salience than to illustrate more generally how the class content of policy perspectives often occupy a secondary position even where it is explicitly addressed. The ISP does seek to address and promote the interests of labour even if in compromise with capital. But its particular pre-occupations, with their origins in flec-spec analysis rather than South African realities, imply an undue neglect of the nature and power of large-scale capital. Specifically, there is the potential error of overlooking the continuing pressure for the promotion of the MEC through mega-projects, its main agenda, even as these are veiled by simultaneously publicising the advance of small-scale enterprises.[21] By the same token, strategies based upon the capabilities of the 'Fordist' MEC tend to be precluded.[22]

However, it is not our intention to put forward alternative policy proposals. They would almost certainly prove outdated before they hit the printing press. However, our analysis does allow a policy strategy to be developed in brief, in principle and in very broad terms, from which more detail can be added.[23] Further, our starting point is taken from the material realities to be found in South Africa. The evolution of the MEC has left the economy with both strengths and weaknesses. The strengths arise out of the productive and infrastructural capacities that have been built up around its core sectors. The weaknesses arise from the failure of this to be vertically integrated forward into the rest of the economy. As explained in previous chapters, the reasons for this have shifted over time but the result has been an internationally uncompetitive consumer goods industry and limited capacity across a range of intermediate and capital goods. In addition, the scope of infrastructural provision, broadly interpreted to include the full range of what are normally public utilities as well as housing, health, education and welfare, is extremely limited as a consequence of the inheritance of apartheid.

In line with the proposals emanating from MERG (1993), we place considerable emphasis upon a state programme of public expenditure to provide social and economic infrastructure. This forms part of a strategy

---

[21] This currently continues to be the line adopted by the IDC in a remarkable reprise of its role under the apartheid system.

[22] It is presumed here, in part by extrapolation from past experience, that new mega-projects are neither commercially nor socially warranted. This cannot be proved on the information available. Lack of open public scrutiny is, however, an index of the likely weaknesses of the projects concerned.

[23] We do leave aside many major issues, such as rural development.

to provide for basic needs. The problem of how to finance such a programme is less acute than the formation of the political, social and institutional capacity to carry it out. Nor is this simply a matter of granting priority of the state over the market. For satisfactory participation in the market requires the prior provision of such infrastructure and market demand will be stimulated by the programme.

The second major component of our strategy is to intervene selectively to ensure greater coherence in the economies of scale and scope that have previously been neglected. This will inevitably raise issues of state vs market, if not only around ownership. But this should be a subsidiary issue, concerned with the most practicable way of ensuring that industrial and other strategies are indeed formulated, implemented and monitored.

We are all too aware of the deficiencies and omissions in putting forward these two policy perspectives; even in this simple form, they already rule out or cut against other proposals. First, there are other strategic issues: gender, re-incorporation of the 'homelands', the southern African region, technology, the environment, macroeconomics balance, etc. These issues need to be addressed and made prominent in any strategy and are often open to neglect. However, because our approach builds upon the strengths of the economy and the basic needs of the majority, there is less necessity for, although no guarantee against, these goals being progressively sacrificed to the logic of commercial criteria and other interests. However, although it is too early to judge its ultimate fate, the evolution in principle and practice of the Reconstruction and Development Programme (RDP 1994), has already been heavily circumscribed and even marginalised.[24]

Secondly, while our proposals could be interpreted as another set of policies, they are attuned to what we have taken to be the central issue: the restructuring and balance of class interests. The policies are designed to push forward the organisation and representation of the interests of labour against the power of financial and productive capital. This is to occur without avoiding conflict with the latter, whether this be done implicitly or not by others, by seeking compromise with large-scale capital or relying upon the cushioning effect of a middle strata of professionals and small-scale capitals. We are mindful that the system of apartheid evolved around the construction of a class of large-scale Afrikaner capitalists through compromise with English capital. The prospects for creating a black counterpart seem as bleak as they are undesirable. But unless the interests of labour are placed foremost, the most likely outcome would appear to be a limited incorporation of only a little less limited section of the black population.

[24] See, for example, Adelzadeh and Padayachee (1995) and Fine (1995).

REFERENCES

Abedian, I., and B. Standish (1985) 'Poor Whites and the Role of the State: The Evidence', *South African Journal of Economics*, vol. 53, no. 2 (June).

—— (eds) (1992) *Economic Growth in South Africa: Selected Policy Issues*, Cape Town: Oxford University Press.

Addleson, M. (1990) 'Decentralisation Incentives, Industrialists' Plans and the Location of Manufacturing Activity', *South African Journal of Economics*, vol. 58, no. 2 (June).

Adelzadeh, A., and V. Padayachee (1994) 'The RDP White Paper: Reconstruction of a Development Vision', *Transformation*, no. 25.

Adler, T. (ed.) (1977) *Perspectives on South Africa: A Collection of Working Papers*, Johannesburg: African Studies Institute, University of Witwatersrand.

Aglietta, M. (1979) *A Theory of Capitalist Regulation: The US Experience*, London: New Left Books.

Alam, M. (1989) *Governments and Markets in Economic Development Strategies: Lessons from Korea, Taiwan and Japan*, New York: Praeger.

Alcorto, L. (1990) 'Financial Groups and Monopoly Power', unpubl. chapter of D.Phil. thesis, Institute of Development Studies, University of Sussex.

Alexander, G. (1935) 'The Disabilities of the Dairy Industry in South Africa: A Criticism', *South African Journal of Economics*, vol. 3, no. 3 (Sept.).

Ally, R. (1990) 'The Bank of England and South Africa's Gold, 1886–1926', unpubl. Ph.D. thesis, University of Cambridge.

—— (1991) 'War and Gold – The Bank of England, the London Gold Market and South Africa's Gold, 1914–19', *Journal of Southern African Studies*, vol. 17, no. 2 (June).

Amsden, A. (1989) *Asia's Next Giant – South Korea and Late Industrialisation*, Oxford University Press.

Archer, S. (1981) 'The South African Industrialization Debate and the Tariff in the Inter-War Years' in *The Societies of Southern Africa in the 19th and 20th Century*, vol. 11, London: Institute of Commonwealth Studies, University of London.

—— (1987) 'South Africa's Industrial Experience in Perspective' *Social Dynamics*, vol. 13, no. 1 (June).

Auty, R. (1991) 'Creating Competitive Advantage: South Korean Steel and Petrochemicals', *Tijdschrift voor Economische en Sociale Geografie*, vol. 82, no. 1.

—— (1993) *Sustaining Development in Mineral Economies: The Resource Curse Thesis*, London: Routledge.

Bain J. (1951) 'Relation of Profit Rate to Industry Concentration in American Manufacturing 1936–40', *Quarterly Journal of Economics*, vol. LXV, no. 3 (Aug.).

Baker, P. *et al.* (eds) (1993) *South Africa and the World Economy in the 1990s*, Cape Town: David Philip.

Balasubramanyam, V., and S. Lall (eds) (1991) *Current Issues in Development Economics.*

Baldwin, R. (1992) 'Are Economists' Traditional Trade Policy Views Still Valid?', *Journal of Economic Literature*, vol. XXX, June.

Bardhan, P. (1993) 'Symposium on Democracy and Development', *Journal of Economic Perspectives*, vol. 7, no. 3 (summer).

Barrett, R., and F. Deyo (1987) 'Similarities and Differences' in Deyo (ed.) (1987a).

Beinart, W. (1994) *Twentieth Century South Africa*, Oxford University Press.

Bell, T. (1975) 'Productivity and Foreign Trade in South African Development Strategy', *South African Journal of Economics*, vol. 43, no. 4 (Dec.).

Bienefeld, M., and D. Innes (1976) 'Capital Accumulation and South Africa', *Review of African Political Economy*, no. 7 (Sept./Dec.).

Black (1991) 'Current Trends in South African Industrial Policy: Selective Intervention, Trade Orientation and Concessionary Industrial Finance', Economic Trends Working Paper (November).

—— (1992) 'Industrial Strategy: Lessons from the Newly Industrialized Countries' in Abedian and Standish (eds) (1992).

—— and J. Stanwix (1987) 'Manufacturing Development and the Economic Crisis: Restructuring in the Eighties', *Social Dynamics*, vol. 13, no. 1 (June).

Bonner, P. *et al.* (eds) (1993) *Apartheid's Genesis, 1935–1962*, Johannesburg: Ravan Press and Witwatersrand University Press.

Bozzoli, B. (1978) 'Capital and the State in South Africa', *Review of African Political Economy*, no. 11 (Jan./April).

—— (1981) *The Political Nature of a Ruling Class: Capital and Ideology in South Africa, 1890–1933*, London: Routledge and Kegan Paul.

—— and P. Delius (1990) Editors' Introduction: 'Radical History and South African Society', *Radical History Review*, vols. 46–7.

Bradford, H. (1987) *A Taste of Freedom: The ICU in Rural South Africa, 1924–1930*, New Haven: Yale University Press.

—— (1994) '"Getting Away with Murder" : "Mealie Kings", the State and Foreigners in the Eastern Transvaal, c. 1918–1950' in Bonner *et al.* (eds) (1993).

Brand, S. (1976) 'Alternative Patterns of Industrial Development in South Africa' in Truu (ed.) (1976).

Brenner, R., and M. Glick (1991) 'The Regulation School and the West's Economic Impasse', *New Left Review*, no. 188 (July/Aug.).

BTI (various years) *Annual Report*, Pretoria: Board of Trade and Industry.

—— (1945) *Investigation into the Iron, Steel, Engineering and Metallurgical Industries,* Board of Trade and Industries, Report no. 286, Cape Town: Government Printer.

—— (1988) *A Policy and Strategy for the Development and Structural Adjustment of Industry in the Republic of South Africa*, Board of Trade and Industries Report no. 2614, Pretoria: Government Printer.

Burmeister, L. (1990) 'State, Industrialisation and Agriculture Policy in Korea', *Development and Change*, vol. 21, no. 2 (April).

Business Day.

Busschau, W. (1945) 'The Expansion of Manufacturing Industry in the Union', *South African Journal of Economics*, vol. 13, no. 3 (Sept.).

Callinicos, A. (1987) *Making History: Agency, Structure and Change in Social Theory*, London: Polity Press.

Cammack, P. (1989) Review Article: 'Bringing the State Back In?', *British Journal of Political Science*, vol. 19, no. 2 (April).

Cartwright, A. (1964) *The Dynamite Company: The Story of African Explosives and Chemical Industries*, London: Macdonald.

CEAS (1992) *Sectoral Data Series – Manufacturing*, Central Economic Advisory Services (Computer Disk).

—— (1993) *The Restructuring of the South African Economy: A Normative Model Approach* (Central Economic Advisory Service), Pretoria: Government Printer.

Cell, J. (1982) *The Highest Stage of White Supremacy: The Origins of Segregation in South Africa and the American South*, Cambridge University Press.

Census on Mining (1987), Pretoria: Central Statistical Service.

Central Statistical Service (1990) *Bulletin of Statistics*, Pretoria.

Centre of African Studies (1983) *Southern African Studies – Retrospect and Prospect*, University of Edinburgh.

Chandler, A. (1990) *Scale and Scope: The Dynamics of Industrial Capitalism*, Cambridge, MA: Belknap Press.

Chang, H. (1991) 'From a "Child" to a "Giant"', mimeo, Faculty of Economics, University of Cambridge.

—— (1993) 'Was Selective Industrial Policy in East Asia Unsuccessful? – Some Comments on the World Bank's *The East Asian Miracle*', mimeo, University of Cambridge.

—— (1994) *The Political Economy of Industrial Policy*, London: Macmillan.

Cho, L., and Y. Kim (eds) (1991) *Economic Development in the Republic of Korea: A Policy Perspective*, Honolulu: East-West Center.

Choo, H. (1990) 'The Educational Basis of Korean Economic Development' in Lee and Yamazawa (eds) (1990).

Christianson, D. (1990) 'Democracy, Rationality and Advanced Technologies: The Case Against Nuclear Power in South Africa', *Politikon*, vol. 17, no. 1, June.

Christie, R. (1984) *Electricity, Industry and Class in South Africa*, Albany: SUNY.

—— (1991a) 'Antiquated Industrialisation: A Comment on William Martin's "The Making of an Industrial South Africa"', *International Journal of African Historical Studies*, vol. 24, no. 3.

—— (1991b) 'Propaganda, Reality, and Uneven Development: A Rejoinder to Bill Martin', *International Journal of African Historical Studies*, vol. 24, no. 3.

Chung, V. (1990) 'Korean Economic Growth and Financial Development' in Lee and Yamazawa (eds) (1990).

Clark, N. (1987a), 'From Dependence to Defiance: State Intervention in a Capitalist Economy: The South African State Corporations', unpubl. Ph.D. thesis, Yale University.

—— (1987b) 'South African State Corporations: The Death Knell of Economic Colonialism?', *Journal of Southern African Studies*, vol. 14, no. 1 (Oct.).

—— (1994) *Manufacturing Apartheid: State Corporations in South Africa*, New Haven: Yale University Press.

Clarke, S. (1978) 'Capital, Fractions of Capital and the State: Neo-Marxist Analyses of the South African State, *Capital and Class*, no. 5 (summer).

Coleman, F. (ed.) (1983) *Economic History of South Africa*, Pretoria: HAUM.

Competition Board, *Annual Report 1980–1990*, Pretoria: Government Printer.

——, *Published Investigations Nos 1–24, 1980–1990*, Pretoria: Government Printer.

Crush, J. *et al.* (1991) *South Africa's Labor Empire: A History of Black Migrancy to the Gold Mines*, Cape Town: David Philip.

Cumings, B. (1981) *The Origins of the Korean War*, vol. I: *Liberation and the Emergence of Separate Regimes, 1945–1947*, Princeton University Press.

—— (1990) *The Origins of the Korean War*, vol. II: *The Roaring of the Cataract*, Princeton University Press.

Curry, J. (1993) 'The Flexibility Fetish', *Capital and Class*, no. 50 (summer).

Davies, R. *et al.* (1976) 'Class Struggle and the Periodisation of the State in South Africa', *Review of African Political Economy*, no. 7 (Sept./Dec.).

Davies R. (1979) *Capital, State and White Labour in South Africa, 1900–1960: An Historical Materialist Analysis of Class Formation and Class Relations*, Brighton: Harvester.

De Kock, W. (1951) 'The Influence of the Free State Gold Fields on the Union's Economy', *South African Journal of Economics*, vol. 19, no. 2 (June).

Dewar, D. *et al.* (1986) 'Industrial Decentralization Policy in South Africa: Rhetoric and Practice', *Urban Studies*, vol. 23, no. 5 (Oct.).

Deyo, F. (ed.) (1987a) *The Political Economy of the New Asian Industrialism*, Ithaca, NY: Cornell University Press.

—— (1987b) 'State and Labor: Modes of Political Exclusion in East Asian Development' in Deyo (ed.) (1987a).

Dickman, A. (1973) 'The Financing of Industrial Development in South Africa', *South African Journal of Economics*, vol. 41, no. 4 (Dec.).

—— (1991) 'Costs of Industrial Decentralization in South Africa', *South African Journal of Economics*, vol. 59, no. 2 (June).

DMEA (various years) *Annual Report*, Pretoria: Department of Mineral and Energy Affairs.

Dollery, B.E. (1983) 'Some Evidence of the Goals of Firms in South African Manufacturing Industry', *Studies in Economics and Econometrics*, University of Stellenbosch, Bureau for Economic Research, no. 3.

Dornbusch, R. (1992) 'The Case for Trade Liberalisation in Developing Countries', *Journal of Economic Perspectives*, vol. 6, no. 1, winter.

Du Plessis, P.G. (1977) 'Concentration of Economic Power in the South African Manufacturing Industry', unpubl. Ph.D. thesis, University of Stellenbosch.

—— (1978) 'Concentration and Economic Power in South African Manufacturing', *Studies in Economics and Econometrics*, University of Stellenbosch, Bureau for Economic Research, no. 3.

—— (1979) 'An International Comparison of Economic Concentration', *South African Journal of Economics*, vol. 4, no. 3 (Sept.).

Dubow, S. (1989) *Racial Segregation and the Origins of Apartheid in South Africa, 1919–36*, London: Macmillan.

Eckert, C. (1991) *Offspring of Empire: The Koch'ang Kims and the Colonial*

Origins of Korean Capitalism, 1876–1945, Seattle: University of Washington Press.

Edwards, A. (1991) 'South Africa's Gold Industry: A Blessing or a Curse?', Johannesburg: Council for Mineral Technology (MINTEK).

Ehrensaft, P. (1985) 'Phases in the Development of South African Capitalism: From Settlement to Crises' in Gutkind and Wallerstein (eds) (1985).

Enos, J., and W. Park (1988) *The Adoption and Diffusion of Imported Technology: The Case of Korea*, London: Croom Helm.

Escom (1990) *Statistical Review 1989*, Johannesburg: Escom.

Evans, H. (1990) 'Outward Orientation: An Assessment' in Milner (ed.) (1990).

Evans, P. *et al.* (eds) (1985) *Bringing the State Back In*, Cambridge University Press.

—— (1992) 'The State as Problem and Solution: Predation, Embedded Autonomy, and Structural Change' in Haggard and Kaufman (eds) (1992).

Fallon, P. *et al.* (1993) *South Africa: Economic Performance and Some Policy Implications*, Washington, DC: World Bank, Southern African Department.

Fine, B. (1982) *Theories of the Capitalist Economy*, London: Edward Arnold.

—— (1987) 'Segmented Labour Market Theory: A Critical Assessment', Birkbeck Discussion Paper in Economics no. 87/12, reproduced in shortened form as *Thames Papers in Political Economy*, spring 1990.

—— (1990a) *The Coal Question: Political Economy and Industrial Change from the Nineteenth Century to the Present Day*, London: Routledge.

—— (1990b) 'Scaling the Commanding Heights of Public Sector Economics', *Cambridge Journal of Economics*, vol. 14, no. 2 (June).

—— (1992a) 'Linkage, Agency and the State: The Case of South Korea', SOAS Economics Working Paper, no. 2.

—— (1992b) *Women's Employment and the Capitalist Family*, London: Routledge.

—— (1993a) 'Economic Development and Technological Change: From Linkage to Agency' in Liodakis (ed.) (1993).

—— (1993b) 'The Military-Industrial Complex: An Analytical Assessment', *Cyprus Journal of Economics*, vol 6, no. 1 (June).

—— (1994) 'Coal, Diamonds and Oil: Towards a Comparative Theory of Mining', *Review of Political Economy*, vol. 6, no. 3 (July).

—— (1995) '"Politics and Economics in ANC Economic Policy": An Alternative Assessment', *Transformation*, no. 25.

—— and L. Harris (1985) *The Peculiarities of the British Economy*, London: Lawrence and Wishart.

—— (1987) 'Ideology and Markets: Economic Theory and the "New Right" ' in R. Miliband *et al.* (eds), *Socialist Register*, London: Merlin Press.

—— and C. Poletti (1992) 'Industrial Policy in the Light of Privatisation' in Michie (ed.) (1992).

Fourie, F. (1987) 'Issues and Problems in South African Competition Policy', *South African Journal of Economics*, vol. 55, no. 4 (Dec.).

Fourie, F., and M.Smit (1989) 'Trends in Economic Concentration in South Africa', *South African Journal of Economics*, vol. 57, no. 3 (Sept.).

Frankel, S. (1938) *Capital Investment in South Africa: Its Course and Effects*, Oxford University Press.

Fransman, M., and R. Davies (1977) 'The South African Social Formation in the

Early Capitalist Period Circa 1870–1939: Some Views on the Question of Hegemony' in Adler (ed.) (1977).

Freund, B. (1989) 'The Social Character of Secondary Industry in South Africa: 1915–1945' in Mabin (ed.) (1989).

Fridjon, M. *c ·l.* (1986) *Conspiracy of Giants: The South African Liquor Industry*, Cape Town: Divaris Stein.

Frost, D. (1990) 'Mechanisation in the South African Gold Mining Industry', *Labour Research Services*, Report, Cape Town (Sept.).

Gelb, S. (1987) 'Making Sense of the Crisis', *Transformation*, no. 5.

—— (1989) 'The Origins of the South African Reserve Bank, 1914–1920' in Mabin (ed.) (1989).

—— (ed.) (1991) *South Africa's Economic Crisis*, London: Zed Press.

Gerber, L. (1973) *Friends and Influence: The Diplomacy of Private Enterprise*, Cape Town: Purnell.

Geyer, H. (1989a) 'Apartheid in South Africa and Industrial Deconcentration in the PWV Area', *Planning Perspectives*, vol. 4, no. 3 (Sept.).

—— (1989b) 'Industrial Development Policy in South Africa – The Past, Present and Future', *World Development*, vol. 17, no. 3 (March).

Gool, S. (1983) *Mining Capitalism and Black Labour in the Early Industrial Period in South Africa: A Critique of the New Historiography*, Lund, Sweden: Studentlitteratur.

Greenaway, D. (1991) 'New Trade Theories and Developing Countries' in Balasubramanyam and Lall (eds) (1991).

Gregory, T. (1962) *Ernest Oppenheimer and the Economic Development of Southern Africa*, Cape Town: Oxford University Press.

Gutkind, P., and I. Wallerstein (eds) (1985) *Political Economy of Contemporary Africa*, Beverly Hills: Sage.

Hagart, R. (1967) 'The Formative Years: A Recollection', *Optima*, vol. 17, no. 3 (Sept.).

Haggard, S., and T. Cheng (1987) 'State and Foreign Capital in the East Asian NICs' in Deyo (ed.) (1987a).

Haggard, S., and R. Kaufman (eds) (1992) *The Politics of Economic Adjustment*, Princeton University Press.

Haggard, S., and S. Webb (1993) 'What Do We Know about the Political Economy of Economic Policy Reform?', *World Bank Research Observer*, vol. 8, no. 2 (July).

Hamilton, C. (1986) *Capitalist Industrialisation in Korea*, Boulder, CO: Westview Press.

Hara, Y. (1990) 'Agricultural Development and Policy in Modern Japan' in Lee and Yamazawa (eds) (1990).

Hindess, B. (1987) *Politics and Class Analysis*, Oxford: Blackwell.

Hindson, D. (1987) *Pass Controls and the Urban African Proletariat*, Johannesburg: Ravan Press.

Hirschmann, A. (1977) 'A Generalized Linkage Approach to Development with Special Reference to Staples' in Nash (ed.) (1977).

Hocking, A. (1987) *Paper Chain: The Story of Sappi*, Bethulie: Hollard.

Hofmeyr, J. (1994) *An Analysis of African Wage Movements in South Africa*, Research Monograph no. 9, Economic Unit, University of Natal.

Holden, M. (1990) 'Costs of Decentralisation: A Theoretical and Empirical Analysis', *South African Journal of Economics*, vol. 58, no. 2 (June).

Holloway, J., and S. Picciotto (eds) (1978) *State and Capital: A Marxist Debate*, London: Edward Arnold.

Hong, W., and L. Krause (eds) (1981) *Trade and Growth of the Advanced Developing Countries in the Pacific Basin*, Seoul: Korea Development Institute.

Horwitz, R. (1967) *The Political Economy of South Africa*, London: Weidenfeld and Nicolson.

Houghton, D. (1973) *The South African Economy*, Cape Town: Oxford University Press.

—— and J. Dagut (1972) *Source Material on the South African Economy: 1860–1970*, Cape Town: Oxford University Press.

IDC (1990) *Modification of the Application of Protection Policy: Policy Document*, Industrial Development Corporation, Sandton.

—— (1992) *Sectoral Data Series – Manufacturing*, Department of Economic Research and Development, Pretoria: IDC.

—— *Annual Report*, (various years), Industrial Development Corporation, Sandton.

Innes, D. (1983) 'Monopoly Capitalism in South Africa', *South African Review*, no. 1.

—— (1984) *Anglo American and the Rise of Modern South Africa*, London: Heinemann.

—— and M. Plaut (1978) 'Class Struggle and the State', *Review of African Political Economy*, no. 11 (Jan./April).

Input-Output Tables (various years), Pretoria: Central Statistical Service.

ISP (1993) 'Meeting the Global Challenge: A Framework for Industrial Revival in South Africa' in Baker *et al.* (eds) (1993).

Jenkins, R. (1991) 'The Political Economy of Industrialization: A Comparison of Latin American and East Asian Newly Industrializing Countries', *Development and Change*, vol. 22, no. 2 (April).

Jessop, B. (1985) *Nicos Poulantzas: Marxist Theory and Political Strategy*, London: Macmillan.

—— (1990) *State Theory*, London: Polity Press.

Jewslewicki, B., and D. Newbury (eds) (1986) *African Historiographies: What History for Which Africa?*, Beverly Hills: Sage.

Joffe, A. (1987) 'The State and Capital Accumulation in South Africa: An Assessment of the Kleu Report', unpubl. M.Phil. paper, Institute of Development Studies, University of Sussex.

Johnson, C. (1987) 'Political Institutions and Economic Performance: The Government-Business Relationship in Japan, South Korea, and Taiwan' in Deyo (ed.) (1987a).

Johnstone, F. (1976) *Class, Race and Gold: A Study of Class Relations and Racial Discrimination in South Africa*, London: Routledge and Kegan Paul.

Jones, L., and I. Sakong (1980) *Government, Business and Entrepreneurship in Economic Development: The Korean Case*, Cambridge, MA: Harvard University Press.

Jones, S. (ed.) (1992) *Financial Enterprises in South Africa since 1950*, London: Macmillan.

—— (1992) 'Union Acceptance: The First Merchant Bank, 1955–73' in Jones (ed.) (1992).

—— and A. Muller (1992) *The South African Economy, 1910–90*, London: Macmillan.

Jourdan, P. (1990) 'Strategies for the Regional Planning of the Minerals Industry in Southern Africa', unpubl. Ph.D. thesis, University of Leeds.

Kahn, B. (1987) 'Import Penetration and Import Demands in the South African Economy', *South African Journal of Economics*, vol. 55, no. 3 (Sept.).

—— (1991a) 'The Crisis and South Africa's Balance of Payments', in Gelb (ed.) (1991).

—— (1991b) 'Sectoral Impact of Exchange Rate Policy in South Africa', ET Working Paper (Nov.).

Kaplan, D. (1974) 'The Politics of Industrial Protection in South Africa, 1910–1939', *Journal of Southern Africa Studies*, vol. 1, no. 1 (Oct.).

—— (1977) 'Class Conflict, Capital Accumulation and the State: An Historical Analysis of the State in Twentieth Century South Africa', unpubl. Ph.D. thesis, University of Sussex.

—— (1979) 'Relations of Production, Class Struggle and the State in South Africa in the Inter-War Period', *Review of African Political Economy*, no. 15/6.

—— (1987) 'Machinery and Industry: The Causes and Consequences of Constrained Development of the South African Machine Tool Industry', *Social Dynamics*, vol. 13, no. 1.

—— (1990) *The Crossed Line: The South African Telecommunications Industry in Transition*, Johannesburg: Witwatersrand University Press.

Kaplan, M. (1986) *Jewish Roots in the South African Economy*, Cape Town: Struik.

Kaplinsky, R. (1992) 'South African Industrial Performance and Structure in a Comparative Context', revised paper presented to the Industrial Strategy Project meeting, 6–10 July, Johannesburg.

Karshenas, M. (1995) *Industrialisation and Agricultural Surplus: A Comparative Study of Economic Development in Asia*, Oxford University Press.

Kawakami, T. (1992) 'Markets and Government: The Korean Case', *Journal of International Economic Studies*, no. 6 (March).

Kay, C. (1991) 'Reflections on the Latin American Contribution to Development Theory', *Development and Change*, vol. 22, no. 1 (Jan.).

Keys, D. (1993) *The Key Issues in the Normative Economic Model*, Pretoria: South African Reserve Bank.

King, W. (1962) 'South Africa's Growing Money Market', *Optima*, vol. 12, no. 3 (Sept.).

Kleu Report (1982) *Report of the Study Group on Industrial Development Strategy*, Pretoria: Government Printer.

Kleu, S. (1973) 'Industrial Policy', in Lombard (ed.) (1973).

Kohama, H. (1990) 'Japan's Economic Development' in Lee and Yamazawa (eds) (1990).

Kohli, A. (1994) 'Where Do High Growth Political Economies Come From?: The

Japanese Lineage of Korea's "Development State"', *World Development*, vol. 22, no. 9 (Sept.).

Koncacki, Z. *et al.* (eds) (1991) *Studies in the Economic History of Southern Africa,* vol II: *South Africa, Lesotho and Swaziland,* London: Cass.

Kraak, G. (1993) *Breaking Chains: Labour in South Africa in the 1970s and 1980s,* London: Pluto Press.

Krikler, J. (1993) *Revolution from Above: Rebellion from Below: The Agrarian Transvaal at the Turn of the Century,* Oxford: Clarendon Press.

Krueger, A. (1981) 'Export-Led Growth Reconsidered', in Hong and Krause (eds) (1981).

—— (1984) 'Comparative Advantage and Development Policy 20 Years Later' in Syrquin *et al.* (eds) (1984).

Krugman, P. (1983) 'Free Trade: A Loss of Theoretical Nerve', *American Economic Review,* vol. 83, no. 2 (May).

—— (1994) 'Introduction' in Krugman and Smith (eds) (1994).

—— and A. Smith (eds) (1994) *Empirical Studies of Strategic Trade Policy,* Chicago University Press.

Kubicek, V. (1991) 'Mining: Patterns of Dependence and Development, 1870–1930' in Koncacki *et al.* (eds) (1991).

Lacey, M. (1981) *Working for Boroko: The Origins of a Coercive Labour System in South Africa,* Johannesburg: Ravan Press.

Lachman, D. (1974) 'Import Restrictions and Exchange Rates', *South African Journal of Economics,* vol. 42, no. 1 (March).

Laight, J. (1955) 'Some Thoughts on the Protection of the South African Manufacturing Industry', *South African Journal of Economics,* vol. 23, no. 3 (Sept.).

Lall S. (1991) 'Explaining Industrial Success in the Developing World' in Balasubramanyam and Lall (eds) (1991).

—— (1993a) 'What will make South Africa Internationally Competitive?', Aspen/IDASA Conference on South Africa's International Economic Relations in the 1990s.

—— (1993b) 'Introduction: Transnational Corporations and Economic Development' in Lall (ed.) (1993).

—— (ed.) (1993c) *Transnational Corporations and Economic Development,* London: Routledge.

Lazar, J. (1987) 'Conformity and Conflict: Afrikaner Nationalist Politics in South Africa, 1948–1961', unpubl. Ph.D. thesis, University of Oxford.

Leach, D. (1992) 'Absolute vs. Relative Concentration in Manufacturing Industry, 1972–1985', *South African Journal of Economics,* vol. 60, no. 4 (Dec.).

Lee, C. (1990) 'The Role of the Trade in Korea's Economic Development' in Lee and Yamazawa (eds) (1990).

—— and I. Yamazawa (eds) (1990) *The Economic Development of Japan and Korea,* New York: Praeger.

Lee, E. (1979) 'Egalitarian Peasant Farming and Rural Development: The Case of South Korea', *World Development,* vol. 7, nos 4/5.

Lee, Y. (1992) 'The Expansion and Restructuring of the Steel Industry: The Case of POSCO and BSC', unpubl. Ph.D. thesis, University of London.

Levy, B. (1981) 'Industrialisation and Inequality in South Africa', Working Paper no. 36, Southern Africa Labour and Development Research Unity, University of Cape Town.

—— (1992) 'How Can South African Manufacturing Efficiently Create Employment? An Analysis of the Impact of Trade and Industrial Policy', Southern Africa Department, World Bank (January).

Lewis, D. (1993) 'Markets, Ownership and Industrial Competitiveness', mimeo, Industrial Strategy Project, Cape Town (June).

Lewis, S. (1990) *The Economics of Apartheid*, New York: Council on Foreign Relations Press.

Liodakis, G. (ed.) (1993) *Society, Technology and Restructuring of Production*, Athens: V. Papazissis.

Lipton, M. (1986) *Capitalism and Apartheid: South Africa, 1910–1986*, Aldershot: Wildwood House.

—— and C. Simkins (eds) (1993) *State and Market in Post-Apartheid South Africa*, Johannesburg: Witwatersrand University Press.

Little, I., T. Scitovsky and M. Scott (1970) *Industry and Trade in Some Developing Countries*, Oxford University Press.

Lombard, J. (ed.) (1973) *Economic Policy in South Africa: Selected Essays*, Cape Town: HAUM.

Luedde-Neurath, R. (1985) 'State Intervention and Export-Oriented Development in South Korea' in White and Wade (eds) (1985).

—— (1986) *Import Controls and Export-Oriented Development: A Reassessment of the South Korean Case*, Boulder, CO: Westview Press.

Lumby A. (1976) 'Tariffs and Gold in South Africa, 1866–1939', *South African Journal of Economics*, vol. 44, no. 2 (June).

—— (1977) 'Tariffs and the Printing Industry in South Africa, 1906–1939', *South African Journal of Economics*, vol. 45, no. 2 (June).

Lumby A. (1983) 'The Development of Secondary Industry: The Second World War and After' in Coleman (ed.) (1983).

Lundahl, M. (1992) *Apartheid in Theory and Practice: An Economic Analysis*, Boulder, CO: Westview Press.

Maasdorp, G. (1990) 'Introductory Survey', *South African J. of Economics*, vol. 58, no. 2 (June).

Mabin, A. (1986) 'At the Cutting Edge: The New African History and its Implications for African Historical Geography', *Journal of Historical Geography*, vol. 12, no. 1 (Jan.).

Mabin, A. (ed.) (1989) *Organisation and Economic Change*, Southern African Studies, vol. 5, Johannesburg: Ravan Press.

MacDonald, M., and W. James (1993) 'The Hand on the Tiller: The Politics of State and Class in South Africa', *Journal of Modern African Studies*, vol. 31, no. 3 (Sept.).

Main, H. (1975) 'The Reynders Commission and the Mining Industry', *South African Journal of Economics*, vol. 43, no. 1 (March).

Marais, G. (1960) 'Tariff Protection, Industrialisation and the Balance of Payments, with Special Reference to the Union of South Africa', *South African Journal of Economics*, vol. 28, no. 1 (March).

Marks, S. (1986) 'The Historiography of South Africa: Recent Developments' in Jewslewicki and Newbury (eds) (1986).

—— and R. Rathbone (eds) (1982) *Industrialisation and Social Change in South Africa: African Class Formation, Culture and Consciousness, 1870–1930*, New York: Longman.

—— and S. Trapido (1979) 'Lord Milner and the South African State', *History Workshop Journal*, no. 8 (autumn).

Martin, W. (1990a) 'The Making of an Industrial South Africa: Trade and Tariffs in the Interwar Period', *International Journal of African Historical Studies*, vol. 23, no. 2.

—— (1990b) 'Region Formation under Crisis Conditions: South vs Southern Africa in the Interwar Period', *Journal of Southern African Studies*, vol. 16, no. 1.

—— (1991) 'Developmentalism: The Pernicious Illusion, A Response to Renfrew Christie's "Antiquated Industrialisation" ', *International Journal of African Historical Studies*, vol. 24, no. 3.

Mason, E. *et al.* (1980) *The Economic and Social Modernization of the Republic of Korea*, Cambridge, MA: Harvard University Press.

Mavroudeas, S. (1990) 'Regulation Approach: A Critical Appraisal', unpubl. Ph.D. thesis, University of London.

McCarthy, C. (1988) 'Structural Development of South African Manufacturing Industry', *South African Journal of Economics*, vol. 56, no. 1 (March).

McGregor, R. (ed.) (1987) *Privatisation in South Africa*, Cape Town: Juta.

—— (1990) *Who Owns Whom: The Investors' Handbook*, 10th edn, Johannesburg: Juta.

Mendelsohn, R. (1991) *Sammy Marks: ' The Uncrowned King of the Transvaal '*, Cape Town: David Philip.

MERG (Macroeconomic Research Group) (1993) *Making Democracy Work: A Framework for Macroeconomic Policy in South Africa*, Cape Town: Centre for Development Studies.

Meth, C. (1990) 'Capital Goods, "Dependence" and Appropriate Technology' in Nattrass and Ardington (eds) (1990).

Michie, J. (ed.) (1992) *The Economic Legacy, 1979–1992*, London: Academic Press.

Milner, C (ed.) (1990) *Export Promotion Strategies: Theory and Evidence from Developing Countries*, New York: Harvester/Wheatsheaf.

Minerals Bureau (1988) *Minerals Bureau Report B6/88 – Commodity Export Price Indices (CEPI)*, Pretoria: Department of Mineral and Energy Affairs.

—— (1991) *Minerals Bureau Bulletin vol. 4*, Pretoria: Department of Mineral and Energy Affairs.

Moll, T. (1990) 'Output and Productivity Trends in South Africa: Apartheid and Economic Growth', unpubl. Ph. D. thesis, University of Cambridge.

—— (1991) 'Did the Apartheid Economy "Fail"', *Journal of Southern African Studies*, vol. 17, no. 2 (June).

—— (1992) 'Macroeconomic Policy in South Africa: Apartheid and After', SOAS Working Paper no. 11 (March).

—— (1993) 'Macroeconomic Policy in Turbulent Times: Apartheid and After' in Lipton and Simkins (eds) (1993).

Moore, M. (1985) 'Economic Growth and the Rise of Civil Society: Agriculture in Taiwan and South Korea' in White and Wade (eds) (1985).

Morrell, R. (1988) 'The Disintegration of the Gold and Maize Alliance in South Africa in the 1920s', *International Journal of African Historical Studies*, vol. 21, no. 4.

Morris, M. (1979) 'The State and the Development of Capitalist Social Relations in the South African Countryside: A Process of Class Struggle', unpubl. Ph.D. thesis, University of Sussex.

—— (1987) 'Social History and the Transition to Capitalism in the South African Countryside', *Africa Perspective*, vol. 1, no. 5/6 (Dec.).

Murray, M. (ed.) (1982) *South African Capitalism and Black Political Opposition*, Cambridge: Schenkman.

—— (1988) 'The Triumph of Marxist Approaches in South African Social and Labour History', *Journal of Asian and African Studies*, vol. 22, nos. 1/2 (Jan./March).

Nam, C. (1990) 'Export Promotion Strategy and Economic Development in Korea', in Milner (ed.) (1990).

Nash, M. (ed.) (1977) *Essays on Economic Development and Cultural Change in Honour of Bert F. Hoselitz, Economic Development and Cultural Change*, supplement to vol. 25.

Nattrass, J. (1988) *The South African Economy: Its Growth and Change*, Cape Town: Oxford University Press.

Nattrass, N. (1989a) 'Apartheid and Profit Rates: Challenging the Radical Orthodoxy', *Indicator SA*, vol. 7, no. 1 (summer).

—— (1989b) 'Post-War Profitability in South Africa: A Critique of Regulation Analysis in South Africa', *Transformation*, no. 9.

—— (1992) *Profits and Wages: The South African Economic Challenge*, London: Penguin.

—— (1994a) 'Constrained Choices and Creative Challenges: Strategic Unions and Social Democracy in South Africa', paper presented at the Journal of Southern African Studies Conference, York University.

—— (1994b) 'Economic Restructuring in South Africa: The Debate Continues', *Journal of Southern African Studies*, with responses from J. Sender and R. Kaplinsky, vol. 20, no. 4 (Dec.).

—— (1994c) 'Politics and Economics in ANC Economic Policy', *African Affairs*, vol. 93, no. 371 (July).

—— (1994d) 'South Africa: The Economic Restructuring Agenda – A Critique of the MERG Report', *Third World Quarterly*, vol. 15, no. 2.

—— and E. Ardington (eds) (1990) *The Political Economy of South Africa*, Cape Town: Oxford University Press.

Newbury, C. (1989) *The Diamond Ring: Business, Politics, and Precious Stones in South Africa, 1867–1947*, Oxford: Clarendon Press.

Nolan, P., and K. O'Donnell (1987) 'Taming the Market Economy? An Assessment of the GLC's Experiment in Restructuring for Labour', *Cambridge Journal of Economics*, vol. 11, no. 3 (Sept.).

Norval, A. (1962) *A Quarter of a Century of Industrial Progress in South Africa*, Cape Town: Juta.

Ocampo, J. (1986) 'New Developments in Trade Theory and LDCs', *Journal of Development Economics*, vol. 22.

O'Meara, D. (1983) *Volkskapitalisme: Class, Capital and Ideology in the*

Development of Afrikaner Nationalism, 1934–1948, Cambridge University Press.

Ogle, G. (1990) *South Korea: Dissent within the Economic Miracle*, London: Zed Books.

Ovendon, K., and T. Cole (1989) *Apartheid and International Finance: A Program for Change*, Harmondsworth: Penguin.

Pack, H., and L. Westphal (1986) 'Industrial Strategy and Technological Change: Theory versus Reality', *Journal of Development Economics*, vol. 22, no. 1.

Palmer, G. (1958) 'The Development of a South African Money Market', *South African Journal of Economics*, vol. 26, no. 4 (Dec.).

Pearsall, C. (1937) 'Some Aspects of the Development of Secondary Industry in the Union of South Africa', *South African Journal of Economics*, vol. 5, no. 4 (Dec.).

Phillips, E. (1974), 'State Regulation and Economic Initiative: The South African Case to 1960', *International Journal of African Historical Studies*, vol. 7, no. 2.

Phimister, I. (1991) 'Secondary Industrialisation in Southern Africa: The 1948 Customs Agreement Between Southern Rhodesia and South Africa', *Journal of Southern African Studies*, vol. 17, no. 3 (Sept.).

—— (1993) 'Unscrambling the Scramble for Southern Africa: The Jameson Raid and the South African War Revisited', *South African Historical Journal*, no. 28 (March).

Piore, M., and C. Sabel (1984) *The Second Industrial Divide: Possibilities for Prosperity*, New York: Basic Books.

Posel, D. (1983) 'Rethinking the "Race-Class Debate" in Southern African Historiography', in Centre of African Studies (1983), *Social Dynamics*, vol. 9, no. 1 (June).

—— (1991) *The Making of Apartheid, 1948–1961: Conflict and Compromise*, Oxford: Clarendon Press.

Przeworski, A., and F. Limongi (1993) 'Political Regimes and Economic Growth', *Journal of Economic Perspectives*, vol. 7, no. 3 (summer).

Ratcliffe, A. (1975) 'Export Policy in Perspective', *South African Journal of Economics*, vol. 43, no. 1 (March).

RDP (1994) *The Reconstruction and Development Programme: A Policy Framework*, Johannesburg: Umanyano Publications.

Report of the Committee of Inquiry into the Textile and Clothing Industries (1983) *The Policy of Protection in Regard to Textiles and Clothing* (Steenkamp), Pretoria: Government Printer.

Reynders Commission Report (1972) *Report of the Commission of Enquiry into the Export Trade of the Republic of South Africa*, RP 69/72, Pretoria: Government Printer.

Reynders, H. (1975) 'Export Status and Strategy', *South African Journal of Economics*, vol. 43, no. 1 (March).

—— and J. van Zyl (1973) 'Foreign Trade Policy' in Lombard (ed.) (1973).

Richards, C. (1935) 'Subsidies, Quotas, Tariffs and the Excess Cost of Agriculture in South Africa', *South African Journal of Economics*, vol. 3, no. 3 (Sept.).

—— (1940) *The Iron and Steel Industry in South Africa*, Johannesburg: Witwatersrand University Press.

268 *The Political Economy of South Africa*

Rodrik, D. (1992) 'The Limits of Trade Policy Reform in Developing Countries', *Journal of Economic Perspectives*, vol 6, no. 1, winter.

Rogerson, C. (1982) 'Apartheid, Decentralization and Spatial Industrial Change' in Smit (ed.) (1982).

—— (1987) 'Decentralisation and the Location of Third World Multinationals in South Africa' in Tomlinson and Addleson (eds) (1987).

—— (1988) 'Regional Development Policy in South Africa', *Regional Development Dialogue*, special issue.

—— (1994) 'Flexible Production in the Developing World: The Case of South Africa', *Geoforum*, vol. 25, no. 1 (Feb.).

Rosenthal, E. (1960) *Industrial Development Corporation of South Africa Limited, 1940–1960: The Story of the First Twenty Years*, Johannesburg: International Development Corporation.

Roux, A., *et al.* (1991) 'Financing Economic Development in South Africa', mimeo.

Rustomjee, Z. (1990) 'Regulating South Africa's Corporate Oligopoly', unpubl. M.Phil. thesis, Institute of Development Studies, University of Sussex.

—— (1991) 'Capital Flight from South Africa, 1970–1988', *Transformation*, no. 15.

—— (1993) *The Engineering Sector in South Africa*, report prepared for the Cosatu/Economic Trends Industrial Strategy Project, March.

Sacob (1990) *A Concept for the Development of a New Industrial Policy for South Africa*, Johannesburg: South African Chamber of Business.

Samuels, L. (1959) 'Some Aspects of Industrial Development in South Africa', *South African Journal of Economics*, vol. 27, no. 3 (Sept.).

Scheepers, C. (1982) 'The International Trade Strategy of South Africa', *South African Journal of Economics*, vol. 50, no. 1 (March).

Schirmer, S. (1994) 'The Struggle for Land in Lydenburg: African Resistance in a White Farming District, 1930–1970', unpubl. Ph.D. thesis, University of the Witwatersrand.

Sender, J. and S. Smith (1986) *The Development of Capitalism in Africa*, London: Methuen.

Shin, J. (1992) 'Catching-Up and Technological Progress in Late-Industrialising Countries', M.Phil. thesis, University of Cambridge.

Singh, A. (1977) 'UK Industry and the World Economy: A Case of De-Industrialisation', *Cambridge Journal of Economics*, vol. 1, no. 2 (June).

Smit, D. (ed.) (1982) *Living Under Apartheid: Aspects of Urbanisation and Social Change in South Africa*, London: George Allen and Unwin.

Smith, R. (1945) 'The Size of the South African Industrial Unit', *South African Journal of Economics*, vol. 13, no. 4 (Dec.).

South African Labour Statistics (1990) Central Statistical Services, Pretoria.

South African Statistics (1990) Pretoria: Central Statistical Services.

South Africa's Mineral Industry Yearbook (SAMI), various years, *Minerals Bureau*, Braamfontein: Department of Mineral and Energy Affairs.

Steinberg, D. (1988) 'Sociopolitical Factors and Korea's Future Economic Policies', *World Development*, vol. 16, no. 1 (Jan.).

Stewart, F., and E. Ghani (1991) 'How Significant Are Externalities for Development', *World Development*, vol. 19, no. 6 (June).

Streeten, P. (1993) 'Markets and States: Against Minimalism', *World Development*, vol. 21, no. 8 (Aug.).

Suarez-Villa, L., and P. Han (1990) 'The Rise of Korea's Electronics Industry: Technological Change, Growth, and Territorial Distribution', *Economic Geography*, vol. 66, no. 3 (July).

Syrquin, M., *et al.* (eds) (1984) *Economic Structure and Performance*, New York: Academic Press.

Tajika, E., and Y. Yui (1990) 'Japan's Public Policies for Investment' in Lee and Yamazawa (eds) (1990).

Tomlinson, R. (1990) *Urbanization in Post-Apartheid South Africa*, London: Unwin Hyman.

—— and M. Addleson (eds) (1987) *Regional Restructuring under Apartheid: Urban and Regional Policies in Contemporary South Africa*, Johannesburg: Ravan Press.

Trade Monitor (1993) Trade Policy Monitoring Project, University of Cape Town, no. 3, August.

Trapido, S. (1971) 'South Africa in a Comparative Study of Industrialisation', *Journal of Development Studies*, vol. 7, no. 3 (April).

Tregenna-Piggott, J. (1976) 'Concentration and South African Industry', Occasional Paper no. 5, Economic Research Unit, Department of Economics, University of Natal.

—— (1979) 'Economies of Scale in South African Manufacturing Industry', *Studies Economics and Econometrics*, no. 6, University of Stellenbosch, Bureau for Economic Research.

—— (1980) 'An Assessment of Competition Policy in South Africa', Occasional Paper no. 8, Economic Research Unit, Department of Economics, University of Natal.

Truu, M. (ed.) (1976) *Public Policy and the South African Economy*, Cape Town: Oxford University Press.

Turrell, R. (1987) *Capital and Labour on the Kimberley Diamond Fields, 1871–1890*, Cambridge University Press.

UNIDO (1992) *Industry and Development: Global Report, 1992/93*, Vienna: UNIDO.

Union Statistics for Fifty Years (1960) *Union Statistics for Fifty Years: Jubilee Issue, 1910–1960*, Pretoria: Bureau of Census and Statistics.

Van der Merwe, W. (1992) 'IDC Megaprojects are an Essential Ingredient of Growth', *Business Day*, (26 Aug.).

Van Liemt, G. (1988) *Bridging the Gap: Four Newly Industrialising Countries and the Changing Industrial Division of Labour*, Geneva: International Labour Office.

Verhoef, G. (1992) 'Afrikaner Nationalism in South African Banking: The Cases of Volkskas and Trust Bank' in Jones (ed.) (1992).

Viljoen Commission Report (1958) *Report of the Commission of Enquiry into Policy Relating to the Protection of Industry*, UG36/58, Pretoria: Government Printer.

Viljoen, S. (1983) 'The Industrial Achievement of South Africa', *South African Journal of Economics*, vol. 51, no. 1 (Jan.).

Wade, R. (1985) 'State Intervention in Outward-looking Development: Neoclassical Theory and Taiwanese Practice' in White and Wade (eds) (1985).

—— (1990) *Governing the Market: Economic Theory and the Role of Government in East Asian Industrialisation*, Princeton University Press.

Webster, E. (1985) *Cast in a Racial Mould: Labour Process and Trade Unionism in the Foundries,* Johannesburg: Ravan Press.

Wellings, P., and A. Black (1986) 'Industrial Decentralization under Apartheid: The Relocation of Industry to the South African Periphery', *World Development*, vol. 14, no. 1 (Jan.).

White Paper (1985) *Industrial Development Strategy in the Republic of South Africa*, WPG85, Pretoria: Government Printer.

White, G., and R. Wade (eds) (1985) *Developmental States in East Asia*, Brighton: Institute Development Studies (research report).

Wilkins, I., and H. Strydom (1978) *The Super-Afrikaners*, Johannesburg: Jonathan Ball.

Wolpe, H. (1972) 'Capitalism and Cheap Labour-Power in South Africa: From Segregation to Apartheid', *Economy and Society*, vol. 1, no. 3 (Nov.).

Woo, J. (1991) *Race to the Swift: State and Finance in Korean Industrialization*, New York: Columbia University Press.

Wood, E., and T. Moll (1994) 'Capital Flight from South Africa: Is Underinvoicing Exaggerated?', *South African Journal of Economics*, vol. 62, no. 1 (March).

Worger, W. (1987) *South Africa's City of Diamonds: Mine Workers and Monopoly Capitalism in Kimberley, 1867–1895*, New Haven: Yale University Press.

World Bank (1993) *The East Asian Miracle: Economic Growth and Public Policy, A World Bank Policy Research Report*, Oxford University Press.

Wright, H. (1977) *The Burden of the Present: Liberal-Radical Controversy over Southern African History*, Cape Town: David Philip.

Yudelman, D. (1983) *The Emergence of Modern South Africa: State, Capital, and the Organized Labour on the South African Gold Fields, 1902–1939*, London: Greenwood.

Zarenda, H. (1975) 'Tariff Policy: Export Promotion versus Import Replacement', *South African Journal of Economics*, vol. 43, no. 1 (March), pp. 111-22.

—— (1977) 'The Policy of State Intervention in the Establishment and Development of Manufacturing Industry in South Africa', unpubl. MA thesis, University of the Witwatersrand, Johannesburg.

Zhao, D., and J. Hall (1994) 'State Power and Patterns of Late Development: Resolving the Crisis of the Sociology of Development', *Sociology*, vol. 28, no. 1 (Feb.).

INDEX

ABSA, banking group, 175
African Explosives and Chemical Industries (AECI) *see* Anglo-American Corporation
African National Congress (ANC), 3, 64
Afrikaner Broederbond, 131
Afrikaner capital: 4, 8, 11, 14, 64, 112, 130, 138, 145, 147, 164; development, 148-52; disjuncture with English capital, 180, 218, 222; finance, 13, 156-7, 161; interpenetration with English capital, 155, 160, 162, 164, 168, 172, 195-6, 206, 226, 230, 253; off-shore, 177; state support, 121, 136, 153, 158-9, 181, 188, 193, 220; tariff favouring, 190
agencies, concept: 7, 19, 23, 25, 38-9, 52, 55, 236; class, 27; the state, 29
aggregate effective demand, 27
agriculture: 149; access to black labour, 127; Afrikaner, 13, 124, 148; co-operatives, 117; forced-export, 129; protection, 128
Alam, M., 31, 36-7, 39, 42-3
Alcorto, L., 99
Alexander, G., 129
aluminium: 172; smelting, 164, 185, 202
Amsden, A., 33-4, 36-8, 41-2, 44, 46
Anglo-American Corporation (AAC): 10, 98, 102-3, 105, 108, 111-13, 135, 143, 153, 155, 157, 160-2, 172-3, 177, 182, 188; AECI, 80, 159, 169, 178, 211, 232; highveld plant, 164; Union Acceptances Ltd, 156

Anglovaal: 98, 103, 108, 111, 173; history, 141
Angola, war, 168, 233
anti-semitism, 136
apartheid system: 22-3, 206, 216-17, 233, 243, 253; characterisation, 65; crisis, 4, 11, 13, 24, 196, 198, 211; demise, 63; historiography, 21; imperatives, 92, 246; labour system, 13, 213, 242; liberal view, 22, 90; macroeconomic policy, 246; Marxist view, 22; MEC symbiosis, 244; policies, 12, 147, 178; post-apartheid economy, 209, 218, 235; state, 110, 179; structures, 5; weaknesses, 6
armaments industry: 108, 159, 166, 243, 246; exports, 233; production, 178
Armscor, 166, 178, 195, 232
authoritarianism: 46, 61, 63; autonomy, 65-6
automated teller machines, 105
Auty, R., 32, 248

Bain, J., 99
balance of payments: constraints, 186, 193; pressures, 219; problems, 6-7, 24, 28; targets, 246
banking, 103
Bantu border areas, lack of infrastructure, 194
Barclays Bank, 151, 153
Barlow Rand, 182
Barrett, R., 39
beer: 245; market, 114
Bell, T., 220

271